RHETOR RESPONSE

RHETOR RESPONSE

A Theory and Practice of Literary Affordance

PETER H. KHOST

UTAH STATE UNIVERSITY PRESS
Logan

Published by Utah State University Press
An imprint of University Press of Colorado
245 Century Circle, Suite 202
Louisville, Colorado 80027

Manufactured in the United States of America

The University Press of Colorado is a proud member of the Association of University Presses.

The University Press of Colorado is a cooperative publishing enterprise supported, in part, by Adams State University, Colorado State University, Fort Lewis College, Metropolitan State University of Denver, Regis University, University of Colorado, University of Northern Colorado, Utah State University, and Western State Colorado University.

∞ This paper meets the requirements of the ANSI/NISO Z39.48-1992 (Permanence of Paper)

ISBN: 978-1-60732-775-2 (paperback)
ISBN: 978-1-60732-776-9 (ebook)
https://doi.org/10.7330/9781607327769

Library of Congress Cataloging-in-Publication Data

Names: Khost, Peter H., author.
Title: Rhetor response: a theory and practice of literary affordance / Peter H. Khost.
Description: Logan : Utah State University Press, [2018] | Includes bibliographical references and index.
Identifiers: LCCN 2017045689| ISBN 9781607327752 (pbk.) | ISBN 9781607327769 (ebook)
Subjects: LCSH: English language—Rhetoric—Study and teaching (Higher)
Classification: LCC PE1404 .K499 2018 | DDC 808/.0420711—dc23
LC record available at https://lccn.loc.gov/2017045689

The University Press of Colorado gratefully acknowledges the generous support of Stony Brook University's College of Arts and Sciences toward the publication of this book.

A version of chapter 5 was previously published as "'Alas Not Yours to Have': Problems with Audience in High-Stakes Writing Tests, and the Promise of Felt Sense" in the *Journal of the Assembly for Expanded Perspectives on Learning* and is presented here with permission.

Cover credit: *Orpheus* (pen and black ink on chalk paper), by Gustave Moreau (1826–1898); photo: René-Gabriel Ojéda; Musee Gustave Moreau, Paris, France; © RMN-Grand Palais / Art Resource, NY.

For Aida and Armon

CONTENTS

ACKNOWLEDGMENTS

Thank you so much Michael Spooner; I will always be grateful to you for believing in me. Thank you to Darrin Pratt, Rachael Levay, Laura Furney, Beth Svinarich, Cheryl Carnahan, Dan Pratt, Charlotte Steinhardt, Kylie Haggen, and everyone else involved at Utah State University Press and University Press of Colorado. Sincere gratitude to my past, present, and future students at Stony Brook University in HON 105: Modes of Knowledge; WRT 302: Living through Texts; and EGL/WRT 614: Rhetor Response Theory, especially my spring 2017 graduate students: Jess Hautsch, Meghan Buckley, Jackie Henry, Steve Kroll, Caitlin Duffy, Jon Heggestad, Sarah Nicole Fisher Davis, and Bernie Krumm.

My extreme gratitude to Gene Hammond. Thanks to Sondra Perl, Kristina Lucenko, Roger Thompson, Robert Kaplan, Duane Roen, Dave Hyman, Nicole Galante, Janet Larson, Rachel Hadas, Lenny Cassuto, Stefan Hyman, Gary Halada, Joonna Trapp, Bradley Peters, Marilyn Zucker, Rebecca Mlynarczyk, Gordon Whatley, Jamie Utitas, Edna Patton, and Frank Gaughan—my collaborator in the earliest published iteration of rhetor response theory, "literaturing composition" (Gaughan and Khost 2007, 10–16). Shout-outs to my Dartmouth sisters Faith Kurtyka and June Griffin and to the rest of my workshop crew: Bob Lazaroff, Lauren Esposito, and Shawn Garrett. Thank you Joan Richardson for not laughing me out of your office on my first day in the English PhD program you were chairing at the CUNY Graduate Center, when I naively told you my aim was to invent a literary/rhetorical theory. Thanks to Karlianne Seri for research assistance. Thank you Jilleen May and Adam Schultheiss for your unwavering helpfulness and pleasantness over the years.

To my parents, Judith Syron Schuddeboom and Henry P. Khost Jr., thank you for a lifetime of unconditional love and support; most of what I have to offer in this book and in general I learned from you, especially (and most important) how to open my heart to others. Thank you Kees Schuddeboom; Deborah Evers Khost; Virginia Syron and Elaine Young; Greg, Jackie, and Maeve Khost; Alex, James, and Oliver Khost and Amanda and Oomi Wilder; Danielle and Henry F. Khost; Hedayat, Behi, Avid, and Arvin Izadpanah; Mary Ann Keirans; the Penney family; Heather Evers; and Hakim Maloum. Thanks to my Syron and Khost grandparents (in memory).

Aida and Armon, you have my deepest love and gratitude for blessing my life every day. Thank you for making this book possible and for bearing with me during the writing of it. Man kheili aasheghetoon hastam.

PREFACE

در دل من چیزی ست، مثل یك بیشه نور، مثل خواب دم صبح.

(There is something in my heart, like a grove of light, like slumber at the break of dawn.)

—Sohrab Sepehri, "In Golestaneh"

Here is a partial history of how I think this book may have been conceived. Parts of the rest of the book say more about this explicitly and implicitly. In a way, perhaps the whole book is about how it was conceived or, more accurately, is still being conceived. I have been intermittently following a hunch (i.e., thinking, analyzing, inventing) with gradually increasing awareness and frequency over almost exactly the past twenty-five years. Honestly, I think I may have been variously in touch with this fuzzy energy my entire life, even possibly in utero, but let's start at the spark of conscious awareness in the most familiar sense.

In my first year as an undergraduate at Fordham University in the early 1990s, my English composition course required me to write a research paper on any topic of my choosing. I composed a patchwork of decontextualized excerpts supporting the pitifully vague position that humans now rely less on instinct than they used to, presumably to our detriment. I am half sorry and half glad to no longer have a copy to reference it more specifically; that work was tapped out on a typewriter, believe it or not. I can remember that I drew on Emerson, who is one of my father's favorites. There was also Nietzsche's *Birth of Tragedy* and most likely some poetry and mystical writings. My aim had been to convince readers to be more instinctual, under the weak assumption that this is both a clear and an attainable goal.

Only many years later, after having marked in countless margins traces of my hunch hinted in further reading, would I realize and revise my hunch-following accordingly, that it isn't instinct but intuition that I am interested in. Not for abstract or scientific reasons but perhaps to sharpen my personal insight and for self-validation, because more than any other trait, intuition has been my greatest strength (and still is), yet it remains marginalized in my culture and perhaps especially in my profession. Also because philosophical, literary, and especially philosophically literary texts had long since been my go-to source of affirmation (though I didn't know it as such for a long time) that I was not absurd or secretly dumb behind my good grades or damaged from that slip-on-ice head injury I never told anyone about until now, which caused me to see something like peripheral blinking parentheses for much of a school day in third grade. I was always good enough, often very good, at the conventional intellectual tasks, but I seldom seemed to go about doing them in conventional ways or for conventional reasons. I loved reading but regularly took the liberty to ignore items on assigned reading lists that didn't suit my interests in favor of my own eclectic choices, even sometimes to the detriment of my performance (but never really all *that* much, in truth). My intuition was perpetually on the trail of something urgent yet unnamed to me, and if a book came my way that didn't carry the scent, I had a pile of alternatives to dig into instead. But I sometimes felt guilty for doing this and was often insecure about my unconventional ways, and literally not until preparing to write this book did I feel confident or did I confide in anyone (save for a very few kindred spirits) about any of this.

In those days, the old Duane Library on Fordham's Rose Hill campus was a thing of real beauty: a stone and stained-glassed neo-gothic church converted into a temple of books, with floating spiral staircases inside that ascended into the spires, wooden card catalogs, and rooms off of rooms off of rooms in the basement in which you could brick yourself up behind hardcovers and drink in volumes of whatever you pleased. (Regrettably, the building's interior has since been modified and is no longer a library.) Some of my colleagues believed it to be haunted, and others thought it housed a gateway to a secret underground tunnel system. There one day, while tracking down a copy of *Lady Chatterley's Lover*—which had not been assigned to me and was not part of a course I never took by the faculty's genuine Lawrence expert, whose "energy" I "sensed" mismatched mine despite our mutual appreciation of the savage pilgrim—I was engaged by a librarian I had seen from time to time mumbling to himself. Clad in faded gabardine and prematurely gray, he projected an air of having shelved books there for ages. He asked and then scoffed to learn about my searching for Lawrence. Then he murmured to me, verbatim, "There are only three great novelists: Tolstoy, Dostoevsky, and Turgenev."

I could not then phrase my understanding of that episode in such clear terms as now, but from that moment it began to dawn on me how my reasons for and ways of reading literary texts often differed from the reasons and ways of most other readers of whom I was aware. That may be especially true of the outspoken and authoritative readers, who were doubtless among the sources of my aforementioned guilt and insecurity. Whereas they tended to privilege the interpretive *meaning* of literature—leading them to judgments of greatness of books and authors, like our Russophilic librarian—I was always looking for what literature could *do for me* and what *I could do with it*, regardless of its meaning or greatness (or lack of greatness). I might have known or cared little to nothing about a text's author, the period in which the text was written, or its reception by critics; I might even have supposedly misread it; yet I could often nevertheless derive personal uses and values from that text. Much later, I would begin to consider this use value in rhetorical terms: what I could do with a literary text *beyond* personal applications of it. In cases of public usage, I would of course need to learn about the text's history and background to be sure to repurpose it respectfully, but this additional conventional step would not necessarily restrict my approach to conventional ends. My non-interpretive rhetorical uses of literature may be lowbrow if not despicable appropriations to make, according to some people's standards. But those are not universal or even the best standards in the world, nor does it seem I am the only person to have taken this kind of approach to texts, nor am I going let the specter of convention scare me off (anymore).

One more thing: Fordham's Duane Library is also about 500 feet away from Collins Auditorium. There in the 1960s my father, an undergraduate trumpeter in the pit, met my mother, a local Bronx-girl singer (and ringer in this case), during rehearsals of a production of *Kiss Me, Kate* at the then all-male Fordham College. In this musical, a Shakespearean text plays a rhetorical supporting role to the front-stage drama, which ironically takes place largely backstage, about a divorced couple. All of this remarkably portends lifelong aspects of my relationships with literary texts and of my relating these texts to life. These relations are the origins and much of the content of my book. I was antedated by, born out of, and born into texts. I have borne them myself. I have lived through texts and used them in ways and combinations that are unique to my experience. I can fruitfully take from and give of these texts with disregard for their interpretive meaning without doing them any harm.

I'll bet the same is true of you, dear reader, and I believe you can become a better rhetorical *user* of literary texts through increased awareness, confidence, and practice in the act. I am not saying that anybody should selectively use literary texts with disregard for their interpretive meaning all or even most of the time, but this may be worth trying at least some of the time. I would like to help you start or keep going at that, in part by awakening (i.e., seeking to better understand) my own practice of this act that I call *literary affordance*, which is the heart of my theory of *rhetor response*. Welcome, then, to my "grove of light."

RHETOR RESPONSE

1
INTRODUCTION

Has it ever happened, as you were reading a book, that you kept stopping as you read, not because you weren't interested, but because you were: because of a flow of ideas, stimuli, associations? In a word, haven't you ever happened to read while looking up from your book?
—Roland Barthes, *The Rustle of Language*

Although this book enters a long- and hotly contested subject area, it is not a polemic. Rather, it is an invitation to approach this area—of institutional, pedagogical, and personal relations between literature and writing—from a new angle. I acknowledge that acceptance of this invitation opens my own text up to approaching from new angles, but I welcome that phenomenon, which of course would happen even if I didn't. In fact, that probability supports my book's claims about thc usability of texts beyond their authors' intentions, except my focus here is on "literary" texts, not nonfictional ones. My primary target audiences are college writing program administrators (WPAs), faculty and scholars in English and writing studies, and graduate students in both disciplines. Secondary readers include undergraduates of all kinds, high school English and composition teachers and their students, education scholars, and intellectual public audiences. I name these parties not only so they will feel personally invited to participate in this text but also to suggest that they belong in each other's company, in theory as well as in practice. This book seeks to prompt dialogue both within and among these groups that I believe often function too separately from each other in relation to the content addressed herein.

In short, my book proposes a case for studying and making rhetorical uses of literary texts. I believe that doing so can open up many powerful and pleasurable learning opportunities, especially regarding oneself in relation to one's lived contexts. I refer to these uses as *affordances*, after a term derived from ecological psychology for applications that emerge in a given context, whether intended (e.g., sitting on a chair)

DOI: 10.7330/9781607327769.c001

or not (e.g., standing on a chair to reach something). I wish to broaden the knowledge and expectations of readers—especially readers who may seek, or who teach those who seek, no more from literary material than entertainment—of what they can do with literary texts, partly by disregarding what the text or its author intends and what the text's conventional reception indicates is an acceptable interpretation. Another way to put this is: allowing oneself to be unconcerned with the text's meaning, regardless of who or what may determine that meaning. This disregard need not be impudent or permanent, and it can be useful in certain situations without damaging whatever meanings may otherwise be associated with the text.

People will generally acknowledge that literary texts can powerfully affect audiences, and with some prompting, many people can also identify an example that has made a notable impact on them individually. However, relatively few may realize that they may also do something with such material, with value for themselves and others. That is to say, although it is well-known that literature *says* things and, to a lesser degree, that it *does* things, rarely do we consider what *audiences* can *do* with literature: what functions it can be made to serve beyond being experienced and analyzed. My book approaches literary material, then, not to be interpreted but to be used, both as intended (i.e., what I call an *apparent* affordance) and not as intended (i.e., *subtle* affordance). Making affordances of texts as such reconceives reading as an active, applied, and creative practice. Other reader-focused theories have made a somewhat similar shift, but with rare exception they are mostly still concerned with what texts *mean*. I am pursuing texts as means to *other* ends.

A considerable influence on my thinking, from whom I eventually diverge in this way, is Louise Rosenblatt, who explains that "literature provides a living through, not simply knowledge *about* [its subjects]: not information that lovers have died young and fair, but a living-*through* of Romeo and Juliet," for example (1995, 38, emphases added). These italicized prepositions help explain my approach. Whereas an interpretation is a response *to* a text that is *about* the text, a literary affordance is a response to something *else* (e.g., a rhetorical situation), which emerges *through* a text (e.g., as a lens or a way of being). My book invites and tries to help readers reflect on their processes of *living through* literature in the latter way, not just during text-oriented current acts of reading or shortly thereafter but also in applications made continuously intermittently afterward in life-oriented situations that may have nothing to do with the literary text, its author or period, or its conventional reception. To expand on this introduction's epigraph by

Barthes, with some texts you look up from your book and keep reading indefinitely, even unconsciously.

So let's imagine that you have "lived through" *Romeo and Juliet* or some other text you may connect with better. What might you *do* with that experience, for yourself and for others? Note the shift in emphasis from the stereotypical complaint to English majors, "what are you going to do with *that*?" to an invitation to all kinds of readers of literature, "what are you going to *do* with that?" I am not claiming that this approach is necessarily any better than conventional treatments of texts, but I also don't think it's any worse. That depends on the context. Though formal literary interpretation is not something most people often find themselves doing in the course of life, living *through* literary texts *is* something they do throughout life's duration, from bedtime stories to last rites. Add to this the talk we hear in the womb and our eulogies and obituaries, and we can see that "our little life / Is rounded with a sleep" that is textual.[1] That is to say, people live narrative and rhetorical lives, amid the discourse of other people and sources, to which they constantly respond with the use of any number of tools or tactics. I intend to show that these tools and tactics can and do include repurposed texts or textual features: what I call literary affordance, a skill that can be improved if individuals become more aware and are supported in the practice. For this reason I would like to see *affordance* become a familiar counterpart to *interpretation* in educational (and other) contexts. This practice has the potential for widespread appeal, since by definition affordances are useful, and in this case they can also be artful. In other words, making affordances of literature is not restricted to situations in which texts or their meanings are the central preoccupation—which, as I just said, are rare occurrences in most people's lives—yet these affordances also potentially deeply engage people with literary content.

Before going further, I want to clarify some key terms and issues. For starters, I will spare my readers and myself from surveying the copious definitions of rhetoric from its thousands of years of theorizing. For present purposes we can take the word to mean the use of sign systems in contexts, with recognizable results. My deliberately passive phrasing here leaves room for the existence of *unintended* rhetorical effects (a debatable concept, I realize). My vagueness about determinants of effectiveness seeks to accommodate widely varying situations. So potentially any effect in any circumstance may be found to have value, even in the unconscious (again, I know: debatable). Detailed accounts of the meanings of *affordance* are offered in chapters 2 and 3, until which we can provisionally equate the term with words like *use*, *application*, or *appropriation*. Literary affordances, then, are applications of features of literary texts to unrelated rhetorical situations.

Throughout the book I distinguish between what I call *interpretive* meaning and *cultural* meaning, with my focus squarely attending to the former. This designation seeks to indicate the kinds of meaning texts accrue through interpretation as literary artifacts, whether by consideration of authorial intent, elements of the text itself, critical reception, or some combination of these and other such scholarly emphases. The latter designation, *cultural* meaning, seeks to indicate the kinds of meaning texts accrue through existence as artifacts associated with various identity or subjectivity groups. Though these two kinds of meaning are of course not mutually exclusive, my book's encouragement of provisional disregard for textual meaning is meant to apply only to *interpretive* meaning. In other words, I do not recommend ignoring *cultural* meanings of texts. Expressions of literary affordance, therefore, should always seek to maintain respect for cultural meanings of texts—a potentially complicated matter that might be best addressed on a case-by-case basis by stakeholders in given rhetorical situations. Discussions about why and how to determine such cultural respect can yield important outcomes and may even comprise the main point of an educational exercise in rhetor response theory.

When I speak of *students* in my book, I tend to mean *readers* generally, and by that I also mean audiences, viewers, listeners, fans, gamers, and so on. Although I prefer the more capacious *rhetoric and composition* to *writing studies*, my book employs the latter name to identify the academic discipline more recognizably for non-specialist readers; however, I occasionally use *composition* in place of *writing* for historical or situational accuracy. When I use the terms *literary studies*, *literature* (as a field), and *English*, I often mean the aggregate of people, places, and activities that belong to English departments or the equivalent, minus that of writing and rhetoric (which may or may not also be housed there). The term *literature* (as a text) might mean multiple works, an entire single work, or only one or some of a single work's features, as the topic at hand may involve no more than a given theme, character, or just an image or a line from a text. I use *work* and *text* interchangeably, despite my appreciation for Roland Barthes's (1986, 56–64) distinction between the terms. So for the sake of ease, I may employ the metonymic terms *literature* or *material* as stand-ins for the part(s) they represent. Furthermore, by *literature* I mean any published or public text or artifact that is not nonfiction. This includes but is not limited to novels, stories, poems, works for the stage, art or design pieces, myths, graphic novels, comics, fairy tales, feature films, TV shows, songs, fanfiction, and video games. My examples in this book are drawn from what is more traditionally thought of as *literature* per se, but that is only because this material is most familiar and appealing to me personally, not because I believe it inherently possesses or deserves special status above these other forms. I am unconcerned with high/low distinctions among these genres in any general sense.

Let it be clear that I do not wish or call for affordances to replace interpretations in educational or any other settings, nor do I believe they ever could. Rather, I am proposing the investigation and making of affordances as other things to do with literary texts, with different methods, results, and values—which some, if not many, readers have already done with varying degrees of awareness and development. I am also suggesting that my approach may carry appeal to some people in some contexts that literary interpretation does not tend to carry (or not as much). This is partly because the study of literary affordance as I present it here involves greater attention to oneself and one's situational/rhetorical existence than to the text in question, the latter of which interpretation tends to emphasize. But I want to nip in the bud the dichotomy already beginning to form here, despite myself, between interpretation and affordance. It seems likely to me that making effective affordances of texts involves some degree of their interpretation (or at least analysis) and that unique affordances can also inform interpretations (or analyses). This view follows Steven Mailloux's (1997, 379) convincing position, variously articulated throughout his career, that "rhetoric and interpretation are practical forms of the same extended human activity: rhetoric is based on interpretation; interpretation is communicated through rhetoric." So I do not present my rhetor response theory as competing with interpretive or analytical modes of textual engagement but rather as pursuing different ends as each other from related origins.

Further, I do not presume that making an affordance of literary material will or should *work* for anyone with any text at any time, putting aside for now what it might mean for an affordance to "work" as such (see chapters 3 and 6 on that point). In fact, I generally recommend that, apart from being provided with some basic awareness, guidance, and encouragement, individuals be enabled to develop affordances as organically as possible (i.e., of their own volition and in their own ways). My aim in this book consists far more of inviting awareness and development of the inherent occurrence of literary affordances in many readers than to argue for a specific hierarchy or course of action for them. Furthermore, I would hope that the effectiveness of literary affordance be determined (i.e., assessed), if at all, not against a supposed universal standard but in relation to elements of its corresponding rhetorical situation: purpose, audience, and exigence.[2] These elements necessarily change across time and space, as presumably do readers' approaches to texts, albeit probably less constantly. Finally, throughout the book when I refer to an "approach" to texts, I am inviting a focus on the nature of the *phenomenon* of approaching rather than on the spatial, temporal, and causal connotations of the word *approach*.

A famous example of an affordance made from a literary source is Freud's concept of the Oedipus complex. For his entire mature career, Freud explained this theory of the child's unconscious sexual desire for the child's parent of the opposite sex explicitly in terms of the ancient Greek myth of Oedipus, best known to Freud and most others from the Sophocles play *Oedipus Rex*. Freud derives many rhetorical benefits from this framing technique, including that his difficult and controversial theory becomes easier to understand and remember (through both narrative and naming), as well as initially more palatable (through the somewhat distancing indirection of analogy). He also gains the insinuation of timelessness to the phenomenon he is pointing out by locating it in a text from as far back as the fifth century BCE.

But it is insufficient and inaccurate to consider Freud's affordance of this myth to be merely an analogy or an explanatory tactic (not that those are insignificant effects). The myth also had a considerable or even essential *generative* role in Freud's formulation of his groundbreaking theory, as well as his worldview. Shortly after his father's death, Freud, who was deeply attached to his mother and was intimately familiar with *Oedipus Rex*, began writing about the Oedipus complex as such. We can intuit from a letter he wrote to a friend at the time that Freud possessed a predisposition to read and generalize his own (childhood) experience *into* the play, a work that was known until that point more for its themes of fate and morality than for its element of incest: "I found in myself a constant love for my mother, and jealousy of my father. I now consider this to be a universal event in early childhood" (1985, 17). During those same years Freud writes in *The Interpretation of Dreams*: "The action of the [Sophocles] play consists now in the gradually intensified and skillfully delayed revelation—comparable to the work of a psychoanalysis—that Oedipus himself is Laius' murderer, but also that he is the son of the murdered king and Jocasta" (1999, 202). Freud continues: "His fate moves us only because it could have been our own as well . . . It was perhaps ordained that we should all of us turn our first sexual impulses towards our mother, our first hatred and violent wishes against our father" (1999, 202).

Freud's *response* as a reader of *Oedipus Rex* was hardly "just" (or for that matter even much of) an interpretation of the play's meaning; rather, it was an emergent and abiding assemblage of his own emotional, familial, social, professional, and aesthetic experiences. Moreover, the affordance he made of the text became the basis of a remarkable rhetorical accomplishment and an extraordinarily influential, if disputed, contribution to psychology. I have to add, finally, that the idea of the psyche itself is another example of a literary affordance. Many centuries before *psyche* became the semantic root and conceptual foundation of *psychology*, Psyche was a classical literary character, whose story makes such an extremely apt analogy for representing the unconscious that today it serves this purpose entirely transparently to most people. Whether we know it or not, when we think of psychological subjects, we are thinking *through* or *in terms of* the story of Psyche. As such, this literary affordance is not only analogical to but also constituent of our thinking. This distinction is key to understanding the potential power to be derived from making and studying literary affordances, as well as the considerable extent to which higher-order reasoning in general relies on metaphor and narrative.

As I have indicated and as the Oedipus complex example demonstrates, literary affordance can and does happen *organically*, which is to say un- or semi-consciously, unintentionally, or of its own volition, so to speak. Many elements seem to have been mutually present at the right time and place for Freud to have found/created what he did in/from the Sophocles play, even though he may not have been consciously intending for this to happen. You might say such a discovery is providential, but I also believe that one's circumstances and especially one's awareness can be influenced (without too much interference) in such a way as to increase the likelihood of one's finding/creating an affordance in a literary text, not to mention taking rhetorical advantage of it. (As for this matter of slashes, I am going to shift now to only employing the latter usage with the assumption that the former is subsumed therein; I say more about this in chapters 2 and 3.) Let me begin to explain this claim by returning to my initial example of a chair.

One may not know in advance that one is going to activate the latent stand-on-ability[3] of a chair, but if one is aware that one somehow needs to reach an object at a height and then goes looking for a means to do so, then one may indeed be more apt to make an affordance of a chair by standing on it (which was not intended by the chair's maker). Among other factors less significant to my purposes—such as the person's height and the size of the chair—a combination of one's will (conscious or not), one's awareness (including "only" through one's intuition), and the situation or context brings the affordance into emergence. One of my hopes for this book is that its readers will join me in developing ways to influence students' circumstances as such, in order for these students to make literary affordances of their own and to study this phenomenon in general. I do not presume to have this theory and practice finished, only perhaps a head start in working on it explicitly.

In chapter 2 I offer a selective overview of affordance theory in its original and most directly successive formulations, respectively, by psychologist James Gibson and by some of his most prominent scholarly beneficiaries in the area of ecological psychology. To establish a foundation for my application of the term *affordance* to literary and rhetorical purposes, I offer definitions, key terms, examples, ambiguities, and debates surrounding that concept. I also ask and answer a pair of significant related questions: are affordances made or found, and are affordances percepts or concepts?

Chapter 3 integrates an eclectic selection of scholarship that unwittingly suggests an opening for literary affordance in the theory and practices of reading, writing, and rhetoric. It also answers a number of important related questions. Rather than develop my theory into a method to be followed strictly, I offer literary affordances as a general *approach* to working with texts, which warrants and welcomes variation because of its applied, contextual, and personal qualities. With this approach, readers become rhetors by making applications of literary content to situations they are engaged in, which may very well be unrelated to the literary text, its author, and its reception history. It is essential to note that with literary affordance, no claim is made to the interpretive *meaning* of the "source" text from which this application emerges but only to the text's *use value* in another, "target" context. So because literary affordance lays no claim to a text's interpretive meaning, correctness seems an inappropriate evaluative criterion here (as opposed to effectiveness and respectfulness, for example). But I acknowledge that my stating this cannot and need not necessarily prevent teachers from introducing literary affordance along with restrictions, and it certainly does not stop anyone from rejecting the approach altogether. I am not arguing that anyone *must* use my theory or must do so for a particular reason or in a specific way; rather, I am inviting readers to consider whether, why, and how they and the personnel they oversee might take it up and to join the conversation either way. For my readers who do not make it to or all the way through chapter 3 (though I implore you to please hang in there), let me now declare that my theory does not license an *anything-goes* treatment of texts. I will make it clear that the *going* indicated by the phrase *anything goes* is always relative to a rhetorical situation and that any failure to "go" (i.e., to be rhetorically effective or culturally respectful) should be taken up on a case-by-case basis relative to the given context. Although it is not a generalizable finding, I will mention anyway that to date, I have received no offensive affordances from the hundreds of students with whom I have practiced this approach. That's not to say it cannot happen, only that it may not be worth fixating on ahead of time.

Chapter 4 addresses a diverse institutional readership that may be interested in rhetor response theory. I propose literary affordance as a supplement to conventional literary-interpretive and writing-instructional practices for educators and students to consider, especially if they have little, no, or conflicted stakes in such conventions. Possible applications include research opportunities for scholars and graduate students, units of study for advanced undergraduates, and assignments or assignment options for others at the postsecondary and secondary levels. My case incorporates a concise history of the ongoing (but in some places nonexistent) institutional "divorce" proceedings between English and writing studies, as well as a response to current scholarship from the latter field on disciplinary expertise, independence, and content. I warn against an unwitting partial reversal of marginalization that writing has long suffered by English, of which I now see potential signs, as well as missed opportunities to possibly improve professional and pedagogical aspects of both fields through a reconciliation of sorts. Two example literary affordances are made of Shakespeare's *The Tempest*.

Chapter 5 offers an original demonstration of literary affordance in theorizing an alternative approach to argumentation and the rhetorical audience. My case makes rhetorical uses of the famous Orpheus myth to critique high-stakes English language arts tests and the narrow approach to textuality they and other exams like them reflect. My objections: these pervasive, highly influential tests impose on students a reductive and potentially unethical attitude toward audiences through an insistently narrow view of argumentation, and they squander much of the wonder and power of literature on rote and resented evaluations that disadvantage teachers as well as learners. In contrast, I want to open up approaches to reading and to rhetorical engagement (and to narrow the perceived distance between these acts) by encouraging writers to increase their holistic awareness (i.e., felt sense) of audience indeterminacy, on the one hand, and of the potential power of literary content in their lives (including through its appropriation by readers), on the other hand.

In chapter 6 I address the issue of why to study and practice literary affordance, and I offer explanations of how I have taught literary affordance and my rhetor response theory, as well as a significant related activity called *autotextography*, which I have assigned at both the undergraduate and graduate levels. Autotextography is presented as a kind of writing-to-learn investigation into past affordances that one has made un-/semi-consciously or unintentionally. One result of this systematic inquiry can be to establish methods and aims for subsequent making of conscious/intentional affordances, including by adaptation of prior affordances one has come to understand though autotextography. The exercises and examples I offer are not meant to be prescriptive but rather descriptive and invitational of potential actions by other practitioners of the approaches I am endorsing in this book. The final section of chapter 6 variously seeks to distinguish the acts of literary affordance and literary interpretation from each other, specifically with regard to teaching writing but with easy application to other contexts. Readers who are seeking a (relatively) shorthand clarification of this vital distinction between affordance and interpretation might skip ahead to this passage at the end of the book and then, it is hoped, backtrack through the supporting theory and numerous examples and explanations throughout the rest of the book.

Interspersed between each pair of the book's chapters is a short interchapter in which I demonstrate my technique of autotextography, which again represents an important precursor activity to literary affordance and is an essential conceptual tributary to rhetor response theory. In these accounts, I briefly narrate and analyze what a particular literary text or set of texts has done for me and how these effects have become assimilated into my rhetorical and pedagogical repertoire. My hope for these interchapters is to support the hypothesis that literary texts often do things to readers that they are not aware of or not wholly aware of and which may be unintended by the authors and irrelevant to interpretive norms. I also seek with these interchapters to model a generative writing and research practice that can usefully and satisfyingly discover and repurpose those effects in unrelated rhetorical situations.

There are many reasons why I would like my readers to consider theorizing, practicing, and promoting literary affordance and autotextography, not the least of which is that they can be highly rewarding experiences. I am focusing on literature in the book partly because I believe people are already inclined to make affordances of nonfictional texts, under different names of course (i.e., we are more accustomed to *using* rather than *interpreting* nonfiction). I focus on literary texts also because literature does things nonfiction arguably does not do (1) as often or as much, (2) in the same ways, or (3) as well. Those things include moving our emotions, stretching our imaginations, and becoming interwoven with or assimilated into our own life narratives. I believe these and other such effects should not be off limits to rhetorical inquiry and application for any reason, let alone for antiquated, unproductive, and often unwanted divisions between the disciplines of English and writing. Some of the more tangible potential benefits I envision for taking up literary affordance in educational and scholarly contexts are as follows.

WPAs stand to gain a viable, cost-free bargaining chip for respectfully engaging their many literarily inclined instructors in writing-studies and rhetorical training. In turn, these often-contingent faculty members gain a sanctioned opportunity to incorporate their literary expertise into their teaching of writing and to generate scholarship from that. Graduate English studies can better help its students prepare for today's faculty jobs, many of which require teaching writing and do not offer support for scholarship. Undergraduate English studies gains a practical means by which to potentially appeal to a wider population of students than it often ordinarily does, or at least English faculty will have new material to consider for their teaching and scholarship. Students of all levels and disciplinary concentrations gain a technique for developing analytical understanding of themselves as consumers and producers of texts, which my instructional experience shows can be empowering in a number of ways. Secondary school teachers and students, education scholars, and public audiences gain new insights and inroads into the value of the liberal arts, which may help counteract the current trend of declaring the humanities and their former crowned jewel, literature, to be fallen.

INTERCHAPTER 1
The Allegory of the Save

I first encountered and started *using* the Orpheus myth shortly after my parents divorced when I was seven years old. A musty paperback of summarized Greek myths was kept in a bookcase in my brother's and my room beneath a window (which reappears in my final interchapter), whose shade we liked to keep drawn because our neighbors', the Paines', window was directly across and near enough to easily see in. I privately reread the story of Orpheus many times in those days. It grabbed and held me like no other myth in the book or any other story did, I think because of my cognitive dissonance in simultaneously admiring and criticizing Orpheus. Only many years later did I realize that this story and especially this dissonance significantly influenced my worldview, and years after that I began shaping my pedagogy in terms of that influence.

Orpheus has long been celebrated for his artistry, courage, and deep love for his wife, Eurydice. This love is what drew me to him—or, more specifically, the thwarting of his love by her loss. As the story goes, tragedy strikes these newlyweds when Eurydice dies suddenly. But Orpheus, the greatest mortal poet and musician, suffers such grief that he resolves to rescue his wife from death. So he charms his way into the underworld using his lyrics and lyre and convinces the gods to restore her life, their one condition being that Orpheus must not look backward during his and Eurydice's ascension from the underworld. Of course that is exactly what Orpheus does in a moment of doubt, thereby losing his wife forever. Afterward, he fails to reenter the underworld, he is killed, and his dismembered head continues to mourn aloud until Apollo eventually quiets it.

I could never fathom why Orpheus turned around during the ascension. To be clear, it is neither his burning doubt nor his desire to confirm his wife's presence that I had trouble understanding; those natural impulses are easy to grasp, even for a seven-year-old. Rather, what have always caused me genuine frustration are Orpheus's self-preoccupation and his (consequent?) resourceless-ness in that moment of crisis. He did

DOI: 10.7330/9781607327769.c001b

not need to turn around to confirm Eurydice's presence; he could have simply called back to her (or just waited). But when faced with the threat of a repeated separation from his wife, he failed to speak with her about the difficulties they were certainly both experiencing, and they paid a fatal price for that.

I had no idea as a child that I was reading and rereading my own story refracted through the Orpheus myth: not just for the similarity of a gifted language user suffering at the breakup of his family but also for the lack of communication about that crisis. As divorces go, that of my parents went better than most seem to do: they are civil to each other, my two brothers and I have remained close with each of them and with each other, and both parents went on to marry again, to lovely people with whom they are much happier. This is why I do not say I experienced a trauma per se (i.e., in comparison with people who unfortunately suffer far worse), but relative to my own experience the divorce was certainly difficult. I shared with Orpheus fears of repeated separation, which were not talked about and which seemed perilous to face directly, but my rhetorical response to this situation differed importantly from that of my mythological counterpart.

I have never blamed my parents or myself for the divorce, and I do not recall ever wishing they would get back together. Rather, the crisis for me (at least as far as I know) came from the shock of my suddenly shattered reality and from the anguish my parents' separation seemed to cause (1) them for their worries about us kids, which I wished to absorb; (2) a brother older enough to have gotten mad, whom I wanted to keep close; and (3) a younger brother, whom I wanted to protect from all harm. So (doubtless, I admit, also as a projection or denial strategy) I assigned myself the task of trying to please these loved ones above all else: a doomed mission that may have played out mostly in my mind and which for a long time I often also unsuccessfully applied to relationships with other (sometimes undeserving) parties. The major difficulty I encountered was communicating about—and thereby, in my case at least, understanding—loss and its attendant anxieties. For all my talents and good intentions I could not, of course, spare my loved ones (or myself) from the conflicts that inevitably arose.

But I still became quite capable at pleasing. The best way to accommodate another's desires, I intuitively discovered, is to make their desires your own desires, and the best way to do that is to not even be aware of the conflation. To this day, I cannot tell whether I simply have very few desires of my own or whether I have repressed them to the point of inaccessibility. I have decided that ultimately the difference does not matter.

The service to others of which I speak was almost always done willingly, so I can peacefully leave it at: what's the difference? Regardless, below are four pieces of evidence that help explain why Orpheus became my negative heuristic in this case and how that literary affordance originated my pedagogical theory.

First, when I was a boy I knew that my strong linguistic intelligence greatly (and understandably) pleased my parents. I aced tests and attended seminars for gifted children. I won school awards in English and published poetry and newspaper columns. My youth's episodes in oft-recited family lore highlight my corrections of adults' grammar, my deconstruction of a question about a given year's Halloween being "the best ever" by my insistence that such could not be determined "because there haven't been all of the Halloweens yet," and an admired family friend's prediction that I would "do something great" in life, which still hangs over me today (will this book finally do the trick?). So many things like this came easily to me and were pleasing to my parents that the role I played in each case—which I rarely resented or resisted, if I was even aware at the time—was mostly that of a conduit from what came naturally to me to what was pleasing to others. Note the "I" here is more of a function than an essence, which is a kind of a basic truth about my subjectivity that could be said to be rhetorical and which explains the genesis of this book and its theories.

Second, not long after the divorce, a family-friend artist drew a caricature of my mother, brothers, and me, which hung in our home for a time. My mother was portrayed as talking too long on the phone, my one brother as drumming virtuostically, the other as joyfully baking, and me . . . as vacuuming the house. My signature trait—as obvious to the caricaturist as a big nose would be—was an over-eagerness to please. Note: vacuuming did not reflect any special dedication to cleanliness; rather, it reflected (accurately) that my character manifests primarily as a relation to the needs and desires of others. To this day, whatever I can do to help I will often do as a reflex, without consideration of preference on my part—usually because I do not possess one. Incidentally, for this reason I could never help but misinterpret Jacques Lacan's claim that a person's desire is always for the Other's desire as an apt account of how other people's desires stood in for my own absent desires. Unlike what Lacan probably means, I have generally not wished to be the object or recipient of the other's desire but rather a supporter of their desire. Surely this trait, coupled with my talent for language, at least in part led me to become a writing teacher—a job in which (as I approach it) I mainly serve the needs of others without need (arguably) of conveying much content.

Third, the only distinct memory I have of the day on which my parents announced their divorce to my brothers and me is of a private moment afterward in which, despite not being religious, I genuinely prayed for the first time. My prayer was to be able to absorb my brothers' pain, to experience it *in their place* (a telling metaphorical phrase, given Eurydice's position in the Orpheus myth). I have never told anyone of this episode, and I recount it now only as a significant example of my situationally derived tendency to serve others without consideration of my own needs (or whether the others wish to be served).

Fourth, as an adult I was told by a reliable source—supporting what I had already suspected in my bones—that my conception (what a word!) might have been in part a deliberate attempt to improve the circumstances of my parents' marriage at the time. (I should note: this may have been a one-sided, unspoken, and/or only retroactively realized attempt.) If so, then there's nothing wrong with or unusual about such a plan; it is widely believed that a baby brings happiness into a home. And though the happiness I did bring to my family could not keep our home together, this potentially explained history nevertheless helps me understand why, as an especially intuitive child born into this specific alleged context, I may have come to prioritize service to others in my approach to life, whether by nature or nurture or both. It also helps explain why I would come to "relate"—as my students like to say—to Orpheus's desperation to save Eurydice and to denounce his rhetorical failure to prioritize her need over his own desire. Both the similarity and the difference are key to the value of this relation.

My point here has not been to lament my failure to save anyone but rather to reveal some of the key processes by which I came to understand my past (i.e., familial) rhetorical situations and to approach my present and future (i.e., pedagogical) ones through the use of a fictional text whose meaning has nothing directly to do with these issues. Without having contrasted my choices with those of Orpheus over the course of many years, I genuinely believe I would not have achieved the awareness I now enjoy and can put to good use for myself and for others in life. Why this particular text, among others that might have prompted a similar affordance? The answer may not (and need not) be wholly or even mostly rational, but one rational reason is because it was there at the right time and it contained such features as to emerge with my abilities in the way it did. Having been revealed as such an important tool for me, this text might now more easily be repurposed for use by others in any number of ways, including the rhetorical use of it I pursue in chapter 5.

2
AFFORDANCE THEORY

Thinking, analyzing, inventing . . . are not anomalous acts; they are the normal respiration of the intelligence. To glorify the occasional performance of that function, to hoard ancient and alien thoughts, to recall with incredulous stupor what some doctor universalis thought, is to confess our laziness or our barbarity. Everyone should be capable of all ideas, and I understand that in the future this will be the case.

—Jorge Luis Borges, "Pierre Menard, Author of the *Quixote*"

This chapter goes into considerable detail about affordance theory and at times quotes important passages at length. Understanding this concept in general is central to understanding my book's application of the term to literary and rhetorical purposes, and I am hoping this chapter might suffice as a standalone introduction to the concept for those who are unfamiliar with affordance theory and who are not likely to research it otherwise on their own. That being said, I am not attempting to provide an exhaustive overview of all the literature on this subject, which is vast and dispersed across disciplines and decades; rather, I have selected a modicum of sources that have appeared to me as most relevant for present purposes. Indeed, there are many more excellent sources that could have made this cut, which I have had to neglect. Perhaps some readers of my book will continue the task of reviewing and forging connections with this compelling area of scholarly inquiry.

A number of definitions of *affordance* by experts from other contexts are provided below, but I want to establish my own amateur formulation for present purposes: affordances are uses individuals make of objects, events, concepts, or environments through relation to their discoverable features.[1] These uses may be conscious or unconscious and originally intended (e.g., sitting on a chair) or unintended (e.g., standing on a chair to reach something).[2] The concept of affordances was introduced by James J. Gibson (1904–79), a prominent American psychologist

DOI: 10.7330/9781607327769.c002

known primarily as a visual perception researcher and a pioneer of ecological psychology. To be reductive, we can think of this sub-discipline (also known as environmental psychology) as the study of psychology from a social-constructionist point of view, its basic principle being that experiential, environment-bound *relations* are central to psychological experience (as opposed to only or primarily mental processes, for example). This situational emphasis should make it easy to see why I believe ecological psychology has much to offer the study of rhetoric (i.e., situational negotiation). Gibson's oft-cited scholarship is still influential in psychology today, in addition to other fields such as design, engineering, cognitive science, computer science, and kinesthesiology. What seems to have generated the most interest beyond his home discipline has been Gibson's theory of *affordance*, which is a nounal neologism (from the verb *to afford*) he coined himself (1966, 285, 1977, 67, 1979, 127).

Gibson's theory naturally took on greater complexity the more he (and others) worked on it. The idea first appeared in little more than a paragraph in a book (Gibson 1966), followed by an edited collection chapter in 1977, followed by a revised and expanded account in his book *The Ecological Approach to Perception* (Gibson 1979), which is the most commonly cited version, often mistaken as the earliest reference to affordance. Gibson studied *physical* properties, principally of visual perception, and much of his work is highly technical in its orientation toward the science of environmental influences on cognition; however, as a student of William James's student Edwin Holt at Princeton, he also seems to have inherited something of a (pragmatic) philosophical inclination (Heft 2001). Gibson first coined the term *affordance* as a replacement for the too philosophically laden word *values*, and in this earliest formulation the concept's resemblance to my pedagogical and rhetorical appropriations of it comes through clearly, as italicized here:

> The simplest affordances, as food, for example, or as a predatory enemy, may well be detected without learning by the young of some animals, but in general learning is all-important for this kind of perception. The child learns what things are manipulable and how they can be manipulated, what things are hurtful, what things are edible, what things can be put together with other things or put inside other things—and so on without limit. He also learns *what objects can be used as the means to obtain a goal, or to make other desirable objects, or to make people do what he wants them to do.* (Gibson 1966, 285, my emphasis)

I am inviting readers, especially educational practitioners and theorists, to join me in making an abstract application of affordance theory to texts, a move for which I have found relatively little precedent.[3] After all, textuality is often the best "thing" one can "manipulate" in order "to make people do what [one] wants them to do." But most ecological psychologists would resist, if not denounce, such a move away from the material realm. For example, eleven years after his first formulation of affordance theory, Gibson still maintains (as his work does indefinitely) a focus on the physical environment. A new concept of referential uniqueness, however, does appear here: "The affordance of anything is a specific combination of the properties of its substance and its surfaces taken with reference to an animal . . . The combination of properties is uniquely related to the animal or species being considered" (Gibson 1977, 67). Two years later Gibson (1979, 127) offers a succinct account of affordances that takes for granted the relationality as "the complementarity of the animal and the environment." For my purposes, readers should consider *animal* and *person* to be interchangeable.

In developing his theory, Gibson acknowledges the influence of cognate concepts from Gestalt psychology such as Koffka's "demand character" and Lewin's "invitation character" or "valence." He explains: "The valence of an object [in such theorists' view] was bestowed upon it in experience, and bestowed by the need of an observer. Thus, Koffka argued that the [hypothetical] postbox has a demand character only when the observer needs to mail a letter. He is attracted to it only when he has a letter to post, not otherwise. The value of something was assumed to change as the need of the observer changed" (Gibson 1979, 138). In some ways, these other terms also suit my purposes, as I maintain that a reader's needs (and abilities, interests, situation, and so forth) contribute to her or his making of literary affordances. But Gibson's reason for parting from the Gestaltists and his reason for coining *affordance* lead to the reason why I rely on his term rather than Koffka's or Lewin's. To be precise, I favor a modification of Gibson's theory posited by Anthony Chemero (2003, 2009), as discussed below, but to get there it helps to understand the "crucial difference" (Gibson 1979, 138) Gibson identifies between his *affordance* and the Gestaltists' *valence* (etc.). That is the belief that affordances are not only phenomenal (i.e., experiential), but they are also at the same time substantial (i.e., physical). On this point there is considerable ambiguity and inconsistency in affordance theory and therefore, of course, disagreement. In a review essay, G. P. Ginsburg (1990, 352) asserts that affordance "does not have a precise and unvarying definition, even within Gibson's own writings."

I think the trick to understanding affordance as simultaneously phenomenal and physical is to ignore the physicality of the given object in isolation and to think of that object instead only in relation to the given animal. So it's not just a chair but a chair in relation to someone who wishes to sit or in relation to someone who needs to change a lightbulb or someone taming a lion or scrounging up firewood (let's say it's a wooden chair), and so on. The chair's physical properties remain the same in each of these cases, but its affordance changes relative to the context.

Gibson (1979, 127–28, original emphasis) explains that you cannot measure the physical properties of an affordance "with the scales and standards used in physics"; rather, "they have to be measured *relative to the animal.* They are unique for that animal. They are not just abstract physical properties. They have unity relative to the posture and behavior of the animal being considered." Note that the affordance of standing on a chair to change a lightbulb includes features of the object (e.g., stand-on-ability), unique qualities of the individual (e.g., the need for light by which to see), and social elements of the environment (e.g., darkness and, say, a sense of vulnerability that comes with it). In parting with the Gestaltists, Gibson (1979, 139) provides another example and returns to the hypothetical postbox (a favorite among affordance scholars, as we will see again below): "I prefer to say that the real postbox (the *only* one) affords letter-mailing to a letter-writing human in a community with a postal system . . . To feel a special attraction to it when one has a letter to mail is not surprising, but the main fact is that it is perceived as part of the environment." Let me foreshadow my subsequent applications of this theory by pointing out in Gibson's example signs of intention, exigence, and relations in a social system. For me, these coexisting elements make affordance a rhetorical subject—at least in its abstract (i.e., non-material) applications. In Gibson's terms, I think the important takeaway is that affordance is an inextricably *environmental* quality.

Examples like the ones above often work best to clarify this complex theory, but the following selection of definitions from prominent affordance scholars may also help. Experimentalist William H. Warren (1984, 683) writes, "An affordance is the functional utility of an object for an animal with certain action capabilities. Specifically, it is the combination of environmental properties that supports some activity for a particular animal." Another experientalist, Leonard S. Mark (1987, 361), identifies affordances as "specific environmental properties that must obtain in order to support an action." James G. Greeno (1994, 340) applies a situationalist lens to his view of affordances, describing them as "conditions for constraints" on activity that may or may not occur, depending on a variety of factors. Harry Heft (2001, 123), who among other things has been an influential Gibson historian, defines affordances as "the perceived functional significance of an object, event, or place for an individual." Theorist and experimentalist Thomas A. Stoffregen would disagree with a number of others (Turvey 1992; Reed 1996; Michaels 2003; Kirlik 2004) who locate affordances strictly in the environmental part of what is often identified as the "animal-environment system." He argues that "affordances do not inhere in either the animal or the environment, taken separately, but emerge only out of relations between the animal and environment" (Stoffregen 2004, 80). This "emergent" quality includes "all of the things that a given animal (or multiple animals, in the case of social affordances) can do in a given environment or situation" (Stoffregen 2004, 79).[4] Stoffregen's views here and elsewhere (2013) seem to align with those of Chemero, a theorist who offers the best bridge I have found to my interests in affordances.

For Chemero (2003, 187), an affordance "is neither of the person, nor of the environment, but rather of their combination." His approach modifies Gibson's original views by taking advantage of the aforementioned ambiguity or inconsistency in those early formulations. To repeat, although Gibson often characterizes affordances as qualities of a given object, he also wavers in this view, stating, for example, "an affordance is neither an objective property nor a subjective property; or it is both if you like. An affordance cuts across the dichotomy of subjective-objective and helps us to understand its inadequacy. It is equally a fact of the environment and a fact of behavior. It is both physical and psychical, yet neither. An affordance points both ways, to the environment and to the observer" (1979, 129). Heft (2001, 132) asks what anyone might ask here: "How is it possible to have it both ways? If a property exists relative to a perceiver, then isn't its existence dependent on the perceiver? Conversely, if a property is independent of a perceiver, then how can it be relational with respect to a perceiver?" Chemero (2009, 145, 147) answers that affordances come into being through their relationality: they are "relations between [people's] abilities and features of the environment" or "of a situation." Chemero (2013, 187) offers the example of one person being taller than another, noting that the feature "taller-than" does not exist a priori in either person but requires both of them in juxtaposition for it to function.

I personally feel no need to try to prove this relationality true in the capital T, metaphysical sense. My interests are rhetorical, so I am content just to come away from these considerations with an emphasis on the partial user-contingency of affordances. That is, we find value in them because we use them, they relate to us, and this relation is reciprocal and dynamic. Greeno explains this symbiosis in the following passage (as you read, replace the word "environment" with "text" to get a head start on understanding my applications of affordance theory):

> An affordance relates attributes of something in the environment to an interactive activity by an agent who has some ability, and an ability relates attributes of an agent to an interactive activity with something in the environment that has some affordance. The relativity of affordances and abilities is fundamental. Neither an affordance nor an ability is specifiable in the absence of specifying the other. It does not go far enough to say that an ability depends on the context of environmental characteristics, or that an affordance depends on the context of an agent's characteristics. The concepts are codefining, and neither of them is coherent, absent the other, any more than the physical concept of motion or frame of reference makes sense without both of them. (Greeno 1994, 338)

Two more ideas in addition to "relation" are important to my applications: "feature placing" and "ability." Following Chemero, we can take *feature placing* to mean the capacity for placing (i.e., identifying) features of a given situation, as distinguished from identifying properties of entities. For example, when it is raining, raininess is a situational feature that an observer can (or cannot) "place" (i.e., identify). Chemero points out that "it" in the phrase "it is raining" is not an entity but a situation (2003, 185; see also 2009, 139–40). *Ability* has already appeared in the quotation just above from Greeno, whom Chemero does not reference despite their overlapping views. We can think of *ability* as meaning the "functional properties" or the actions of an animal "that came to play the role they do in the behavioral economy of the animal because . . . they were helpful in helping the animal (or its ancestor) survive, reproduce, or flourish. Yet, even in circumstances identical to those in which they were helpful in the past, functional properties can fail to become manifest; there can, that is, be a malfunction" (Chemero 2003, 190). I will add that rarely are contemporary circumstances identical to past ones; that is, contexts are constantly shifting.

So to put this all together (with my appropriations in brackets for transitional purposes), for theorists at the farther end of the *relational* camp such as Chemero, Stoffregen, and Greeno, an affordance is not a property of an environment [literary text] or of a person [reader] but rather a person's [reader's] ability to make uses of objects or environments [literary texts] by placing (i.e., identifying) and activating useful features in them. Finally, I interpret Chemero's point about "malfunction" [misreading] to suggest that although affordances tend to be "normative," as William Noble (1981, 73) observes, they can also be aberrant (Chemero 2003, 190), which is not necessarily to say *wrong*. Scholars have emphasized the study of normative and physical affordances, such as climbing stairs (Warren 1984) or sitting on chairs (Mark 1987), which is fine. But my approach is more interested in *aberrant* affordances, such as (to remain with the present examples) sliding down stairs or standing on chairs, and *abstract* affordances, such as placing features of literary texts in unrelated rhetorical situations in one's life. Multiple examples of this will follow in the book, but one we have seen so far, in the introduction, is Freud's affordance of plot and character features in Sophocles's play *Oedipus Rex* for conceiving and expressing his psychoanalytic theory.

TRANSITIONING TOWARD LITERARY AFFORDANCES

In this section I transition toward appropriating the above theories for rhetorical situations in chapter 3, where I propose that affordances be made of abstract concepts (i.e., literary texts) as distinguished from material percepts, of which they are ordinarily made and theorized. From what I can tell from my outsider's point of view, with the exception of aforementioned outliers and a few other socially oriented theorists (e.g., Costall and Still 1989; McArthur and Baron 1983), most scholars who study affordances seem to have subscribed to the view that they *just are* properties of environments, not relations (e.g., Turvey 1992). Noble (1981, 76) explains this attitude effectively by contrasting it with a kind of approach I am drawn to instead: "In a pragmatic account, meaning is realized in practice—an object's affordance, therefore, indeed its existence, is in relation to its use (to its being addressed, or noticed, or employed) by organisms. Gibson frankly would reject that view as being in some way 'mentalistic.'" In this way it might also be objected that what I am talking about is interpretation, not affordance; after all, it might be said, affordance pertains to direct perception of physical environments, not to referential conception of abstract ideas. But I am not talking about interpretation of textual meaning and not even wholly about referential concepts; I'm talking about emergent textual utility that is (partially or initially) experienced or perceived directly, bodily, and situationally. See chapters 3 and 6 for more on this distinction.

It appears there already exists considerable sensitivity about misuses of the concept of affordance. The sizable bibliography on affordance theory is rife with supposed corrections of misunderstandings of the term's meaning. For a helpful example, I turn to an insightful and sometimes humorous blog called *Notes from Two Scientific Psychologists,* which focuses on ecological psychology, embodied cognition, and empirical research in these areas. In one of a series of posts on affordances, bloggers Andrew D. Wilson and Sabrina Golonka (2013) address the subject of misuses of the term. Though they offer only one citation, they seem to assume that their target audience would agree or take their word for it that the affordance-misnomer problem is widespread. In short, they argue that if one does not employ a specific set of empirical methods in studying affordances, then one is not actually studying affordances. The team of experimenters they single out in their lone example used pictures of objects instead of objects themselves in their study, leading to faulty results, say Wilson and Golonka. Interestingly, the bloggers begin their post with a still shot and corresponding quotation from a famous scene in the cult film *The Princess Bride*. In this fictional scene, a delightful character calls out a despicable character for repeatedly misusing the word *inconceivable*. Any fan of this beloved romantic comedy can likely quote the passage verbatim: "You keep using that word. I do not think it means what you think it means." Wilson and Golonka's joke works by insinuating a replacement of *inconceivable* with *affordance* in the present context. This may be a thematically appropriate and lighthearted way to begin what amounts to a corrective of a singular, specified research project. But let's look more closely at the rhetorical functioning of Wilson and Golonka's repurposing of this literary text.

I cannot determine if the bloggers are being ironic or if they have just missed the fact that they begin their critique of a supposedly erroneous study of image-based affordances by making an image-based affordance of their own (albeit of a different kind). Of course, Wilson and Golonka would not grant that what I am calling an affordance is indeed an affordance, but putting aside nomenclature, they could not rightly deny that they do *use* a literary text to achieve situational effects that emerge in a partly bodily way (e.g., laughter, feelings of levity), which is to say, through direct experience.[5] This is not just a funny way to begin their post, then; it is also a rhetorically savvy appropriation of a fictional text. That's because any reader familiar enough with the film to get the joke should also be able to transfer (consciously or not) to the context of Wilson and Golonka's critique the effect the quotation has in its original cinematic context: an acknowledgment of the awkwardness of correcting a peer's error. Readers of the blog who are not familiar with *Princess Bride* do not experience the affordance. Now we could debate whether the rhetorical function Wilson and Golonka derive from their cinematic reference inheres in the film itself or does not exist until the bloggers bring it to the film or is an effect that emerges among the relations of the filmic environment, the bloggers, and their rhetorical audience. We could also pinpoint specific textual features and calculate degrees of audience awareness (i.e., abilities) that are required for establishing functional perception of the literary affordance. But I don't think these steps are necessary for my point to come through, which is: whatever one calls the act, it's hard to deny that Wilson and Golonka have made rhetorical use of observable features of a literary text in relation to a situation that does not involve interpretation of that text. I call that literary affordance.

I have managed to find some research that gives me hope I am not entirely out on a limb in appropriating affordance theory for abstract application. Greeno (1994, 336), an educational psychologist, examines verbal conversation in drawing connections between situation theory and affordances, the latter of which he says establish "conditions in the environment for constraints to which the agent is attuned." This notion of attunement to linguistic contexts seems promising to me, but Greeno's empirical, quantitative research agenda ultimately bears no resemblance to my theoretical speculations. In a very different context, Phil Turner (2005, 798) connects affordance theory to Heidegger and offers what seems to me a promising conclusion: "For Heidegger, equipment is context . . . A thing is identified by its use—that is, we identify it through its affordances or significances—so as equipment is context, affordance and context must be synonyms." This idea seems apt because I can imagine a reader approaching a literary text as a tool that has significance (or not) in relation to a given rhetorical context. But Turner goes on to seek applications of this notion to interactive computer systems, which is a tangent I cannot pursue. Even Gibson (1979, 137), in passing, seems to leave open the possibility for abstract applications of his theory: "When vocalization becomes speech and manufactured displays become images, pictures, and writing, the affordances of human behavior are staggering" because, after all, "speech, pictures, and writing still have to be perceived." But Gibson says nothing more here about *how* spoken, pictorial, and written texts are perceived. I will argue that such experience is both direct (i.e., perceptual, experiential) and indirect (i.e., conceptual, referential) and that understanding this double nature is key to unlocking the value of literary affordances.[6]

Perhaps this double nature is a reason why experimental psychologists tend to avoid what I have been calling *abstract* affordances. It's much easier to study percepts than concepts with validity and reliability, and the sciences live and die by these measures.[7] But Noble (1981) sees a challenge here for affordance theory.[8] To illustrate his point, he returns to "the muddle of the mailbox" (see above, this chapter), introducing a new variable to the hypothetical. If postal workers were to go on strike unbeknownst to a would-be letter mailer, then the functional affordance of the mailbox would dissolve, even though its perceptual affordance would remain intact for this person. So to correctly perceive this affordance (and others like it), there appears to be a prerequisite that entails a cooperative linguistic community conveying the necessary information. Noble (1981, 73) notes that Gibson and others ignore or dismiss this sociolinguistic dimension,[9] which requires that "we leave the realm of the purely biological-behavioral and enter the world of cultural rules and roles" in which "the relationship between persons and objects is now complexly mediated by a normative structure that is not connected with the visible affordances of objects per se." In other words, "To 'correctly' perceive the mailbox's affordance is to assent to a set of social rules about uses and abuses of a mailbox. We are doing more, when we map into the meanings of social objects, than successfully identifying their affordances; we are *going along with* culturally sanctioned ways of perceiving such objects" (Noble 1981, 73, original emphasis). It is only a short distance from here to related issues of power, erasure, and agency, and Noble makes this humanistic leap with deftness and vividness:

> If I, as an urban guerilla, perceive the mailbox as a symbol of the power of an oppressive bureaucracy that sanctions my ways of making contact with the world (prohibiting the use of the mailbox as a receptacle for a bomb—and even certain kinds of literature), then I am in no wise assenting to its meaning for the culture, and hence the "correct" perception of it as a cultural object. The perception of all socially (linguistically)-sustained objects has this normative character. In perceiving a (culturally-valued) thing as an 'X' I automatically exclude perceptions of it as a 'Y' or a 'Z.' (Noble 1981, 73)

My theory of literary affordance seeks to honor and make way for (make off with?) Y and Z readings, which is not to dishonor or block X readings. I invite readers to approach texts, if they wish, as Noble's urban guerrilla perceives the mailbox or, more accurately in many cases, to acknowledge that they have already approached texts as such. The point is not to go out of your way to invent literary affordances (though there's no harm in doing so) but to become aware of them if/when/as they emerge in your relational transactions with texts, to accept and to act on them, and to keep your eyes open for them with an evolving understanding of how they can work. Literary affordances may or may not occur often for you, and their significance may vary by occasion or by your or another's estimation. Actively welcoming them might increase their frequency and significance, and closing yourself off to them might stunt or prevent their emergence. It might also require on your part considerable determination and practice to maintain your resolve when the rest of the culture sees an ordinary mailbox and you see opportunity for guerrilla action. I hope to be of service, then, in making some progress toward naming, understanding, and promoting literary affordance. But there is much more work to be done in the area. Two related questions must be taken up before turning explicitly to *literary* affordances: are affordances made or found, and are affordances percepts or concepts?

Are Affordances Made or Found?

Chemero and the other "relational" theorists mentioned above help us answer this question with relative ease: affordances are neither made nor found; they emerge. Or perhaps it's not so easy as that because depending on how you look at it, affordances may actually be thought of as somewhat both made and found. This complication stems from the matter of how technical one wants to be with one's language. Readers of my book can find many instances in which I casually refer to *making* affordances from a literary text or *finding* them through acts of reading and writing. If I wanted to be more technical in these cases, I should say (as I sometimes do) that affordances have *emerged*, as in: *affordances emerged from relations among the reader's perceptual and conceptual abilities and certain features of a literary text, relative to rhetorical situations in her environment.* But a theory that seeks to be practiced widely, including by nonspecialists, should keep this kind of language to a minimum. So I am content to say in most circumstances simply that affordances are made or found. Besides, as far as abstract concepts go, there is no escaping metaphorical language, so settling for *make* and *find* seems reasonable so long as there is accompanying awareness of the figurative status of these terms. Take the previous sentence, for example, which speaks of going, escaping, and settling where no going, escaping, or settling is *literally* happening. And the sentence now just prior to this one (and for that matter, this one as well) speaks of speaking where no *actual* speech is happening.

If users of the phrase (and tactic) *literary affordance* possess awareness of the kind of metaphor theory glossed just above and elaborated in chapter 3, then I think the casual usage of *make* and *find* should suffice where technical language would be distracting. What I mean by "awareness" is remembering to transcend the false dualism inherent to the concepts of making or finding. Or, inversely, *awareness* here can be thought of as remembering the holism inherent to the concept of emergence. In the introduction to their collection *Doing Things with*

Things, Alan Costall and Ole Dreier offer a clear explanation of what this means, but in reference to everyday things (which I see no need to distinguish from *texts* for present purposes). Costall and Dreier (2012, 11) encourage readers to think of *things* "not as fixed and independent of human beings, but as themselves transformed, even coming into being, within ongoing human practices, and which, in turn, transform those practices." From such a holistic standpoint, things or texts are not *out there* and we *in here*; rather, they and we (among other things) are co-constituent of the same lived environment and the same rhetorical functions that emerge uniquely from each relation within it. Gibson (1979, 8) offers several helpful explanations of this point of view: "The words *animal* and *environment* make an inseparable pair. Each term implies the other. No animal could exist without an environment surrounding it. Equally, an environment implies an animal (or at least an organism) to be surrounded." And later: "There has been endless debate among philosophers and psychologists as to whether values are physical or phenomenal, in the world of matter or only in the world of mind. For affordances as distinguished from values, the debate does not apply. Affordances are neither in the one world or the other inasmuch as the theory of two worlds is rejected. There is only one environment, although it contains many observers with limitless opportunities for them to live in it" (Gibson 1979, 138).

Any student of literature, or even someone who has recently discussed a movie, say, with other people, already knows that multiple simultaneous and valid interpretations of a common text are possible, perhaps even likely. The same phenomenon is true, and probably to a greater degree, when it comes to affordances. Affordances, or for now we can just say *uses* of texts, will emerge for readers relative to the situations in which they think, feel, and communicate; and those situations and corresponding points of view are never the same for any two or more people, even those involved in the same transaction. Noble introduces the helpful phrase "discursive ecology" to account for the interactive user-contingency of things and phenomena. These objects and events, *as* objects and events, occupy our attention necessarily because we *use* or *engage* in them:

> Saying that objects and events are held in discursive ecologies means that none of these things exists by itself. For artefacts (or their equivalent, arranged events) this is obvious, because such things are produced/performed by people for purposes, and human purposes arise via discursive practices. Therefore, artefacts and arranged events are further expressions of discursive practices. They cannot possibly exist outside of such

> practices. But even naturally occurring objects and events do not exist alone. They attract attention, they are used, named, and roped into courses of action. People get emotional about them in various ways and from time to time (consider the sacred rites of any community, or the annual flooding of the Nile). The natural landscape is also held, therefore, within the discursive practices of people. (Noble 1993, 388)

Why does the made/found/emergent issue matter? One reason is that your opinion on this may affect the conditions (or even the existence) of your discursive ecologies and the utility affordances may carry for you in them, as the following hypotheses propose. If you believe that affordances can only fall into your lap, then you may experience them less actively, less expansively, and less frequently than otherwise. On the contrary, if you believe affordances can be made of just anything at any time, then you may experience them less personally, less persuasively, and less deeply than otherwise. However, if you believe affordances are emergent from relations among your abilities and an object's or a text's features, then you may be more likely to experience them as acts of your own agency in a socially constructed context. Another reason why this issue matters is because powerful forces exist that want to and often do control your relationships to objects and texts (and related discourse), and you may wish to know where and how to derive tactics such as affordance making for negotiating these forces. In chapter 5 I critique a notable example of such a powerful controlling force—high-stakes writing tests—and I employ a literary affordance to help make my case.

Are Affordances Percepts or Concepts?

Similar to the question of made/found is the percept/concept question, and on this subject I similarly call for transcending the either/or formulation. To be reductive, percepts can be thought of as direct sensory apprehensions of stimuli. Concepts can be thought of as indirect cognitive processing of that energy through mental categories and the often-linguistic products thereof. It may be easier to think of these functions simply as perceiving, marked by directness or immediacy, and conceiving, marked by indirection or representation. I hope it would not be controversial to assume that literature engages both of these functions in readers. After all, we certainly experience literary texts on sensory levels, which accounts for much of their potential to move us, and innumerable cognitive processes bring order and meaning to these sensations and related discourse. However, even in such an inclusive formulation, a faulty dualism still lingers in intimations of linear sequencing (i.e., first one feels, then thinking takes over), which may belie a more accurate account of human cognitive experience in which feeling is not subsumed by thought and the two forces are variously coexistent or co-influential. The most recent supporting scholarship cited below in this section contends that cognition is simulational and necessarily embodied.

Let's begin with views on affordance and perception held by Gibson and some of his respondents. At the heart of Gibson's ecological innovation is his contention that an experience's potential for action is perceived directly, a view that counters the dominant cognitive model, which requires mental processing or representation for such understanding to occur (Chemero 2003; Heft 2001). In Gibson's (1979, 134) own words, "You do not have to classify and label things in order to perceive what they afford." Noble (1993, 391, original emphasis) helps explain this idea using the hypothetical context of rock throwing: "I do not go through the business of seeing a rock and then *interpreting* it as a throwable object. I see its detachability, its graspableness and thus its throwableness all at once, Gibson-style. And presumably I see those properties as a function of the context for action: the need to throw a missile—say at a marauding band." Heft (2001, 130) clearly agrees: "Affordances are percepts rather than concepts"; they are "part of the ongoing flow of immediate experience specified by perceptual information," as distinguished from concepts, which are abstractions based on that flow. Stoffregen and Bruno Mantel (2015, 257) say they "understand perception as being active; it is something that people do, rather than something that happens to them." William W. Gaver provides a clear overview of the competing cognitive and ecological views in the backdrop of these testimonies:

> The cognitive approach suggests that people have direct access only to sensations, which are integrated with memories to build up symbolic representations of the environment and its potential for goal-oriented action . . . In focusing on perception, action, memory and problem-solving "in the head," its descriptions of action in the world, tool-use, perceptually-guided learning, etc., often seem baroque and overly complicated. In contrast, the ecological approach stresses relevant human-scaled objects, attributes and events and the patterns of energy that provide effective perceptual information about them. It eschews detailed accounts of information processing as being unnecessary products of the abnormal situations found in laboratories . . . In this account, affordances are the fundamental objects of perception. People perceive the environment directly in terms of its potentials for action. (Gaver 1991, 79)

Chemero (2013) traces these philosophical and psychological histories, respectively, to the atomistic, structuralist, Cartesian method of

Wilhelm Wundt (emphasizing cognition) and the holistic, functionalist, Darwinian approach of William James (emphasizing embodiment). Interestingly, Chemero proposes a recent convergence of these competing lineages in embodied cognitive science.[10] Benjamin K. Bergen is a cognitive scientist who also tells the histories of these competing schools of thought in the context of his work on embodiment in human understanding of language. He says the first camp supports the "language of thought hypothesis," which maintains that we understand language because we have definitions for words in our minds (these are the mental categories for representation mentioned above). Bergen points out a number of problems with this theory and then introduces an alternative view that has been gradually developing since the 1970s. This camp supports the "embodied simulation hypothesis," which speculates that "we understand language by simulating in our minds what it would be like to experience the things that the language describes" (Bergen 2012, 13). According to this hypothesis, "Meaning . . . isn't just abstract mental symbols; it's a creative process, in which people construct virtual experiences—embodied simulations—in their mind's eye" (Bergen 2012, 16). In this scheme, both conscious and unconscious thought draws on the brain's wiring for perception and action, such that imagining your parents' faces, for example, activates your brain's visual systems, imagining a familiar song activates your brain's aural systems, and the same for the other senses, as well as for thinking of movement and activating the brain's motor systems (Bergen 2012, 14–16). "The idea is that you make meaning by creating experiences for yourself," says Bergen (2012, 16), noting that if this is true, "then meaning is something totally different from the definitional model we started with. If meaning is based on experience with the world—the specific actions and percepts an individual has had—then it may vary from individual to individual and from culture to culture. And meaning will also be deeply personal . . . Moreover, if we use our brain systems for perception and action to understand, then the processes of meaning are dynamic and constructive. It's not about activating the right symbol; it's about dynamically constructing the right mental experience of the scene."[11] So instead of arguing that affordances are either perceptual or conceptual or even that they are both, one might just prefer to think of them as direct, experiential, and situational, in which case they are also personal, creative, and action-oriented.

Why does this matter in the context of reading and producing texts? Because there may be at least as much of a reason to investigate a literary text's role in the discursive and rhetorical ecology of one's life contexts—that is, the text's "potentials for action"—as to investigate the meaning supposedly held by that text or its author or what literature specialists have determined about it through analysis and classification. This is not, however, to denigrate those acts of literature specialists. Although I share Susan Sontag's (1966) and Jane P. Tompkins's (1980, 201–32) objections to the current dominance held by interpretation of texts' meanings, I am ultimately not "against interpretation," as Sontag puts it; rather, I only wish to supplement or provide an occasional alternative to that practice. Sontag (1966, 14) would denounce my approach as a violation because, like interpretation in her view, literary affordance "makes art into an article for use," but I see my approach, instead, as just a different kind of "erotics of art" for which she advocates. Whereas Sontag calls for the audience's presence to the text itself (1966, 13) in order to "serve the work of art" (1966, 12), I call for the same kind of presence, but in service of one's place in a given rhetorical situation that warrants it. I would qualify Tompkins's (1980, 226) insistence that this situation be political in nature by stating that it may, but need not necessarily, be political.

The state of direct (one might say intimate) perception inherent to literary affordances establishes a reader's tacit, immersed, and holistic relationship with a text, from and through which to attend to his or her (rhetorical) environment—a state scientist-turned-philosopher Michael Polanyi (1966b) refers to as *indwelling.* The fact that this experience is, to some degree, unmediated endows literary affordances with an embodied or even a somewhat erotic quality that enables a text's metaphorical function to occur as a natural aspect of a reader's being in the world. As Rosenblatt (1994, 94) explains of the tacit nature of this function, with reference to Robert Burns's famous comparison of his beloved to a red, red rose, "If the reader stops to consider in what logical ways a woman might be 'like' a rose, the metaphor has vanished." I don't disagree with Rosenblatt's point, but I will qualify it by noting the great potential value to be derived from engaging in figurative holistic dialogue with the metaphors that seem to carry the most energy for us as individual readers.

We shall see in chapter 3 how conceptual metaphors permeate people's sense of reality transparently (i.e., unnoticed). One of the ways conceptual metaphors work is by helping us understand complex things in terms of simpler things, including especially by putting abstract concepts in terms of direct bodily experiences (certainly including, but perhaps not limited to, simulation). So I propose that although they may be complex in other ways, features of literary texts (i.e., literary affordances) that readers assimilate through embodied perception may have qualities of this tacit metaphorical simplicity, which perhaps ironically also opens up opportunities for significant dialogue with and through them. If so, then this phenomenon can significantly shape readers' lived experiences—whether small or large, singular or repeated, controllable or uncontrollable, and so forth—including their understanding of and engagement with complex ideas.

INTERCHAPTER 2
When Shall I Marry Me?

For over twenty years I have been carrying around a misreading of a line from Sir Walter Scott's poem "Proud Maisie" because of its usefulness to me. Though I may have gotten the conventional meaning of the poem wrong, there is no denying that my misreading has still had value for me over this time. Furthermore, the occasions in my life on which I could use this value (dozens at least) greatly outnumber the occasions on which I was expected to posit a correct interpretation of the poem (exactly one). Yet until now, I have never confessed to anyone my continued misappropriation of this work—such is the power that conventions assert on one's approach to literature. I mention this all now in hope of playing a counteractive influence. A wrong reading can still be a useful one, and as long as it is not presented as a correct reading, then I believe it can continue to serve its uses.

The setting for my misreading was a literature course I took as an undergraduate at Fordham University, in which I was tasked to analyze a Romantic poem of my choosing. For reasons I could not identify at the time, I selected Scott's "Proud Maisie," a simple lyric of four quatrains about a (probably young) woman walking in the woods. After an initial stanza of narrative framing, the rest of the poem consists of a dialogue—two questions and two answers—between Maisie and a songbird. Maisie wants to know when she will marry, and the bird answers that it will happen when she dies. My misreading applies to Maisie's inquiry: "Tell me, thou bonny bird, / When shall I marry me?" As an undergraduate I was able to recognize the archaic reflexive usage of "marry me" as meaning *marry myself,* but I missed (or ignored) the literal meaning, as in *get married* (i.e., to someone else). Rather, I (mis)took the phrase to mean a state of self-integration, as in *when will I get married to myself* or *achieve a state of personal union* or *be at peace with the conflicting aspects of myself.*

Coincidentally, I happened to be visiting home (which was not far from Fordham) while I was preparing to write my paper about Scott's poem. In keeping with a fond tradition of discussing school projects

DOI: 10.7330/9781607327769.c002b

(especially in English) with both my parents, who are each great readers, I happened to mention my interpretation of the "marry me" phrase to my father. He pointed out, graciously as ever, the conventional reading of this passage, as in *to get married to another person.* I am still unsure if I had previously missed that meaning or if I knew but ignored it in favor of my alternative reading. Either way, after my father's gentle corrective, I did conventionalize my take on the poem for my English paper. But my prior misreading never went away; in fact, I have only continued to poke at it, as one does with a scab.

Why would I have substituted the idea of self-integration for the obvious meaning of matrimony to another person? Why would I have continued to entertain this misreading even after being corrected on it?[1] To the first question, if marriage equates with integration and Maisie seeks to marry herself (*herself* as a direct object here, not a reflexive marker), then she would be seeking self-integration by marrying one aspect of herself to another aspect. That would have been an appealing prospect to younger, nonintegrated me whose parents' separation, unlike my own being, I had no control over. To the second question, as a person who grew up associating marriage with *disintegration* (a word which, by the way, insinuates decomposition and loss of identity after death, as in Maisie's case), I simply found more payoff in my misreading of the poem than in its correct interpretation. The poem does something valuable for me this way (i.e., affordance) that the other way (interpretation) simply does not do.

So there I was visiting home from college, seeking in vain (mostly unconsciously) to integrate the emotional halves of me that split when my parents divorced, similarly to how Maisie—in my mistaken but not illogical reading—seeks self-integration in vain. Both she (if the poem's bird's prediction is right) and I had no choice but to face disintegration instead. My gradual realization of this parallel over the course of the past twenty-plus years has shaped an approach to life that is central to the core of my being, whereby acceptance of indeterminacy now spares me from the threat it could pose nearly everywhere. With awareness and acceptance of the fact that all social experience is infused with separateness (note: even intimacy is nearness, not sameness), I have become better able to cope with difference and distance and to try to help others do the same through communication. In this way, my misreading of Maisie's question serves me as an apt marker of these realizations and a tool with which I can go to work every day at trying to improve relations among people despite (or because of) their inevitable mutual separateness.

3
LITERARY AFFORDANCE

Readers are like nomads poaching their way across fields they did not write, despoiling the wealth of Egypt to enjoy it themselves.
—Michel de Certeau, *The Practice of Everyday Life*

In this chapter I work through a theory of literary affordances, that is to say, a theory of rhetorical responses through literary texts that are incidental to the meanings of these texts. Along the way, I make reference to other theories from a variety of disciplines, which is one of the ways I might unintentionally create some trouble with this book. That's because not only do I neglect any number of ideas and individuals that might well belong here (some knowingly for the sake of space and ease, such as speech act theory, Derrida, or Sedgwick [2003, 123–51], and doubtless many others unknowingly), but I may also fail to provide (accurate) enough context or justification to some people's taste for the ones included in my excerpts and explanations of each inevitably prolific corpus. Furthermore, I put this material to uses and into combinations that may seem awkward or worse to some readers. One reason is that there is simply too much ground to cover; another is that I do not consider my theory to belong to any particular scholarly tradition such that I can be singular and exhaustive in scope. I also wish to present my ideas as organically as possible to their own nomadic origins and purposes. The fact is, I generated my theory of literary affordances primarily by reflecting on my own experiences and later by observing those of my students and mostly only thereafter by wandering (and wondering) about scholarly references that began to appear like constellations as I moved along. This nomad metaphor merits further consideration.

Nomadism is the species' oldest method of fulfilling its need for nourishment; it is distinguished by its migratory character from the stationary alternatives of agriculture and manufacturing, which have their own, different benefits. Nomads relocate with shifting resources, and in the

DOI: 10.7330/9781607327769.c003

distant past these kinds of travelers were known to have navigated by the stars. For such people, reading constellations was a means to an end, an act that seems to me more about applied use value than abstract meaning, though, of course, these same stars were imbued with meanings in other contexts. But in the context of navigation, constellations served as texts in relation to which nomads moved along on paths otherwise unrelated to the stars themselves. The approach to reading and composing I am considering in this book works somewhat similarly, whereby a reader may experience and appropriate literary features that are useful to some rhetorical purpose of theirs, consciously or not and regardless of other related discussions, say, of the meaning of the source material. Furthermore, in thinking about literary affordance I am more interested in getting this theoretical approach to "move along"—relative to some textual constellations aligned in certain ways from my viewpoint—than in establishing any fixed tradition in the name of this theory. I am not setting up a market, let alone trying to corner it, but rather seeking out conceptual nourishment where I can find it. I am also inviting others to share in the navigating and in the findings.

As I say in the preface, my experiences that have coalesced into the working theory presented here have occurred while pursuing a better understanding of an intuition of mine. We shall see how this pursuit has taken me across and askew of any number of fields and periods in a trajectory that has accumulated something of its own cohesiveness without concern (but not without respect) for traditional disciplinary boundaries and agendas. This all goes to say that my thinking here does not emerge from any singular tradition; instead, it draws on various areas in literature, psychology, philosophy, and more. I admit that I was not *taught* most of the theories that I use here, which means, on the one hand, that I was not trained by any systematic process to work with them in particular ways (including *correct* ones) and, on the other hand, that I have not been sanctioned to work with them in any way at all. The truth is, I belong to none of the disciplines on which I am poaching to build my theory, and the result (or even this fact alone) might draw ire from some of the supposed proprietors of these territories. I could write volumes in probably futile preemptive defense of my nomadic appropriations, but instead I will only try to assure readers that in my figurative poaching, no riches have literally been despoiled, no claims to dominion have been made, and no offense has been meant. I am merely passing through and sketching in my travelogue with abstract, not representative, strokes.[1] I am also inviting others to take up such explorations on their own trajectories and to document[2] them in their own ways.

To belabor this migratory metaphor a bit further, let me pause at an important wellspring. It takes the form of a quandary that has occupied many a mind: the question of whether objects are encountered (directly experienced) or created (represented) by perception or, more specific to the present case, if a text has a meaning of its own (whether author-inscribed or in and of itself) or if readers alone impute meaning in marks on pages that do not become *texts* per se until activated as such by the reader's agency. This is a fascinating place to explore, and I will return to it occasionally but again, only in passing through on my way to other destinations. That is because even if I could resolve this phenomenological quandary, which I cannot, it would not make a difference in what I wish to do: to explore possible ways to make *uses* of literary texts, not to debate their interpretive *meaning*. In other words, it matters far less to me whether a text is encountered externally or created internally (or neither of these, which I will soon show is what I believe) than how and why a reader *uses* that text. I am calling this productive (i.e., not passive) reading activity the making of literary affordance or just *affordance*. In chapter 2 I introduced this concept generally; now I take it up in terms of literary texts.

I would like to offer a preliminary example of literary affordance, but first a few words about my examples in general. Although numerous examples appear throughout the book, I am deliberately not presenting a classification of literary affordances, at least not a very thorough one. I can imagine such a thing being expected of a book like this—introduce a new(ish) concept, classify its types, offer examples of each, provide instructions for following suit, and so forth—but there are a few reasons why I resist doing this. For starters, literary affordance seems to be such a variable act that I'm not sure I can pin down all of its permutations. Later, I do employ some terminology to help with understanding literary affordances (e.g., *apparent/subtle*, *intentional/unintentional*), and I occasionally apply provisional rhetorical labels to some examples (e.g., *heuristic*, *framing*, *adaptive*).

But beyond this, my heart is just not in it for a formal classification. That's partly because I worry that classifying literary affordances could have a controlling influence on those who wish to take up the act, and control is the opposite of what I hope to achieve by drawing attention to it (see also footnote fourteen, below, in this chapter). I greatly prefer to invite organic applications and new adaptations of literary affordance than to potentially constrain the act with categories that may limit perception of what is possible.[3] That goes as much for teaching this approach to texts as it does for actually approaching texts.

Furthermore, if the teaching of literary affordance gains traction, then I would like to try to forestall any attempts to develop rigid evaluative standards corresponding to affordance types. I can already imagine the life being sucked out of the act through some would-be universal scoring mechanism: "You scored a 75 on your heuristic affordance." Whereas I generally believe in the benefits of *assessment* through reflection on what has been done, projection of what wants doing, and determination of what, if any, adjustments need making in the interim, I am dubious of the effects of *evaluation* on the basis of fixed standards. Systematically rewarding and punishing individuals through evaluation seems often to narrow expectations, normalize behavior, and suppress such values as engagement, risk taking, and pleasure, which are crucial for better learning and living through texts. All this being said, I do recommend Joseph Harris's (2006b, 34–53) handy classification of textual "forwarding" strategies: *illustrating, authorizing, borrowing,* and *extending*—all, some, or none of or more/other than which may describe any given literary affordance (also see later in this section as well as the section "How Does Literary Affordance Differ from Analogy and Adaptation?" later in this chapter).

As we consider the following example, let's keep in mind a working definition of literary affordance as uses readers make of features of literary texts through rhetorical application of them to unrelated situations. This is what Kristie S. Fleckenstein does, effectively in my view, with Lewis Carroll's image of the bread-and-butter-fly in her 2005 *JAC* article about ethos in the cybernetic era. Before I explain the concept of cybernetic ethics, let me take the opportunity while its meaning may be uncertain to point out *why* (I think) Fleckenstein makes a literary affordance: to make this extremely complicated subject more intelligible and moving and thereby to make her argument about it more convincing. It would be difficult to convince critical thinkers of an argument they do not understand or care about, and probably very few readers (even of the heady journal *JAC*) have an abiding command of what is meant by the neologism *cyberethos.* Literary affordance also makes Fleckenstein's case far more memorable. After all, there is little sense in making an argument that nobody recalls or wants to recall, no matter how convincing it may be. As we shall be able to see later in this chapter, Fleckenstein's literary affordance is a classic example of a conceptual metaphor, whereby an easier to understand idea stands in for a more complex one to improve comprehension, retention, and so on.

Cybernetics is the present condition of many humans in which both abstract and biological experiences are pervasively mediated by technology. Traditional boundaries of identity that we have taken for granted are now blurred or erased by our coexistence with machines and mechanized systems. On the abstract side, Fleckenstein gives the example of interactive hypertext literary formats that allow readers to modify, and therefore become (co-)writers of, the very content they are "reading." Breaking down the boundary between reader and writer creates what she and others call the "wreader" (Fleckenstein 2005, 324). These two previously separate identities dissolve into each other, creating a uniquely mutual and mutable subjectivity. On the biological side, Fleckenstein offers the example of her mother's illness–prompted reliance on an oxygen tank, which, as a requirement for survival, became an inherent aspect of her subjectivity. Here again, boundaries such as those between self and technology and interior and exterior are dissolved. Ethos is an accumulation of associations, wherein the quality of an individual's actions is taken to comprise and reflect that individual's character, which has formative implications on future states of her actions and character, in part through the effect of other people's perceptions of these qualities in that individual. In other words, ethos is an aspect of your character, or just *is* your character, that comprises your actions (including linguistic ones) and how others respond to them.

The related complication Fleckenstein identifies is the question of how to determine good character now that the boundaries of subjectivity are rendered so permeable and unstable by our cybernetic existence. Her answer is cyberethos, which I take to be a kind of continually updating awareness of one's character as dispersed across ever-changing temporal and spatial relations. She describes it as "a means to unite ourselves in an ecology of good character, reconfirming/recreating our identity and connectedness within the larger systems that offer us life, and assuming responsibility for that identity and that life" (Fleckenstein 2005, 342). Fleckenstein's case is as brilliant as it is difficult to understand (i.e., very). Luckily, she seems to be aware of this difficulty and offers a literary affordance to help her readers follow along. Cyberethos, she suggests, can be better understood and remembered by thinking of it in terms of the bread-and-butter-fly from Lewis Carroll's *Through the Looking-Glass.* You don't need to have read this sequel to *Alice's Adventures in Wonderland* to picture the image. Imagine a butterfly made of thin buttered bread slices for wings, a crust of bread for a body, and a sugar cube for a head. This butterfly lives on (i.e., feeds on) weak tea with cream in it. The irony here is that to get its sustenance (multiple meanings here), the butterfly dissolves into the very tea it is consuming. Fleckenstein sees this as "an apt metaphor for this cybernetic age." She explains: "When eating to sustain its life, a bread-and-butter-fly dips its sugar cube head into weak tea and cream only to dissolve and become part of that which it eats. To survive, it blurs its own boundaries, which means that its identity as a bread-and-butter-fly disintegrates. We, too, are bread-and-butter-flies; we live as and amid boundaries that materialize, shift, and disappear, only to rematerialize in new forms" (Fleckenstein 2005, 323).

Note that Fleckenstein's article is not *about* Carroll's novel, the Alice stories, or even literature at all. She is addressing challenges posed to traditional notions of ethos by the shifting and permeable boundaries of subjectivity in today's cybernetic age. Her affordance of a literary text (we can call it the *source text*) serves rhetorical purposes that are unrelated to that source text's meaning. Yet Fleckenstein's choice is hardly random. We have already seen why and how the image she makes an affordance of improves comprehension and retention of her complicated theory. But beyond (or, better, constitutive of but transcending) that improvement, her literary affordance provides readers with an experience of her concept that is appropriately embodied. Thanks to Fleckenstein's affordance, her readers can cognitively simulate (i.e., have a *felt sense* of, not just conceptualize) their own dissolution into a body of liquid as they read of the bread-and-butter-fly consuming and being consumed by tea. For this reason I think, Fleckenstein not only evokes the image for an introductory explanation but also frames the entirety of her article within these terms, drawing on bread-and-butter-fly imagery to shape each of her section headings, which are the building blocks of her logic. To return to Michael Polanyi's concept of indwelling, which appears in chapter 1 and later in this chapter, we can say that Fleckenstein is *attending from* her subject *within* this conceptual-experiential framework. She is not merely looking *at* and pointing *to* a text that exists somewhere outside of her reasoning; she is indwelling that text (i.e., has assimilated it). Carroll's bread-and-butter-fly inhabits Fleckenstein's thinking about cyberethos and vice versa, and her readers experience something of the same by virtue of her affordance. For readers desiring such descriptive terms, Fleckenstein's acts of literary affordance might be called *naming* and *framing*.

A last point on this example is needed to distinguish literary affordance from illustration. We have (speculatively) understood why Fleckenstein uses the image she uses, but why this particular image *from this particular source text?* Fleckenstein could easily have just described a sugar cube dissolving into tea to achieve a clarifying and memorable metaphor for her complex subject. I can think of a number of possible reasons, all, some, or none of which may in fact be the case, and it's possible that an author would not consciously know the answer either, or at least not wholly. Maybe Carroll's novel carries special significance for Fleckenstein, in which case she might be more apt to write about it with particular ease, confidence, and force. Maybe she wants to use a text that is famous for blurring lines between reality and fantasy to match her goal of de-territorializing readers' stable sense of reality. Maybe the inevitable disintegration of the insignificant fictional bread-and-butterfly allows Fleckenstein a low-stakes means of insinuating the high-stakes matter of the dissolution of human subjectivity as we once knew it. Maybe Fleckenstein wishes to entangle her subjectivity somewhat with Carroll's, which could be effective both because he is an author of considerable stature (not that she isn't, of course) and because doing so only further demonstrates her case about the permeability of ethos boundaries. After all, Fleckenstein is, in a small but not insignificant way, rewriting (i.e., *wreading*) Carroll. Maybe she wants to reveal the unexpected depths of consequences of her theory to be found in unlikely places, as she says: "The dilemma of the bread-and-butter-fly is not just an episode in an amusing children's story; blurred boundaries are not merely interesting bits of intellectual play. They are not limited to our interactions with digital or analog technologies. Instead, the reality of the bread-and-butter-fly is life and death, fact and fiction, truth and lie" (Fleckenstein 2005, 325).

Harris offers a similar example to this one in the case of a scholarly book chapter by Robert Pattison that is structured around three fictional figures (Truffaut's wild boy of Aveyron, Gracie Allen's literalist radio skit character, and Homer's Agamemnon) who incidentally "stand for" corresponding levels of illiteracy. Such standing for, according to Harris, functions as "a way into a subject," or a way to "mark hinge points in a text." In the case at hand, these fictional stand-ins "serve as markers of [Pattison's] ideas, steps in his argument, ways of thinking about his subject" (Harris 2006b, 43–44). I wish to note Harris's acknowledgment of the rhetorical value of these stand-ins as comprising more than just examples; they also carry generative, structural, and epistemological significance. They are not something extra or external but rather (at least part of) the very ecology in which Pattison's argument comes into being or expression. Unfortunately, in my view, Harris's terminology somewhat obscures or belies this status by classifying the technique as the "illustrating" mode of textual "forwarding." Although Pattison's approach does illustrate and forward, it seems to me to do more than that, even by Harris's own account.

By now, a good deal of theory and a number of examples have been established to facilitate understanding of literary affordances. To sum up this idea again: one makes a literary affordance when one uses features of a literary text for application to an unrelated, non-literary context. You might think of this as a transitive act of reading beyond the text or, more simply, as a rhetorical performance. But keep in mind that this effect can be achieved unconsciously (unintentionally) as well as consciously (intentionally). I will say more about this below, but if some readers do not agree with me that an unconscious act can be rhetorical, then they can ignore that aspect of my theory; it is not essential, and there is plenty to consider regarding intentional affordances alone. With a literary affordance, one is responding rhetorically *through*—not *to*—a literary text. Or to put it another way, one is issuing a *rhetor's response.* Literary affordance is an act that can influence a rhetorical situation in the conventional sense (i.e., the dynamics of one's transactions in sign systems), as well as one's own perspective on that situation in the first place (in a given case alone or through one's worldview or somewhere in between). To return to the example from my book's introduction, Freud not only expressed his idea of the Oedipus complex in terms of features of Sophocles's play but also conceived the idea and perceived reality partly *through* these features, a process that seems to have originated in unconscious or at least pre-lingual operations for Freud. The same applies to my personal examples in this book and may apply to Fleckenstein and Carroll's bread-and-butter-fly, to Pattison's character references, and perhaps to you and features of whatever literary texts might strike you as generative or descriptive or persuasive and so on, in situations beyond your real-time reading of the text. My experiences suggest that once one becomes aware of literary affordances and their rhetorical power, one may be more likely to make/identify them from/in one's own literary reading and to find them in other people's nonfiction compositions.

Other scholars have done outstanding work on the rhetoricity of literary interpretation (e.g., Mailloux 1989, 1997, 1998; Jost 2004; Fahnestock and Secor 1991), on the rhetoricity of literature itself (too many to reference, but perhaps most notably Booth 1961), and on the limits and possibilities of interpretation (e.g., for a small selection, Eco 1990; Fetterley 1978; Hall 1980). The difference in the present case is that literary affordance is unconcerned with traditions or negotiations of textual reception or with authorial intention or even with textual meaning, which collectively comprise much of the gravitational pull that grounds interpretation. To put this differently, unlike rhetorical hermeneutics, rhetorical literary analysis, and other interpretive theories, a rhetor response approach to literary texts is not *about* those texts; its outcome does not pertain to the text or its reception but to the reader's lived experience in other contexts. A literary affordance is an act taken *through* or *in terms of* the text. It lays no claim to the correctness of any interpretive process or result, either local or general. It only is or is not useful, often as determined in relation to no more than a local (or even "just" a personal) situation and perhaps with conflicting simultaneous assessments (but that's no different than the state of many literary analyses). Some of these issues are taken up again in the following sections, where I answer a number of questions readers may be asking: what about the text's meaning? Why not just call affordance *use* or *appropriation*? Why literature? How does literary affordance differ from analogy and adaptation? Is this any different from reader-response criticism? Is this any different from ethical literary criticism? Can you really do that to a work of literature?

WHAT ABOUT THE TEXT'S MEANING?

I am tempted just to say "what *about* it?" But I'm not courageous enough to pull that kind of a Bartleby move. Herman Melville's character Bartleby happens to be a fairly common source of casual literary affordances. Whenever someone is in the company of readers and a curt refusal has been issued, one can say the refuser has "pulled a Bartleby," and the point may be taken and perhaps a few chuckles will be earned. For the same effect with parents of little children, Bartleby can be replaced with Ferdinand, the reluctant bull of eponymous fame.[4] This idiom of "pulling a . . ." means roughly to do something in the fashion of someone or something else, and it's workable shorthand for a casual kind of literary affordance. For another example, when I was a boy, *Dennis the Menace* was still a familiar cartoon in the newspaper comics section, and skateboarding was extremely popular. Dennis's curmudgeonly neighbor, Mr. Wilson, was known to periodically trip on Dennis's misplaced skateboard and take a hard fall. So when one of my childhood buddies or I took a similarly clumsy fall on our skateboards from a stationary position, it became known as "pulling a Mr. Wilson." These kinds of comparisons do not only point out similarities and thus ironically also create a wake of dissimilarities, as James E. Seitz (1999, 121–28) theorizes; they also establish or deepen relationships. In the example cases, friends exchange lighthearted teasing with the Mr. Wilson epithet, parents commiserate over binge reading with their kids by invoking Ferdinand, and readers share a little pride with each other over getting the Bartleby reference. Where cartoons, children's books, or casual literary jokes are concerned, the stakes tend to be low enough that these literary affordances hardly register, let alone offend anyone for their making. But I am aware that the considerable expansion of this tactic that I am proposing—to instructional practices and even to people's worldviews—is not likely to get so easy a pass from everyone. This chapter section acknowledges a primary area of potential dispute: interpretive meaning.

I can imagine that some readers may understandably be concerned (or worse) about the chance that my approach to literary texts invites and sanctions misinterpretation (or worse). But this is only a concern as far as interpretive *meaning* goes, and I have made it abundantly clear that literary affordances have to do with *uses* of texts, not their meanings. Teachers of this approach should take care to emphasize this point to their learners and their would-be critics. They should also call out affordances that might violate or offend *cultural* (i.e., as distinct from *interpretive*) meanings of texts and respond to any such instances accordingly. As I mentioned in this book's introduction while disclaiming that this is not a generalizable experience, I have so far encountered zero offensive literary affordances in the work of hundreds of university students to whom I have taught this approach. But it is of course feasible that they will occasionally occur. I would like to believe that such instances are opportunities for discussion—teachable moments, as they say—which arguably benefit from being directly sourced from (and therefore presumably motivated by) student's own lived experience. As for instances of literary affordance in non-educational settings, the discourse community that comprises the rhetorical audience can serve a similar role to that of the teacher in my example scenario just above.

Let me be clear: I am not going as far as to say literary texts don't have meanings; I am saying they don't *only* have meanings, and in some contexts it may be more fruitful to speak of their uses instead of (or in addition or in relation to) their meanings. Also, literary affordances may very well be or may lead to meaningful acts, but whatever meaning they create is not necessarily or even likely the same as the meaning of the source text as identified by popular interpretation. Furthermore, making affordances of texts does not harm those texts, though again, I concede that one could potentially do harm to others with affordances, as with anything else. No tool is impervious to misuse. But what could also do harm to some readers of literary texts is to insist on discussing only their meaning. Affordances offer another option. When Robert Scholes (2011, xiv) comments late in his career on the uncanniness of writing in the wake of his prior publications—because feedback on them affects his present-day composing—he cleverly likens the experience to that of Don Quixote during the self-reflexive part two of the eponymous book, which was written after part one had become a widely popular publication. Scholes's affordance of Quixote here is handy, even thought-provoking, but I wouldn't call it meaningful. He is just making rhetorical use of the literary text in a culturally appropriate way. There is no denying, however, that *Don Quixote* itself is a meaningful text, interpretively and culturally. As a reminder not to be absolute with such classifications, I offer a similar case that would be an exception. *Jane Eyre* is a meaningful literary text, of which Sandra Gilbert and Susan Gubar (1979) make an affordance in framing their theoretical book *The Madwoman in the Attic*. Because the latter work became a landmark publication in feminist criticism, Gilbert and Gubar's affordance of Brontë's novel might be said to have some meaning in itself (or at least through metonymy with their success).

To repeat what I stated in the introduction, I do not support affordances of texts that would be illegal, for example, in using them in such a way as to violate copyright—though I do direct readers to Lawrence Lessig's (2009) excellent book *Remix* for a valuable complication of this issue. I am not going to elaborate on this matter or on the potential for cruel or immoral uses of literary texts that some may worry I am making way for with my theory. I generally defer to free speech rights and restrictions on this issue, but the invitation of creative repurposing of fictional materials is not nearly the same as the sanctioning of violent, hateful, or other disagreeable kinds of appropriation of those materials. Also, as I have indicated previously in this chapter and will occasionally return to later, I believe the effectiveness or appropriateness of a given affordance is a relevant issue only with regard to the corresponding rhetorical situation, which above all indicates its reception by audiences. Let's now consider examples of what I have been saying so far: one in relation to objects and one in relation to a literary text, which, after all, is still an object, if not *only* so.

In theorizing about affordances (general, not literary, ones) in relation to meaning and utility, Noble offers helpful hypotheticals involving rocks and a screwdriver. "In the case of the thrown rock," he asks, "is the category of 'missile' the object's meaning? . . . it turns out to be more correct to say, 'This is one way the object can be used', rather than 'This is one thing the object means' " (Noble 1993, 391–92). Noble (1993, 392) elaborates: "An object which bears a certain title, say 'screwdriver', may be used for other purposes, say, to open tins of paint; even to stir their contents. We know as we do this that we are abusing the object . . . But perhaps we do not care; or we are going to do it carefully; or we are desperate." For an object used in such ways, says Noble (1993, 392–93, original emphases), "its *meaning*, say as 'missile' or 'screwdriver', is not, typically, the appropriate way to characterize it. Its *function* or *identification* under its title is more intelligible. 'Identity' is a term for classification that certainly involves meaning . . . Identifying something as X can be seen as an instruction on how it is to be used or understood. But identity is not, itself, meaning. It may turn out that the best characterization of material entities is that they *have no meanings whatsoever*, only that their uses (and abuses) might have meanings for users." Both rocks and screwdrivers can be used powerfully as constructive materials or as weapons, but they might also serve usefully as decorative items, artistic tools, or any number of other purposes that, if actualized, have no bearing on each original item's existential status. In other words, regardless of what purposes a specific rock or screwdriver has been put to, rocks and screwdrivers in general still maintain their other possible functions—even their *intended meaning*, if that must be acknowledged. I see no reason to dwell on the possibility of their appropriation as weapons when they have not been or do not appear to be especially likely to be used as such.

I believe the above points can also be applied to conceptual entities such as texts, and for support in making this transition I turn to philosopher Richard Rorty. He additionally uses an example of a screwdriver in rejecting the views that objects control what people can do with them and that imposition of a reader's subjectivity on texts is undesirable and avoidable: "To my ear, this is like saying that my use of a screwdriver to drive screws is 'coerced by the screwdriver itself' whereas my use of it to pry open cardboard packages is 'willful imposition by subjectivity'" (Rorty 1992, 103). Rorty (1992, 93–94) denies that there is any difference between "getting inside the text itself and relating the text to something else," for in his view "there is no such thing as an intrinsic, non-relational property." He argues that all descriptions (i.e., analyses, uses) of texts should be "evaluated according to their efficacy as instruments for purposes, rather than by their fidelity to the object described" because "interpreting something, knowing it, penetrating to its essence, and so on are all just various ways of describing some process of putting it to work" (Rorty 1992, 92–93).[5] The following passage from Rorty (1992, 105) could serve as a fine partial explanation of literary affordance: "Reading texts is a matter of reading them in the light of other texts, people, obsessions, bits of information, or what have you, and then seeing what happens." With this in mind, let's turn now to an example—and some framing discussion—of a useful literary affordance that makes no claims about the meaning of the original text, John Milton's 1637 poem "Lycidas."

Milton explicitly tells us in its short prologue what the intentions of his poem are: to elegize his recently drowned friend and to criticize corruption in the clergy of the day. Does this announcement from the poet establish the only true meaning of the text? Literary theorists of the intentionalist camp would obviously say yes. Others would object that the poem's meaning is to be found in the text alone or in one's interpretive community. Others would historicize the text to get at its meaning or apply to it one or a number of analytical lenses (e.g., race, class, gender, power, psychology, sexuality), with each camp denying the others' rights to the Truth about the text. I do not wish to enter this debate, but in stepping away from it, I think I can grant all these parties some legitimate claim to the truth about the text, though I doubt many of them would accept a non-exclusive allotment of lowercase "t" truth, let alone from someone with as little authority as I possess.[6] Nevertheless, I offer the following excerpt from William James toward that end: "Any idea that will carry us prosperously from any one part of experience to any other part, linking things satisfactorily, working securely, simplifying, saving labor; is true for just so much, true in so far forth, true *instrumentally*" (1910, 58, original emphasis, but I wish to emphasize that too). James's term *linking things satisfactorily* works fairly well to generally sum up *literary affordance*. Now here is Rorty in a similar vein, from his contribution to the debate following Steven Knapp and Walter Benn Michaels's (1982) well-known attack on the general viability of literary theory in "Against Theory." Rorty (1985, 461) asks seriously, "Why not just put [the text] in a context, describe the advantages of having done so, and forget the question of whether one has got at either its 'meaning' or 'the author's intention?' "[7]

In chapter 6 I will demonstrate again (but from an explicitly pedagogical angle) my version of what Rorty is recommending here, but it pays to have multiple examples of how making literary affordances sometimes entails only a relatively small shift in emphasis away from textual analysis. It would not be much of a stretch to interpret "Lycidas" as a poem *about* grieving. In fact, a quick database title-keyword search turns up at least four articles on this topic, including one which supports a hunch I have long held: that in this poem Milton is working through the well-known stages of grief (Bell 1975); after all, his good friend, who is the poem's subject, had recently drowned. But instead of writing an analysis of this poem's being *about* grief, which is a task few people other than some select English specialists wish to do, what if one could somehow *use* the poem effectively in relation to the subjects of grieving or suffering (just for example)? That would entail *using* features of the text that are, in James's terms, true or advantageous *instrumentally* in relation to one's abilities, needs, and lived context, not necessarily according to any interpretive theory.

Rorty distinguishes these approaches from each other as, respectively, unmethodical (i.e., *affordance* in my terms) and methodical reading (*interpretation*). Like Rorty, I wish to promote unmethodical reading, which is positively charged in his view despite the connotations this label may carry elsewhere. Rorty (1992, 107, my emphasis) describes this kind of reading as "the sort which one occasionally wants to call 'inspired' [and which] is the result of an encounter with an author, character, plot, stanza, line or archaic torso which has made a difference to the critic's conception of who she is, what she is good for, what she wants to do with herself: an encounter which has rearranged her priorities and purposes. Such criticism *uses* the author or text not as a specimen reiterating a type but as an occasion for changing a previously accepted taxonomy, or for putting a new twist on a previously told story." Also like Rorty (1992, 108), I distinguish this approach to reading from the "essentialist" tendencies of "traditional humanistic criticism," which "believed that there were deep permanent things embedded in human nature for literature to dig up and exhibit to us."[8] But perhaps unlike Rorty, I take no issue with anyone's wanting to practice methodical literary criticism in the name of interpretive meaning, even essential meaning, if that is their preference—though chapter 4 explains why I favor literary affordance to this methodical kind of literary interpretation in college *writing* courses. I also emphasize that the kind of reading Rorty has described here participates rhetorically in the reader's social contexts, not just in their personal experience, and Rorty would agree, though perhaps not with my terminology or objectives in this regard.

There are many ways "Lycidas" could be used instrumentally or unmethodically as such, with relation to grief (and other subjects), including an explanation of how the poem has helped a reader recover from trauma or what might be teachable about the poem in such a specific way or why a relevant contrast in therapeutic methods is particularly enlightening. Any of these affordances of "Lycidas" may very well impact the reader/writer's actual experience of being in the world, especially if her connection with some feature(s) of the poem is particularly strong—for example, the Christian or classical allusions, the celebration of nature's powers, or, as in the present reading, coping with loss or trauma. If the reader/writer's own real-world healing from a traumatic loss, and that of his audience, might be aided by means of using the poem, then an emotional affordance will have been made of the poem (again just for example).

Let's take a particular set of lines near the end of the poem, in which Milton is directly consoling his deceased friend: "Hence forth, thou art the Genius [Guardian spirit] of the shore, / In thy large recompense, and shalt be good / To all that wander in that perilous flood" (183–85). This verse is lovely on the ears if nothing else, and it arrives like a breath of fresh air after submersion in 150 or so lines of mourning and disappointment. A conventional interpretation would explain that Milton employs this image to evoke the Christian covenant of the afterlife. So although his mortal existence has expired, Lycidas receives compensation in the "blest kingdom" (177) by means of symbolically performing a beneficent role as protector of "all that wander in that perilous flood," in other words, by being a sort of patron saint of those who venture into the same waters in which he himself was drowned. But what can a reader make of these lines if the lines have gotten under his skin somehow and he is looking for something to do with them other than interpret their meaning? Let's also suppose this reader is neither religious nor an English major, yet he still wants to write about this part of this poem. If this person were to acknowledge that Lycidas's reward is not only religiously but also ironically charged, then that might be a start: poor Lycidas's afterlife reward comes in the form of patrolling the shores of the same sea in which he perished. So far we are still in the realm of interpretation, though we have parted from at least the intentionalist method, as it's highly unlikely that Milton meant to be ironic here. But the following demonstration shows one way, with just one detail, a shift in emphasis toward affordance can occur.

To the non-specialist, nonreligious contemporary reader who happens to be interested in these lines, a project might begin here, in which a Lycidasian relationship with traumatic loss is explored as somehow usable in another context. The task entails understanding something related to trauma through lenses (i.e., images, phrases, and the like) afforded by the poem, *not* proving something about the poem itself. For example, as with Lycidas, suffering may compel one to achieve a kind of mastery of its province in such a way as to be able to benefit others (as the poem's narrator imagines him to do). Lycidas does not merely roam about on the beaches as do, say, the Ancient Mariner or the Flying Dutchman; he also protects others there. This inquiry is moving along with a little more promise now, but it is still not especially novel.

As I have previously said, a public affordance is eventually answerable to the question "why *this* particular text?" Though we have discounted two of Lycidas's fellow oceanic literary ghosts, there is still something of a sub-genre of that-which-doesn't-kill-me-makes-me-stronger literature from which to distinguish this reading. George Herbert's "Easter Wings" comes to mind, for example, as in "shall the fall further the flight in me."

So let's go back to the reader's *relation* to the *features* of this particular text, and to facilitate the pursuit of felt sense in real time, let's also acknowledge that this hypothetical reader is to a large extent really me. Wherein lies the felt sense of a latent affordance? What is it about Lycidas's trauma or redemption in particular that makes it stand out so much for me? For one thing, his loss is felt so deeply by others. The poem reads at times like a list of mourners appearing to pay their respects: the narrator himself, Triton, Camus, Saint Peter, the valleys and their flowers, and "woful Shepherds." None of this is particularly unusual, but Lycidas does repay these mourners by bolstering their faith and security. This feels promising; there's energy here, though it's still vague. Continuing: the poem's consolation is directed mainly at the others, not as much at Lycidas (a familiar story by now, if you have read interchapter 1, above). Again, this is unlike the Ancient Mariner and the Flying Dutchman and for that matter even Herbert's sinner; Lycidas has suffered, too, but he serves to console the others, not himself: "Weep no more, woful Shepherds weep no more, / For Lycidas your sorrow is not dead, / Sunk though he be beneath the watry floar" (165–67). His loss was uncontrollable, but through his absence Lycidas soothes those who share in the loss. Yes, that's it. I had previously put my finger on the idea, but one line too late in the poem. Here it is in full: "Now Lycidas the Shepherds weep no more; / Hence forth thou art the Genius of the shore, / In thy large recompense, and shalt be good / To all that wander in that perilous flood" (182–85). The shepherds no longer weep. That's what I (and probably many other readers) have looked for after traumatic loss. And Lycidas's service *through his absence* (or the absence of his substance, content) is the key to the affordance in my case (see interchapters 1 and 3).

This is all telling, but I feel there is still more at work here. Something in these lines: "your sorrow is not dead, / Sunk though he be." Sorrow over drowning. Sorrow. Drowned. Drowned sorrows. Drowning one's sorrows. Drinking. The numbing consolation of drunkenness. Indeed, a common use of alcohol. I have known it well. In extreme form, alcoholism, it's an abuse. Lycidas has been beneficent after drowning and sorrows. His is not just life after death; it is also learning after loss. Learning *through* loss: a worked-through mastery of the subject. Learned-through loss, sorrows, drowning. Drowning sorrows, loss learning, mastery of the province of one's loss. A watery death. A genius of the shore. I am thinking now of experienced recovering alcoholics who sponsor new survivors of the disease, say, through Alcoholics Anonymous. These individuals are geniuses of the shore if ever there were ones. Like Lycidas, they offer anonymous, experienced service to fellow sufferers. That is nearly precisely my own perceived relationship to loss, others, and service. But only the distance (and difference) experienced through the poem has brought this connection into such clarity for me.

No wonder I have been so drawn to this poem since first encountering it twenty-five years ago but never quite being able to articulate why. No wonder I memorized the poem's entirety while walking my baby boy around the apartment every night during his first sleepless months. "Why *that* poem?" the few people I told would ask, thinking of Milton and his intentions or the content or the genre of the poem—all completely unrelated to children and parenting. But something was keeping me awake at night, and it wasn't only my sleepless infant. For as long as I could retain self-reflexive awareness, I have thought of myself as characterized primarily by serving the needs and desires of others. I was thus well equipped to become a caring father, so it wasn't training that I needed in this case. Rather, the affordance I made of "Lycidas" was the act of coming into fuller awareness of that specific central aspect of my subjectivity and, through that, seeking to refine my skills at serving others in large part through the absence of my own personal content (i.e., desires, needs, subjectivity, and the like). In other words, as I have known my whole life intuitively—and now explicitly—it is far easier to serve others when one possesses or asserts little will of one's own. This is the usefulness of the empty vessel the *Tao Teh Ching* speaks of in another textual passage that has always greatly resonated with me (Tzu 1961, 15). Now I have a clear idea of why. It would be mistaken to think that these issues are not deeply entangled in my career as a teacher of writing: writing is a skill that (in part) serves others' needs and an academic discipline that arguably has relatively little content of its own (see chapter 4 and interchapter 5 on this admittedly debatable point).

So my "Lycidas" affordance has granted me considerable, highly valuable awareness of my own character and approach to life. Beyond this, does it help to posit a figurative expression of my status as a loss-tested, somewhat selfless server of others' desires rather than just to call this what it is literally? In other words, does it make me a better server of others to think of myself as a "Genius of the shore" and of my past trauma as leading to "large recompense"? Yes, I do register a difference here. This difference is difficult to articulate, but it helps to be able to say that I shall continue to try to "be good to all that wonder in that perilous flood," even if this rhetoric manifests more or better through my actions than in any expression I may be able to make of these notions. I know how difficult it can be to connect with other people, and I am determined to help this cause. What does this version of this tactic hold in the way of promise for *other people*? Some benefits of pursuing literary affordances of this kind include a potentially increased awareness of latent, unintended significance, whether "only" personal or also social; a boost in one's perception of such an outcome's value; a way to communicate these ideas more effectively; more hope of making or sustaining a recovery from trauma (in this example case) or some other effect (generally); a deeper connection between one's recovery and one's faith (in this case); a new aspect of the pleasure of the source text, if not also an increase in that pleasure; a greater likelihood and ability to identify such affordances again (a recursive benefit); and a better capability to teach affordance making, including a means of unpacking that placeholder phrase students like to use: "I can relate to it."

We may have gone far afield from the *meaning* of "Lycidas" as Milton meant it or as literary scholars have determined. But I am not interested in assessing my affordance in those terms, which are more suitable for other (i.e., interpretive) approaches to the text. When people speak of meaning in this way, they seem to be suggesting a property of a text that is somehow inherent to it or else to a kind of (discourse) community consensus; either way, it is something that sticks with the text across contexts and lasts over time. My affordance may or may not do that. But in this case, I am not seeking other contexts for it than application to the ones that are closest to my heart, which surprisingly are almost entirely socially constructed: my familial and professional interactions. As for lasting over time, we shall see, but this affordance has developed in me for many years and is likely to adapt further if it continues to find application, as I suspect it will. I think of the outcomes my affordance has yielded as rhetorical. Though these processes and effects may be largely invisible to others (except for their presence now in this book)—as they were invisible to me for years, even while operating as central aspects of my being—the value of such affordances can best be determined by their usefulness to the parties who have stakes in them, who are affected by them, which is hardly just me. That strikes me as a rhetorical situation. Rorty (1992, 92) would agree that readings of texts should be assessed, in his words, "according to their efficacy as instruments for purposes, rather than by their fidelity to the object described." It would not make much sense to speak of this activity as determinant of or determined by the *meaning* of the text.

WHY NOT JUST CALL AFFORDANCE *USE* OR *APPROPRIATION*?

As we have seen, I sometimes employ the words *affordance* and *use* interchangeably. If it helps to grasp or to teach literary affordance, then the word *use* will often suffice where *affordance* would appear; I can live with that occasional substitution. But there are some good reasons why I retain the unfamiliar term *affordance* and why I hope my readers will do the same. For starters, because the word *affordance* is unfamiliar, it draws attention to the fact that something different is happening than what may be expected or conventional. Yes, the word *use* can also indicate unconventional applications, but standard assumptions too easily apply when *use* is paired with many objects, a phenomenon that does not occur with *afford*. If I say, for example, "I *used* a blanket," the assumption would likely be that I did so for keeping warm. But I may have actually used it for coverage in a play "tent" with my son or as an escape device by tying it together with sheets to climb out a window in an emergency. So although I admit that context tends to provide clarity and the phrase "I made an affordance of a blanket" still does not specify the nature of an affordance, I nevertheless maintain that the term *affordance* at least minimizes the chance of a faulty assumption by identifying something unconventional that requires further explanation. In the present case, that is a good thing. In the early going at least, rhetor response theory is going to need the benefit of clear articulation, so identifying affordance specifically for what it is represents an easy and important step in that direction.

More important, if we give up the term *affordance*, then we lose all of its corresponding theory, both that which I accounted for in chapter 2 and that which I have not been able to cover. *Affordance* enables our awareness of highly significant related concepts such as perception, relation, and emergence. *Use*, by contrast, carries no such associations but rather seems consciously instrumental in ways *affordance* was coined to avoid. The word *use* carries an insinuation of intentionality, whereas *afford* does not, especially if one remembers that affordances *emerge* in a discursive ecology rather than are made purposely (at least at first), as specified above. Perhaps not always but often, *use* is associated with an action that has been intended or that originates consciously in the user. Saying "I used the text in my argument" clearly refers to a deliberate act. This usage is so familiar that if I wanted to narrate an unconscious version of the same, I would have to qualify the verb: "I *unconsciously* used the text." Even then, this usage comes across awkwardly because of the deep association we tend to make between *use* and conscious action, so I can easily imagine my interlocutor responding: "what do you mean you *used* the text *unconsciously*?" More likely, my original formulation would have to be something like "the text affected me unconsciously." But this passive construction closes off the very possibility I hope to be opening up with my theory: that we can *actively* make unconscious rhetorical affordances of texts, as I have done with Milton's "Lycidas."[9] If this pairing of "unconscious" and "rhetorical" is too strange for you to accept, then alternatively try something like " . . . we sometimes make unconscious operations through texts . . . " (and you will find you are nowhere stranger than in the realm of psychology).

The difference I am trying to get at in my formulation is that some internal capacity *has worked on* rather than (or in addition to) "merely" *been affected by* the text in question. In other words, I am speculating that reader/rhetors perform internal operations relative to texts, of which we are unaware or only partly aware. These operations, especially if patterned, potentially have ongoing consequences on our perceptions, behavior, and interactions with others, among other things. If these were *fully conscious* operations, then I don't think there would be debate over whether they are rhetorical or not. So if the outcome is the same but the process is unconscious or only partly conscious or, say, intuited through felt sense (see chapter 5), then I am comfortable calling them rhetorical, and I hope others will be too. It may seem that I could avoid this difficulty by simply calling these effects *psychological*, but that label feels too broad and vague to me. That would be like referring to a trauma merely as psychological. It may be that, but it's certainly not *only* that. For one thing, the trauma may also inspire a rhetorical stance through which one approaches and experiences life, probably with varying degrees of awareness over time and across spaces, and which may permanently change one's life, even after a recovery has been made.

So, you might follow up, why not just call literary affordance *appropriation*? Again, I admit there is overlap here, and I do also occasionally use this term as a near synonym. After all, somewhat like appropriation, affordance involves adopting something for personal purposes, as in the familiar example of standing on a chair to reach something at a height. It's not difficult to understand what it would mean to *appropriate a chair* in such a way, but still, this usage feels off, not a close enough fit. I think that feeling can be attributed to at least three connotations that are troublesome in this context. First, *appropriation* suggests taking something into *possession* for one's own. As I state at the outset of this chapter and as I elaborate in the section below titled "Can You Really Do That to a Work of Literature," the *property* of literary ideas is imaginary or theoretical in nature, and therefore so is most taking (up/over/on) of those ideas. The etymology here involving "property" is at most figurative, if relevant at all, in the case of literary affordance, unlike the exception of the *literal* act of appropriation that constitutes plagiarism. Someone who stands on a chair to change a lightbulb is only really borrowing the chair for that purpose, not claiming ownership of it (unless she actively takes ownership of it). The same goes for someone who refers rhetorically to an image in a poem, for example. In fact, it would be odd to raise the question of ownership in the case of the lightbulb changer or the image referrer (as long as proper citation is given in the latter case), as such a concern would not likely seem relevant to any witness of either of these acts.

This leads me to the second aspect of *appropriation* that does not befit literary affordance: negative associations. In general parlance, *appropriation* is so often expressed as *mis*appropriation that the sense of this prefix (which indicates wrongness) tends to linger even without its actual presence, like a phantom limb. Take, for example, the article section titled "Appropriation" in Frank J. D'Angelo's (2009) valuable inventory of inter-textual rhetorical strategies. D'Angelo dedicates most of this passage to highlighting the controversial nature of textual appropriation, as in the case of one artist's deliberate exact photographs of another artist's photographs. Such appropriation often occurs "without permission" and thereby evokes charges of "copying, faking, [and] plagiarism." For support, D'Angelo (2009, 36–38) cites several court cases in which textual appropriators have been prosecuted for copyright infringement. Although I am willing to risk insinuations of figurative poaching (see below, this chapter), I would like to spare literary affordance from the inapplicable negative baggage of litigable subversion,[10] which is another reason for distinguishing *affordance* from *appropriation*.

On an interesting and complicating related note, Steven Mailloux (1997, 383–89) identifies a common trope in epistemological myths whereby the bearers of enlightenment and linguistic mediation tend to be thieves, including Prometheus and Hermes of the classical tradition and Legba of the West African Fon ethnicity. For an alternative myth of this ironic type, which we might call benevolently appropriative, I invite you to consider "Pierre Menard, Author of the *Quixote*" (Borges 1962), in which a twentieth-century Frenchman writes—note: not rewrites or copies but *writes* (as in *creates*)—several verbatim chapters of *Don Quixote*.

This astonishing story by Jorge Luis Borges (1962) blurs the lines of ownership of texts through their rhetorical performance, for lack of a better phrase. Menard's actions suggest that every unique situation renews the rhetorical potential for any text introduced to it. Even if that text remains graphically identical to a previous version, every given speech act necessarily differs (if "only" in impact) from other speech acts. See the epigraph in chapter 2 of my book for a representative statement to these effects by Borges's eponymous character.

The third connotation that makes *appropriation* an imprecise descriptor for what I mean by *literary affordance* is the assumption of intent that seems to inhere in acts of appropriation. The mismatch here closely resembles that which I pointed out several paragraphs above regarding the word *use*. The natural tendency to expect that appropriators have *intended* to make appropriations does not necessarily apply to literary affordance. Although a person certainly *could* intend to make affordances,[11] the expectation is that, at least at first, they tend to emerge unintentionally (or, e.g., unconsciously, semi-consciously, organically, or spontaneously). The opposite applies to appropriation, which *could* happen unintentionally (i.e., unconsciously and so on) but which tends to occur intentionally. If a person were to try to speak of an unintended or unconscious appropriation without being misunderstood, then that person would likely need to specify that, as in *I didn't know it at the time, but I had appropriated the text.* The term *affordance* subsumes that specification as well as the embodied dimensions of perception and simulated cognition (see chapter 2 and the following section of this chapter).

WHY LITERATURE?

I will offer three answers to this question. The first is that where *nonfiction* texts are concerned, we are already accustomed to *using* them, and much has already been written about that, which need not be repeated here. For example, it's completely ordinary to hear "anything you say can and will be *used* against you in a court of law" or "I *used* his article to support my argument." In fact, use (i.e., production) seems to be as much the default approach to nonfictional texts as interpretation (i.e., consumption) is to fictional texts. It is not at all ordinary to hear "I *used* the poem" or "let's *use* that movie." Rather, we tend to say we *read* or *watch* them. There is nothing wrong with such receptive acts of textual engagement, but I wish to explore a more active, applied approach. By encouraging the repurposing of fictional material, however, I am in no way endorsing or condoning the manipulation of its *factual* content. To invoke an example from a minor debate Stanley Fish (1980, 345–47) takes up in print with Norman N. Holland (1975a, 12), it is a *fact* that "A Rose for Emily" is about a reclusive southern woman, not an Eskimo. But to modify and extend Fish's view on the matter, I propose that this fact (of Emily's non-Eskimo identity) does not deny a reader the ability to *use* some feature(s) from Faulkner's story to privately conceptualize or publicly make a point related to indigenous people of the northern circumpolar region—if the reader has reason to pursue that possibility and if a rhetorical situation bears out (or bears with) such an affordance. In fact, because of the stark incompatibility between these two elements, a certain otherwise nonexistent rhetorical leverage might be gained through such a usage of the Faulkner story.

Let it be clear that my approach has nothing at all to do with "alternative facts" or, for that matter, any claims whatsoever to the *truth* of texts—again, because a literary affordance lays no claim to interpretive meanings of source texts. Unlike Fish and Holland, my hypothetical maker of an affordance of "A Rose for Emily" does not care whether Eskimos have anything to do with the *meaning* of that story, only that some feature(s) of the story may be used effectively (and respectfully) in some Eskimo-related context. Furthermore, as I see it, makers of literary affordances do not alter the source texts they work with in applying them to unrelated rhetorical situations.

For readers interested in a kind of parallel version of my approach that *does* pertain to factual material, I recommend Harris's excellent textbook chapter on "Forwarding," which does not exclude fiction but clearly emphasizes nonfictional (i.e., informational) texts. Harris (2006b, 37–38, original emphasis) explains: "As I use the term, a writer *forwards* a text by taking words, images, or ideas from it and putting them to use in new contexts. In forwarding a text, you test the strength of its insights and the range and flexibility of its phrasings. You rewrite it through reusing some of its key concepts and phrasings." At first glance, this tactic appears to be equivalent to literary affordance, but I note several differences. As mentioned above in the section "Why Not Just Call Affordance *Use* or *Appropriation*," the term *affordance* accounts for the experience of a host of embodied, perceptual, ecological, and emergent qualities; *forwarding* does not carry these implications. This point is related to another difference, which is the also aforementioned inclusion of unintentional or un/semi-conscious effects that *affordance* accounts for and *forwarding* does not. Furthermore, my situationally orientated *literary affordance* is not interested in making a "test" of texts' strengths or in rewriting texts, as is Harris's text-oriented *forwarding*.

Finally, whereas Harris focuses on helping his readers become more competent participants in conventional academic discourse, I am hoping to lightly shake up and supplement those conventions. These contrasts do not insinuate any value judgments; they only point out differences in these otherwise relatively similar approaches to textuality.

The second answer to the question "why literature" is that literary texts (broadly defined; see the introduction) uniquely afford the thinking, feeling, and doing of particularly powerful thoughts, feelings, actions—and with some learning and practice we can (better) take advantage of that phenomenon in various rhetorical situations. Marshall Gregory (2009, xiii) describes this quality of literature as "the universal human obsession with stories." In the title of his book, Robert Coles (1989) names this the *Call of Stories.* David Bleich—whose treatment of literature resembles mine (minus his broader argumentative aims)—offers a fine description of why to work with literature in ways similar to what I am proposing:

> Literature is the locus for the organized cultivation of new language elements and habits. It has been traditionally conceived as play or amusement or art or nonsense, but these roles contribute to its importance as a prime occasion for tangibly enlarging mental capacity and strength. Insofar as literature has been treated as a real object and criticism pursued as the local description of that object, the growth of language awareness is essentially inhibited; the decisive subjective action we all take with literature is subordinated, in educational practices and depressing cultural lethargy, to the dissemination of information and the moralistic, coercive demand to read carefully. To treat literature as a symbolic object is to shift our attention from acts of informational perception first to the perceptual initiatives we automatically take with a work, and then to the more deliberate conceptualizations we try to synthesize from these initiatives. (Bleich 1978, 96)

My third answer has to do with how readers' relations with literature (i.e., Bleich's "perceptual initiatives") afford rhetorical responses to their life experiences ("deliberate conceptualizations"). There are doubtless many different ways in which literary affordances emerge and find application to some of our lived situations. I am going to focus on one that seems prominent to me: how literature can function as a kind of conceptual metaphor through which readers variously (including "only" partly) perceive or approach reality. That is to say, if cognition can be equated to one's embodied "experience with the world," as was proposed by way of cognitive scientist Benjamin Bergen in chapter 2, then it's likely that literary thoughts can be especially rich and potentially powerful embodied experiences, and not nearly just in ways that have been intended by authors or favored by critics. These literary experiences may be valuable in and of themselves, as well as through assimilation by one's own life narrative and by application to one's rhetorical situations.[12] As Jennifer Lin LeMesurier (2014, 363–64) finds from her work on metaphor's embodied impact on rhetorical practices, the fundamental interrelationality of discourse and bodies means that "our bodies are trained to navigate the world from stores of embodied, affective attachments to certain affiliations or investments, attachments that make some rhetorical paths more or less appealing than others."

Previously in this chapter I have employed a key term from conceptual metaphor theory without having explicitly identified it as such. This is *source text*, a phrase I use to identify the text from which an affordance emerges through/for its reader. This term is an adaptation of what metaphor scholars refer to as *source domain*, which is one half of a metaphorical equation: the concrete thing in terms of which one thinks of an abstract thing, also sometimes referred to by literary scholars as a metaphor's *vehicle*. A classic example is *war* in the metaphor *argument is war* (Lakoff and Johnson 1980, 4–7). Argument is an abstract concept, which is the other half of a metaphor, known as the *target domain* or sometimes as the *tenor*. Many cultures think of *argument* (target domain) in terms of the more concrete concept of *war* (source domain). For example, it is common to speak of *defending* claims, *attacking* a position, or *shooting down* a point. Constructions of this kind, say metaphor theorists, do not merely describe and simplify complex concepts; they also shape our and our culture's expectations, influence our behavior, and even affect what we do and do not perceive. So if one is conditioned to think of argument in terms of war, as many of us are, then one will be more apt to find combative properties in arguments and to approach and enact them accordingly. To emphasize this point, conceptual metaphor theory pioneers George Lakoff and Mark Johnson (1980) invite their readers to participate in a thought exercise: imagining a contrasting culture in which argument is conceived not in terms of war but in terms of dance. Consider how this would change people's experience of argument and, by extension, of each other in rhetorical situations. It is worth quoting the authors here:

> Try to imagine a culture where arguments are not viewed in terms of war, where no one wins or loses, where there is no sense of attacking or defending, gaining or losing ground. Imagine a culture where an argument is viewed as a dance, the participants are seen as performers, and the goal is to perform in a balanced and aesthetically pleasing way. In such a culture, people would view arguments differently, experience them differently, carry them out differently, and talk about them differently. But

> we would probably not view them as arguing at all: they would simply be doing something different. It would seem strange even to call what they were doing "arguing." Perhaps the most neutral way of describing this difference between their culture and ours would be to say that we have a discourse form structured in terms of battle and they have one structured in terms of dance. (Lakoff and Johnson 1980, 4–5)[13]

I want to introduce two additional important notions from conceptual metaphor theory. The first is that much higher-order reasoning operates largely by means of metaphor. This occurs so universally and transparently that most people rarely ever notice the phenomenon. That is to say, nearly any substantive linguistic expression of abstract concepts will possess metaphorical constructions that are simply taken for granted. Consider, for example, the previous sentence's metaphorical concepts of *substance, expression, possession, construction,* and *taking.* The second important notion is the belief that what makes source domains so effective in helping us understand abstract concepts is that our experience of these source domains is direct and embodied. Again, consider *substance, expression, possession, construction,* and *taking,* which are all understood through embodied experience—in other words, tangibly and therefore easily cognitively simulated. Substance and possession are felt, expressions are heard or seen, and constructions and acts of taking are made physically and spatially. To restate this in terms that will be familiar from the theory presented earlier in this book, source domains function as direct percepts, not as indirect concepts. When I say *argument is war,* the various embodied associations you make with war—potentially including, and in some cases perhaps especially, those of *fictional* origin—impact your understanding of "argument" directly and immediately. You do not need to first process this idea through mental categories to understand it, and what you understand of it is hardly limited to dictionary-style definitions or your thought processes alone (i.e., in the conventional language-of-thought sense, to use Bergen's term from chapter 2). The experience is perceptual, personal, and socially situated. LeMesurier (2014, 364) goes as far as to state, "Our range of rhetorical actions is guided by our embodied memories just as much as [by] our training in argument or analysis."

My point in invoking this theory is to suggest that literary affordances function (at least sometimes) in the way source domains do in shaping our metaphorical perceptions of the world and thereby our higher-order reasoning. To put this in plain terms, the effects that sometimes emerge between literary texts and readers are so powerful and intimate that they directly inform readers' experience with life in such ways as to influence their expectations, behavior, and thoughts, including unconsciously and unintentionally. This would mean that literary affordances, as embodied and constitutive elements of our worldview, can partly determine both our approaches and tactics applied to rhetorical situations. That is—to remain with my working definition of rhetoric from this book's introduction—in contexts in which recognizable effects are achieved through sign systems. I believe readers can derive more power and pleasure, if not increased ethical attunement, from this phenomenon by increasing their awareness of and practice with rhetor response theory.

If it were not so common for lay people to have deep and abiding relationships with literary texts, then I might concede that these matters may be best left to specialists, but the fact is that most adults and probably many children after a certain age have favorite texts or features of texts that particularly stand out for them. Each instance of this standing out is a potential opportunity to learn more about oneself and one's engagement in the world (and therefore the supposed world itself) by examining that literary affordance. Certainly, interpretation can help here, too, but, *especially as it is practiced in school*, that act often serves other purposes and entails conventions that affordances do not require. As Chemero (2009, 140) notes of "placing features" during the act of affordance making: "[in] the placing of a feature, there is no need to know anything about any particular entity. All that is necessary is the ability to recognize a feature of situations," such as raininess when it is raining, for example. One need not be a meteorologist to make use of (e.g., take action in response to) the perception of raininess. This is certainly not to say there is no value in learning about the meanings of fictional texts (of course there is) but only that such learning is not the sole, ultimate, or best first thing to do with texts—especially outside of traditional English courses, which is where non-specialists mostly encounter the literature in their lives.

HOW DOES LITERARY AFFORDANCE DIFFER FROM ANALOGY AND ADAPTATION?

I want to dismiss an assumption that to some readers might come with this heading's question: that literary affordance exists in a category entirely of its own. It doesn't. Rather, it belongs to (among other things) a continuum of tactics that some people call text-to-life applications.[14] Although I disagree with the directionality suggested by that label, which wrongly insinuates that life is not textual in and of itself, I will abide it as a provisional placeholder for announcing this chapter section's intention to address two of literary affordance's closest neighbors in the text-to-life category: analogy (manifest as metaphor or simile) and adaptation. Notwithstanding the commonalities among these tropes, my aim here is to preempt inaccurate and dismissive conflations that occur when someone says that affordance is *just* analogy or is *just* adaptation—with "just" meaning *no different than* or *merely*. First, the *inaccuracy* of such "just" charges stems from the "no different than" usage. Although in many cases literary affordance does take the form of analogy or adaptation, it does not always or wholly do so, for example, in the cases of artistic repurposing of source texts, adaptive performances (see the section "Adaptation" below), or even the standard basic example affordance of standing on a chair to change a lightbulb. Second, as for what is *dismissively* meant by the "just" charge, it may be deeply flawed to criticize anything as "merely" an analogy. That is if such renowned scholars as cognitive scientists Douglas Hofstadter and Steven Pinker are correct in arguing that analogy comprises the very core of human cognition, without which we may not be able to think at all—to say nothing of analogy's distinguished philosophical champions in Plato, Aristotle, Kant, and Nietzsche, as Hofstadter and Emmanuel Sander (2013, 21) point out.

Metaphor and Simile

Literary affordance, metaphor, and simile are all variously somewhat analogical in nature.[15] In the aforementioned text-to-life context, this means that each of these three tropes indicates some kind of a condition of relationality between fictional and real-life experiences. In the previous two sentences I say "somewhat" instead of *outright* and "relationality" instead of *similarity* to draw attention to a relevant problem. In common usage the word *analogy* tends to insinuate a relationship composed necessarily of likeness. In this view, metaphor would be a relationship of likeness expressed as equivalence (e.g., *that story is my life*) and simile, a relationship of likeness expressed as resemblance (e.g., *that story is like my life*). Etymologically and in the case of literary affordance, however, analogy is more complicated than that, perhaps better likened to *comparability*, a word I take to subsume *contrastability*. Or we can say *relationality*, which is my preferred term for indicating the kind of ambivalence I wish to preserve. Far too much scholarship exists on these subjects for me to even scratch the surface of reviewing here. So given the likeliest range of interests of readers reaching this far in my book, I recommend Seitz's superb *Motives for Metaphor* (1999) as a starting point, for its workable overview of metaphor theory (especially as relevant to the teaching of writing), for defending analogical conceptions against dismissive challenges, and for the fact that Seitz opens a passage to my point in this chapter section.

As kinds of analogical expressions, Seitz distinguishes between metaphor and simile in the way I have just done, as functioning, respectively, through relations of equivalence and resemblance. Both Seitz and I are wary of uncritical casual declarations of resemblance that simile seems to enable in readers of fiction, for example, as in *I am just like that character* or *the romance plot was as complicated as my relationship.* Undergraduate and secondary students may be particularly prone to this habit, whereby recognition of superficial or reductive similarities stands as the end point of an examination of reading rather than the starting point to more substantial textual engagement. This is partly why Seitz favors metaphor: the daring proposition of equivalence (i.e., rather than just resemblance) seems more likely to inspire deeper analysis of the relation and therefore, ironically, to wind up inevitably back at difference, thus setting the metaphor into a kind of chasing of its own tail.

Seitz (1999, 125) characterizes this paradox in positive terms, calling it "dialogic metaphor," which is a metaphor that "partially inhibits its own movement toward identification." "Rather than seeking an equivalence whose appeal is so convincing that the reader completely identifies with its fiction," he adds, "the dialogic metaphor seeks an equivalence that [Kenneth] Burke . . . refers to as 'planned incongruity'" (Seitz 1999, 125). Seitz (1999, 125) continues: "Metaphors that retain, rather than eradicate, their incongruities create a dialogic relationship with their readers" through, again in Burke's terms, "the intrusion of 'deliberate misfits.'" Seitz (1999, 125, original emphasis) warns that if, by contrast, metaphorical identification "'goes all the way,' without any recognition of the differences between this and that, then the dialogue between reader and text has ended before it even begins, with no space for the exploration of further relationships: this simply *is* that—and nothing more need be said." To use one of Seitz's examples, when Whitman refers to grass as "the beautiful uncut hair of graves," this formulation evokes a sense not only of likeness between the two compared things but also of difference. Grass is similar enough to hair for the metaphor to make sense, but the image is also too peculiar to register as a perfect equivalency (Seitz 1999, 125–26). Readers can embark on "explorations" of the "relationships" involved in such a dialogic metaphor, which I concede may disrupt part of the tacit magic of metaphor Rosenblatt seeks to preserve in the passage I quoted on page 34. But it might not or it might open up the textual encounter to other kinds of wonderment and utility. So "explorations" of "relationships" remain central to my rhetor response theory, but not for the sake of decoding textual meaning (a point I have made throughout the book and will return to below in distinguishing my approach from that of Seitz).

A key to understanding the usefulness of Seitz's theory to my purposes is his portrayal of readers as participants in the function of dialogic metaphor—to which I would add that this necessarily entails readers' social/rhetorical situatedness. Seitz (1999, 7) claims, "Readers of metaphor are thus asked not simply to discern resemblances between this and that; they are asked to enter a fictional world in which the distinction between this and that no longer obtains," or, as restated later (1999, 108), "much of the persuasive force generated by metaphor derives from its ability to stimulate readers not merely to compare but to cross the thresholds of uncharted fictional territories." Adding helpful specificity to the vague "text-to-life" label, Seitz (1999, 126, original emphasis) argues that such entry into fictional discourse "requires . . . that *readers also be made spectators of their own forms of participation.* It is in this nexus of participation and spectatorship that dialogue is born." To continue my expansion and application of Seitz's point, I say that readers can similarly become aware of the *rhetorical* aspects of the metaphoricity of fiction—both that which can be said to be original to an organic (unintentional) affordance and that which accrues to a created (intentional) affordance.

By no means merely only to demonstrate the inherently self-reflexive nature of metaphor talk, I want to depart from Seitz's use of the term *spectator*, which suggests a passive disposition. To be fair, Seitz does clearly append this passive spectatorial aspect of the metaphorical function to the explicitly active aspect of readerly participation, but I wish to draw attention to an even more dynamic consideration of perception, as theorized by scholars who work with affordance, conceptual metaphor, or simulated cognition (see chapter 2 and elsewhere in this chapter). In some cases at least, I propose that readers who have learned or who naturally come to perceive themselves as participants in metaphorical worlds of fiction can put this capacity (especially any patterns therein) to use for purposes other than decoding the source text. Namely, I mean better understanding and engaging in rhetorical situations that somehow evoke that fictional metaphoricity.

So if it helps anyone to think of literary affordance as functioning similarly (but not identically) to dialogic metaphor, then I don't object to that. As previously noted, my aim is not to close the case on any of the ideas I am offering by establishing definitive boundaries for them but rather to open up possibilities and further inquiry into them, including through cross-pollination of neighboring concepts. But I still insist on distinguishing literary affordance from dialogic metaphor for the sake of reminding my readers of a divergence in aims. Seitz seems to remain focused on author-intended metaphors and thus on bringing the point of textual engagement ultimately back to the source text and its interpretation. This is most evident in his grounding of dialogic metaphor theory in Burke's concepts of "*planned* incongruity" and "*deliberate* misfits" (Seitz 1999, 125–26, my emphases). The deliberate planning in these cases is done by the metaphor's author, not its reader. As we well know by now, my focus addresses metaphorical capacity or rhetoricity *beyond* the source text, regardless of authorial intent.

Adaptation

Adaptation can be considered a kind of literary affordance, one that may place greater emphasis on *creative* than on *rhetorical* aspects of the approach. I say this while fully acknowledging that creative acts are often also rhetorical acts and vice versa; my distinction goes only so far as emphasis is concerned. For example, although a theatrical adaptation of a novel undoubtedly reflects rhetorical decisions such as, let's say, content cutting, casting, and modernization, it is more common to conceive of these phenomena in creative terms such as the effects of plot, acting, and production design. Again, the difference here lies in the placing of emphasis, not in the existence or nonexistence of any of these elements.

Conventional literary and rhetorical theory can already do an excellent job of helping audiences learn about dynamics of adaptation. But I think it's fair to speculate that in many institutional contexts, this kind of learning privileges the moves made by authors, producers, and performers over the conception and performance of actual adaptations by students. In other words, to repeat a now familiar refrain, interpretation of meaning tends to take priority over or entirely eclipse applications of literary texts (i.e., affordance). Furthermore, when students are occasionally invited to generate their own adaptations, the task tends to focus on modes and texts that are pre-selected by the teacher or the curriculum, for example, by reciting *Hamlet* in class (as I did in the twelfth grade) or, rarer than that, by staging a production of the play. There is a time and place for these valuable activities, but so should there be occasion for students to do the same with modes and texts of their own choosing that correspond to their own abilities, identity themes, and rhetorical situations—without obligation to argue for interpretive meanings of the texts in question. Especially if combined with research, peer review, discussion, reflection, and self-assessment responsibilities, such adaptive affordance opportunities can yield positive effects on students' rhetorical knowledge, self-efficacy, and transfer, to name a few significant outcomes. Whether teachers can spare time for this under the pressures of curriculum coverage and test preparation is a matter to be locally determined, of course. But where there is (or could be) capability, desire, and freedom to do so, I hope that English, writing and rhetoric, and other teachers will consider practicing the approach. Readers outside of institutional contexts can presumably do so whenever they wish.

Let me provide a significant and admirable example of adaptive literary affordance to further illuminate the difference between studying past expressions of meaning or even someone else's adaptive affordance and creating one's own adaptation. Once again, I will note that these approaches need not be conceived as mutually exclusive, because they are not; in fact, they may well be mutually complementary. My example is the case of *Theater of War* (TOW) performances, which were begun in 2009 by Theater of War Productions and were still ongoing as of the start of the 2017 summer.

TOW performances are touring, staged readings and subsequent discussions of the Sophocles plays *Ajax* and *Philoctetes* by military veterans or professional actors, intended for military and civilian audiences with the explicit intention of "address[ing] public health and social issues . . . such as combat-related psychological injury, end-of-life care, police and community relations, prison reform, gun violence, domestic violence, sexual assault, and substance abuse and addiction" (Theater of War Productions 2017a). The group says it "uses" and "employs" these particular plays as "textbook descriptions of wounded warriors, struggling under the weight of psychological and physical injuries," noting that the material was originally performed in part by ancient Greek military personnel for audiences including citizen-soldiers. The aim, seemingly both in antiquity and today, is to "forge a common vocabulary for openly discussing the impact of war on individuals, families, and communities . . . [and] generating compassion and understanding between diverse audiences" (Theater of War Productions 2017b).

It is not hard to see how TOW's performances represent an example of adaptive affordance, with their use of classical fictional texts for achieving specific contemporary rhetorical results. Because relatively little adaptation occurs in this sample case, as compared with productions that manipulate source material or alter staging effects to heighten intended effects, TOW performances also offer a good example of what

I call elsewhere in the book *apparent* affordance. Such is an instance in which the intentions (or at least the effects) of a text's affordance maker match or closely resemble the (presumed or known) intentions of the author of the source text (or at least relative consensus about its effects). For example, TOW explicitly says it uses materials that "timelessly and universally depict the visible and invisible wounds of war" to literally *depict the visible and invisible wounds of war* (Theater of War Productions 2017b). There is nothing necessarily less effective or less valuable about an apparent affordance, as distinguished from its continuum counterpart, *subtle* affordance. In fact, an apparent affordance may be the only kind that emerges in a given situation, or it may simply be the best strategy for achieving one's aims. We know that TOW performances have benefited thousands of veterans and their family members as well as many more civilian audience members. So rather than promoting one type over the other (again, noting that these are counterparts on a continuum, not polar ends of a hierarchy), I propose that the apparent/subtle distinction enables fruitful opportunities that could be missed without attention to the concept and its supporting theory.

It is one thing—valuable, to be sure—for students to study the Sophocles plays alone or alongside TOW performances and to analyze how they do what they do and what that means. In a course on literature of war or on violence and culture, for example, that might well be the end of the lesson, if we can safely assume that there is sufficient interest in the topic among the enrollees. It is another thing—also valuable, perhaps as an additional step in the cases just described or as a prior or alternative activity in another, less-specialized context, such as a writing and rhetoric course—for students to try their own hand at making affordances of the Sophocles plays for similar or other results or to select their own literary material and results for enacting adaptive affordance. Among other issues to address in such a unit would be the degree of apparentness or subtlety that has emerged or to aspire to in the affordance maker and how that relates to elements of the rhetorical situation: purpose, audience, and exigence. To help with this, comparisons can be made to other affordances from familiar contexts, like giving a gift of a mixed tape (or these days I suppose it would be a playlist), quoting a literary passage in a significant context (e.g., a yearbook blurb), or simply wearing a piece of clothing that recasts a fictional element (such as the T-shirt I saw with a letter "A" logo printed on front and a number on back with the name "Prynne" above it, in sports jersey style, whose wearer would rhetorically metaphorically *be* Hester, most likely not without an interesting backstory).

IS THIS ANY DIFFERENT FROM READER-RESPONSE CRITICISM?

Yes, rhetor response is different from reader-response criticism, though they share some commonalities. To begin, this is a complicated issue because it's not precise to refer to reader response as a singular thing to which something else can be either similar or not similar. As many others have noted, reader-response criticism is not a unified school of thought but a fairly diverse assemblage of theories grouped together asynchronously because of their common interest in highlighting the role of the reader in the interpretive process: the reader, that is, as opposed to the text, its author, or any of the various interpretive lenses (e.g., race, class, gender, power, psychology, sexuality). I will say more on this below, but first I note that we have already arrived at my key point of departure from reader response, in the phrase above, "the interpretive process."

Although I share an interest with reader-response critics in paying close attention to the reader, I do not do so—as reader-response criticism does—with a focus on interpretation. To me, that signals a return to privileging the text. No one I know of has made this argument better than Jane P. Tompkins (1980, 201, 203), who contends that reader-response critics "have not revolutionized literary theory but merely transposed formalist principles into a new key," because "the assumption that criticism is synonymous with interpretation, the belief that the discovery of meaning is the goal of the critical enterprise, [still] remains unquestioned." Take this passage from Louise Rosenblatt (1994, 18), which might appear to align closely with my views: "In ecological terms, the text becomes the element of the environment to which the individual responds. Or more accurately, each forms an environment for the other during the reading event." I agree to an extent but must note that a "reading event" is a short-lived, text-oriented moment within a long social lifetime of rhetorical situations to which a person constantly responds, including—as I have been arguing—through the lenses or in terms of the most significant texts of that person's life. So whereas "response" in reader-response criticism is a response to a *text*, namely, to interpreting its meaning, "response" in my rhetor response theory is a response to the reader/rhetor's *lived experience* through features of a text, which is a component but not the subject of that same lived experience (or rhetorical situation). In other words, although reader response was revolutionary in its day for shifting the directionality of textual meaning from how authors and texts make it to how readers and their environments make it, I wish to shift the emphasis away from the text altogether. In my scheme, the text plays a supporting role to the reader's lived experience, which is the main player, and *meaning* is not the currency of transactions between them.

Another difference between reader response and rhetor response involves treatment of the reader. At times, some reader-response critics seem to treat the reader as a category, a type, or a hypothetical (as opposed to a unique, real individual) to a greater degree than I am comfortable doing. I certainly believe that subjectivity is both a psychological and a socially constructed phenomenon, but I do not feel that literary affordances can be primarily categorized as symptoms of fixed psychological patterns or products of discourse communities. I prefer to think of the psychological and social dimensions of the reader as contributing factors to tactics developed and applied (consciously and otherwise) in the negotiation of lived experiences or rhetorical situations, which are constantly shifting and not masterable once and for all by any single method or approach. Contrary to this, I often get the feeling from reader-response critics that their aim is still to crack a code for reading as if to arrive at *the* theory or *the* method for how meaning is made, or what I have referred to above as a capital "T" Truth. It should be obvious by now that such is not my aim.

Now on to the matter of the various views assembled under the banner of reader-response criticism. There are far too many scholars of too much diversity included under this banner to review here, so I offer an admittedly very narrow inquiry into only the most prominent reader-response critics who seem to come nearest to my interests: Wolfgang Iser (1989, 1993), David Bleich (1978), Norman N. Holland (1975a, 1975b), and Stanley Fish (1970, 1976). The following is not meant to be an exhaustive or representative review of these scholars, their historical contexts, or even the texts I have singled out but rather only a rough mapping of nearer and farther neighboring constellations relative to my position in this book. So I present the following material through a particular selective lens suited to this purpose. Specifically, I am content only to demonstrate whether and how each of the selected theorists focuses on functions of the reading experience that involve the following: (1) decoding the meaning of texts themselves in the experience of reading, a function I call *decoding*; (2) responding to texts by filling in their gaps or making associations with them, a function I call *responding*; or (3) doing unrelated things with texts after reading them, a function I call *doing things*. As we shall see, even among these theorists who come close to my interests, relatively little attention is paid to *doing things* with texts in the way I mean. I am not saying these scholars *should have* paid more attention to this; I am only pointing out the differences in our purposes. On account of this difference, at the end of the present chapter section—as a kind of transition to the next one, on ethical criticism—I offer a quick account of philosopher Richard Rorty's literary theory relevant to present purposes, despite the fact that Rorty is neither a reader-response nor an ethical literary critic. But like my approach to literature, Rorty's approach also emphasizes doing things with texts, and like me, he trespasses across various fields without conforming to their boundaries and conventions.

Iser

Iser seems to focus predominantly on what I am calling the *responding* function of the reading experience. In fact, he gives us the phrase *filling in gaps*, which I centrally associate with this category. To Iser, texts provide these gaps for readers, and this is the directionality of the relation, not vice versa or otherwise. Although at times his theory possibly gestures toward *doing things* with texts, Iser is clearly most interested in understanding the actions readers undertake during the processes of reading and responding to a text, and these actions relate back to the text rather than to the reader's lived experience. Text and reader occupy roughly equal status in their "interaction," wherein the text sets preconditions for the reader, who transforms these signals or brings them forth and thus creates the text's meaning in the moment of reading. Because literary texts do not make identical reference to real-life situations, they lead to what Iser usefully calls "indeterminacy." When faced with this indeterminacy, the reader has no specific point of reference outside the text by which to determine whether "the text has presented itself rightly or wrongly." So after trying out the multiple perspectives the text offers, the reader can use only her own experiences to judge what the text has presented (Iser 1989, 7). Again, note the text-centrism of this process.

Literary texts are unique, says Iser, because they can stray far beyond ordinary life experiences, thereby exposing readers to opportunities to develop new perspectives or otherwise be changed by the act of reading. (Rorty praises this quality, too.) Iser examines the potential for two extreme reactions stemming from confrontations between the real and the literary worlds: the reader might pronounce the literary world to be fantastical for straying far from her own experience, or she might deem the literary world trivial for merely echoing her own experience. Although the reader possesses agency in this scheme, Iser does not go further to suggest what the reader might do with the text beyond determining its meaning. In other words, the reader is poised to *be* changed by texts, even to have a hand in that, but not necessarily to *effect* change in anything with the text. My aim is to bring attention to that next step in this kind of reasoning. For another sense of how Iser returns the reader and reading process to the *text* where this dynamic might instead have been extended out into the *world*, as I wish to do, we can consider the example he provides of reading serialized novels. During the interruptions between serial iterations, a reader tries to "imagine the continuation of the action" (Iser 1989, 11) and thereby participates in furthering that action as a kind of "coauthor." But to Iser this action is more about filling in textual gaps than about performing lived experiences apart from that. The difference is a matter of emphasis, and Iser is certainly not wrong for pursuing what he chose to emphasize; he just goes in a different direction from where I want to go with my response theory. Among the theorists selected for this modest overview, Iser grants the most authority to the text in guiding the nature of the reader's response. Although each reader in Iser's scheme will fill in the gaps she faces through the text's indeterminacy, the text still maintains control over that process by setting the preconditions for and remaining the end point of the reading experience.

Bleich

Like Iser, Bleich forgoes *decoding* in favor of attending to the *responding* function of reading; however, whereas Iser's filling in of textual gaps says more about the text and its author than about the reader, Bleich's subjective criticism says (much) more about the reader than about the text and its author. Indeed, the reader dominates Bleich's (1978) best-known work of reader-response theory, *Subjective Criticism*, in which he endows the reader with far more primacy and agency in the interpretive act than do any of the other theorists I have selected (and seemingly everyone else, too). The text as a symbolic object (i.e., not its physical being) does not come into existence until the reader creates it as such through the act of response. This radical view recasts interpretation as an act driven by the interpreter's desire to create new knowledge based on her or his ever-shifting "present perception" of the "interpretive occasion" (Bleich 1978, 96). Bleich calls this new knowledge "resymbolization," which I would deem an excellent synonym for *literary affordance* if I didn't want to distance myself from Bleich's grander theoretical claims, as discussed below. But the idea is a compelling one that deserves further attention.

Resymbolization occurs after our "first acts of perception and identification produce in us a need, desire, or demand for explanation" (Bleich

1978, 39). Bleich (1978, 39) continues: "A community of thinkers is both the original synthesizer and the final authority for the resymbolization and its ranges of applicability and value. An adequate explanation may or may not meet the criteria of predictability and repeatability. But if the community finds the explanation satisfactory for its own needs, this alone is enough to render it adequate." To try my hand at a simplification: first, something within a reader in a context motivates a particular response to a text, then the reader and others in this context seek to understand the response and its motives through acts of interpretation, and then this community of thinkers does or does not validate the response relative to its own standards in the given time and place. According to another description by Bleich (1978, 132), this kind of response "is an expression of, and declaration of, self in a local context reflecting a set of local choices, motives, and interests in knowledge." So even though a reader is not beholden to authorial intention (which is irrelevant in Bleich's scheme) or to any objective meaning in a text (which does not exist), the reader's explanation of knowledge derived in response to the text does eventually seek acceptance in a social context.

This last, negotiated aspect of a reader's resymbolization sometimes seems to go forgotten in popular accounts of Bleich's subjective criticism,[16] and it suggests overlap with what I am calling *doing things* with texts. To incorporate terminology from earlier in this chapter, there is a non-dualistic ecological reciprocality to Bleich's (1978, 64) theory of interpretive motives, which he links to a Darwinian view of adaptation for survival. In my own terms, this means that whatever a reader does with a text both emerges from and affects her rhetorical situation (*sometimes* in my opinion but seemingly *always* in Bleich's). The "first acts of perception" Bleich speaks of equate with what I have referred to as *percepts*; resymbolization, as I have said, matches well with literary affordance; and "applicability" and adequacy align with rhetorical effectiveness in my scheme.

These are significant commonalities between Bleich's and my theories; however, a number of differences also exist. I will explain them using my terms from the pairs of equivalencies laid out just above. For one thing, I am not sure that literary affordances always call for "explanation" (i.e., interpretation). My experiences and those of many of my students indicate that initial percepts can linger with no conscious or only semi-conscious recognition for any length of time. For example, I believe my reciting of "Lycidas" to my newborn child served a number of purposes for me despite my not being able (until recently and perhaps only partially) to explain them. Also, I want to retain the possibility that interpretation of causes or motives must not be the reader's only option in responding to an affordance that has emerged (e.g., perhaps direct application might occur, as in my "Lycidas" example). But I admit that this does appear to be the default response. Furthermore, I do not agree with Bleich (1978, 39) that one's interpretive community need be "the original synthesizer and the final authority" in the formulation and application of literary affordances. Sometimes their value might be "only" ever personally synthesized and authorized or personally synthesized and publicly authorized or publicly synthesized and personally authorized. As others have noted, Bleich seems to be understandably intent on precluding charges of solipsism, so perhaps he is more insistent on this point because he has grander visions for his theory than I do for mine.[17]

This brings me to another area of difference between us. Bleich, as with many other theorists invoked throughout this book, seems to aspire to presenting *the* (ultimate, definitive) theory of reading (i.e., interpretation) and insight into a capital "T" Truth, or at least a true method (see the Rorty material below for a critique of the myth of a true method). Bleich is also taking on entire paradigms of thought in science, religion, and other aspects of culture, with a corrective intention to replace them. By contrast, I am only proposing an approach to literary textuality that seeks optional application where it can be useful, enjoyable, or both and which lays no claim to truth or meaning. I do not intend to explain or absorb all acts of reading with my approach, and I am skeptical of any project that tries to do so. Let me offer an example of the kind of grand claim Bleich makes that I am not willing to make despite my sympathy for its main idea. In speculating about the consequences of his subjective paradigm writ large, he states: "When knowledge is no longer conceived as objective, the purpose of pedagogical institutions from the nursery through the university is to synthesize knowledge rather than to pass it along: schools become the regular agency of subjective initiative. Because language use and the interpretive practices that follow from it underlie the processes of understanding, the pedagogical situations in which consciousness of language and literature is exercised establish the pattern of motives a student will bring to bear in his own pursuit of knowledge" (Bleich 1978, 133).

I can imagine (or simply look around and see) far worse than such a vision as Bleich's of a universal educational culture centered around metacognitive and deliberated exchanges of speech acts. And I certainly don't deny Bleich his right to dream in his book (in fact, I applaud it). Furthermore, I respect his relatively rare commitment to balancing theory with pedagogy in seeking to inspire practical applications toward change. But if only from a rhetorical standpoint, I cannot help but think that claims on the scale of the quotation I have provided—which is not an outlier as such—seem to draw the loudest responses from those who find them off-putting rather than those who find them inspiring. That is to say, such declarations seem especially to invite objection, though I suppose that is only a matter of degree, as anything put in print or pixel seems inevitably prone to attack by academics. In other words, paradigms are hard to shift by means of mere individual declaration (see Miller 1998; Scholes 2011, xiv), and the only singular force I know to be able to affect curricular change straight through from P–16 is, unfortunately, capital. Although Bleich's "subjective paradigm shares with Marxism," says Mark Shechner (1979, 155), "its rage against things as they are and the repressive authority that has a stake in them, Bleich is no Marxist." All this being said, I would be pleased to see renewed interest in Bleich's subjective criticism, caveats included, as a part of well-rounded efforts to push back on curricular over-standardization, including critiques of material aspects of institutional treatment of literature and literature experts (see chapter 4 for more on this).

Holland

Bleich and Holland overlap considerably in their subjective theories of readers' responses to literature. But as Bleich and others note, Holland differs in remaining squarely focused on the psychological dimension and in considering a reader's approaches to texts to be more or less fixed rather than variable across contexts. Holland's theory, like Bleich's, falls in the category I call *responding*. Here, the associations readers make in real time while reading texts or other ways they make sense of them occupy the most theoretical attention, as opposed to how readers might do things with that in other situations. But Holland's theory, also like Bleich's, can be said to lean somewhat toward the *doing things* category because he believes readers *use* texts psychologically—however, these are necessarily personally oriented responses and therefore reflect only partly what I mean by the latter category. Holland is primarily interested in how readers' identities shape their experiences with texts. He theorizes how and why readers achieve their own kinds of pleasure or balance when they read literature, and he extrapolates from that general ways many or all readers respond to a text.

Arguably, the most important concept in Holland's work (and certainly the most applicable to my interests) is that of the reader's "identity theme," a theory in which it is easy to find a strong Freudian influence. From the earliest stages of infancy, Holland (1975a, 8) proposes, we establish patterned mechanisms for coping with "the demands of inner and outer reality," and we apply these strategies to all new experiences, including literary experiences. Identity themes are the continuity reflected in one's accumulated ego choices in life, including one's characteristic approaches to textual choices and interpretations. Holland (1975b, 816) explains: "All of us, as we read, use the literary work to symbolize and finally to replicate ourselves. We work out through the text our own characteristic patterns of desire and adaptation. We interact with the work, making it part of our own psychic economy and making ourselves part of the literary work." According to this theory there are three steps or methods by which we supposedly replicate our identities in the texts we read: (1) as acts of defense, we find our biggest fears in texts and repeat our strategies with them; (2) as acts of fantasy, we recreate texts in terms of our own wishes; and (3) as acts of transformation, we try to explain these moves on an intellectual level (Holland 1975b, 816–18). To use terminology from earlier in this chapter, we might think of Holland's theory as proposing that each of us possesses personal metaphors that we live by.

I happen to go a long way with Holland's theory of identity themes, as I have found it to fairly accurately account for many of my and my students' literary affordances. As such, it is a handy concept to employ, as I have consistently done, in teaching reader-based approaches to literature. But several reasons prohibit me from entirely agreeing with Holland's scheme as I understand it. First, people's psychic conditions strike me as necessarily socially constructed, and therefore I am not so sure we can treat them as much as private experiences as Holland's theory generally does. This ecological influence is why I consider unconscious or semi-conscious literary affordances to be rhetorical phenomena (at least partially): negotiation is taking place not just between the self and the text but also among those and one's social contexts or rhetorical situations.

Second, people may not be motivated solely by their psychology, or at least not by a psychological causality reducible to only fears and desires in the conventional sense, and these drives do not seem to be activated every time someone reads fiction. Holland (1975a, 115) argues that if a reader has responded positively to a literary work, then "he must have found something in the work that does what he does to cope with needs or dangers." The reader, in other words, must have been able to synthesize from the text similar desires or defenses that the reader would respond to in real life. While this formula makes sense and I find it to accurately reflect many of my own most significant responses to texts, I cannot be so sure that this *must* occur in all reading experiences.

Third, I am skeptical of Holland's insinuation that a person's identity themes remain fixed across time and contexts. If that were the case, then it would require a great stretch, at best, to account for a reader's different impressions of the same text over multiple readings. For example, I experienced dramatically different responses to Jack Kerouac's *On the Road* upon two readings separated by twenty years. The book greatly exhilarated me when I first read it at nineteen, and it awakened a spatially charged urge for freedom, as I suspect it does for many readers in that age range. But upon rereading the book at age thirty-nine, I found it to be extremely depressing. I suppose one could construct a broad enough identity theme to account for these widely varying readings—something like *desire for satisfaction* (in this case, originally fulfilled and later not)—and then argue that the theme remained consistent while my sense of satisfaction changed over the decades. But that may not be the most useful way of looking at the issue. Notwithstanding such exceptions, I find Holland's theory of identity themes to work quite well as a kind of template for analyzing trends in one's literary affordances. My interchapters are examples of that.

Fish

Like both Bleich and Holland, Fish is considerably more interested in the reader's experience of the text than in the text itself. And like all of the critics covered here, Fish seeks to counteract widespread neglect of the reader in literary theory up to his contemporary period. Among the theorists selected for this modest overview, Fish (eventually) grants the most authority to the reader's social context in guiding the reader's response (through interpretive conventions). There are two versions of Fish's reader-response theory, an earlier and a later, both of which I will consider here but only quickly to arrive at his significant later idea: interpretive communities. Fish's (1970) early work in the area of reader response focuses on the real-time experience of reading, an approach he calls "affective stylistics." Years later, he is still interested in the reader but shifts his focus to theorizing the cultural embeddedness of the reading experience.

Affective stylistics corresponds to the category I call *decoding*, wherein a reader's response consists of deciphering the text's meaning on the page. That may appear to be a conventional approach, but what is unique in this case is that whereas most literary theory considers meaning to be offered by texts, Fish maintains that decoded meanings are instead created by readers of those texts. Fish considers how readers respond to texts line by line, arguing that a description of that response *is* the text's meaning. I want to mention an example that is relevant here but that actually comes from Fish's later piece cited below, which I do for three reasons: it is a clear example of how the reading process creates conditions in which meaning (i.e., intentions, forms) can then be decided by readers, it pertains to the recently discussed Milton poem "Lycidas," and it enables me to look back and ahead in the present book chapter with regard to useful misreading. Fish explains how a reader can *make* (he emphasizes the literal force of this word) one sense of a meaning from a pair of lines from "Lycidas" and then reverse that meaning in the very next line. Knowing already that Lycidas has died, one can read "The willows and the hazel copses green / Shall now no more be seen" to mean that these natural entities (symbols of nature generally) will wither away and disappear out of deep mourning for the loss of their loved Lycidas. But then one reads in the next line "Fanning their joyous leaves to thy soft lays," and one changes the initial meaning. The trees will in fact remain; it is *Lycidas* who will no longer be seeing them (on account of having died). Fish's point in tracing this sequence of formulations is to note that we find in texts what we put in them and only *afterward* ascribe that, as meaning, to the author or the text and then seek to verify that. Intention and form are things we bring to or activate in texts, not vice versa (Fish 1976, 476–80).

I am going to break form for two paragraphs to issue a relevant aside. What I wish to do with this example from Fish is to hold on to his initial interpretation (after the first two lines) that gets dismissed as a misreading (after the third line) and to acknowledge its potential utility as a source or outlet of energy and as a metaphorical category. What I hope to establish is that if textual meaning can be put aside as the sole standard, then even aberrant readings such as Fish's premature pathetic fallacy, above, can have potential use value. This is not to promote the act of misreading but to object to necessary and automatic dismissal of misreadings. Hofstadter, the Pulitzer- and National Book Award–winning cognitive scientist mentioned in the previous chapter section, tells a story of his own misreading that it may help me to recount here. As a math-loving boy, he once thought subscripts such as 1–3 in X_1, X_2, X_3 *indicated some kind of operation analogous to the powering function marked by superscripts (e.g., 1–3 in* X^1, X^2, X^3*), only to be disappointed to learn from his physicist father that subscripts have no such value; they merely distinguish variables from each other. Forty years later, Hofstadter similarly played the disappointing father to his toddler daughter upon* *informing her that a second button on the family dust buster carried no exciting properties like the first one did by powering the machine on and off. Hofstadter points to a number of analogies formed from his connection of these two memories, and he classifies the connections as "a reminding event," an apparently common form of analogy. He is careful to state that these kinds of phenomena are not meaningful in a purposeful or intended way; rather, "they just happen." His point is that cognition at its very core works through the making of analogies; we naturally categorize things according to common essences that we perceive in given times and places (Hofstadter 2006).*

I want to add that aberrant analogies might be put to useful purposes, if "only" toward increased metacognition. Where sufficient energy seems associated with a concept—even incorrect ones such as Fish's disappearing trees or Hofstadter's nonexistent subscript powers—valuable understanding might be derived, since that lived experience may correspond to an analogical construction shaping one's worldview or tactics in a given situation. In other words, circumstances may arise in which that concept may have resonance and may have value to a person. A literal or figurative file might be maintained in which such charged readings (regardless of correctness) can be kept for subsequent consideration. Hofstadter found out that he possessed a category for things one thinks serve a special function but do not, which carried associations with disappointment and father/child relations, among other things. Fish's pathetic fallacy category may indicate a common enough desire for reconciliation with death. In interchapter 2 I describe my own incidentally useful misreading of a poem that also carries associations with loss and desire for reconciliation. But now back to my review of Fish and selected reader-oriented theories.

According to affective stylistics, *response* means "any activities provoked by a string of words . . . attitudes towards persons, or things, or ideas referred to" (Fish 1970, 127). This notably extends beyond just the emotional, as most theorists until that point would have dismissively assumed, and it includes any "mental operation" that occurs in reading as well. So it seems potential does exist here to think about rhetorical actions the reader might perform with the text as a result of reading it, but Fish does not take his theory in that direction. He is content to have made the important shift from what a text means to what readers do to make meaning of texts. Another relatively conservative aspect of Fish's (1970, 145, original emphasis) earlier theory is that he has in mind a particular kind of reader who is not only a competent speaker of the text's language but also "in full possession of 'the semantic knowledge that a mature reader brings to the task of comprehension' . . . [and] has *literary* competence." In other words, Fish isn't thinking of readers in general but of an "ideal" or "informed" reader, someone with traditional literary training already established. There is nothing wrong with that, of course; it is only a point of difference between his and my aims, despite our mutual interest in the lived, perceptual experience of reading.

Fish's later reader-response theory shifts focus to the social contexts in which discussions of textual meaning circulate, with an emphasis on *why* readers generate certain interpretations (rather than *what* those interpretations are). Fish calls these contexts *interpretive communities,* later known as discourse communities. They are not necessarily determined by physical proximity or presence but rather by conventions or shared methods of interpreting that predispose readers to "perform certain acts" that "give texts their shape" (Fish 1976, 481). Interpretive communities are "made up of those who share interpretive strategies . . . for constituting [texts'] properties and assigning their intentions"; these strategies "exist prior to the act of reading and therefore determine the shape of what is read rather than, as is usually assumed, the other way around" (Fish 1976, 483). To put the idea simply, when readers agree in their interpretations of a common text, they do so because they are collectively predisposed to read the text in that way; when readers disagree in their interpretations, they do so because they have read the text from the standpoints of different interpretive communities. This theory of reading seems to fall somewhere between my categories of *responding* and *doing things.* On one hand, the orientation of activity is still text-directed and concerned with interpretation of meaning, and therefore the emphasis remains on response. On the other hand, in this later theory Fish is also in the realm of the rhetorical: texts have socially constructed currency. I agree, but—along the lines of Scholes's (1983) critique of Fish's theory—I do not see such an absolutely determinative effect on what individuals can do with texts in contexts. Their currency can be traded in a greater variety of ways than are acknowledged here.

Rorty

Although Richard Rorty is not a literary critic per se, his theories involving literature are both reader-oriented and pragmatic, and as such they closely align with my interest in promoting the response category I call *doing things.* Neither Rorty nor I address literary critics as our primary audience with our theories of literary textual utility, though we both poach on their territory. We both share an interest with Iser, Bleich, Holland, and Fish in refocusing critical attention on the *reader,* but neither Rorty nor I maintain these theorists' commitment to a *meaning* of the text, whether that meaning be something readers create on their own, whether the text has some say in creating the meaning, or whether the experience of reading itself somehow acts as the text's meaning. Rorty breaks from these and any other theories of meaning and focuses instead on the usefulness of literary texts. He distinguishes his literary critical agenda from what fellow pragmatist Jeffrey Stout (1982) calls intentionalists, on the one hand, and from contextualists, on the other hand, the latter of whom Rorty calls decoders or weak textualists.

By contrast, a strong textualist, Rorty (1982, 151) explains—following Harold Bloom's notion of a *strong misreader*—"brushes aside what the author undertook to signify." This reader's non-methodological approach denies "that there really is a secret code and that once it's discovered we shall have gotten the text right" (Rorty 1982, 152).[18] Furthermore, this reader engages a text "for what he can get out of it, not for the satisfaction of getting something right" (Rorty 1982, 152). Rorty (1992, 103, original emphases) denies the possibility of a right reading altogether: "The thought that a commentator has discovered what a text is really doing—for example, that it is *really* demystifying an ideological construct, or *really* deconstructing the hierarchical oppositions of western metaphysics, rather than merely being capable of being *used* for these purposes—is, for us pragmatists[,] just more occultism. It is one more claim to have cracked the code, and thereby detected What Is *Really* Going On." Rorty's (1982, 151) reader, much like my maker of affordances, "asks neither the author nor the text about their intentions but simply beats the text into a shape which will serve his own purpose. He makes the text refer to whatever is relevant to that purpose. He does this by imposing a vocabulary . . . on the text which may have nothing to do with any vocabulary used in the text or by its author, and seeing what happens." This reader "simply asks himself the same question about a text which the engineer or the physicist asks himself about a puzzling physical object: how shall I describe this in order to get it to do what I want?" (Rorty 1982, 153).

Rorty's positions are worth considering in the original here because my views align rather closely with them and because his prose is so refreshingly clear. One difference in our approaches, however, may be that I believe the making of uses or affordances of literary texts can happen unconsciously or semi-consciously as well as intentionally. It is not clear to me what Rorty's position on this point would be, but this doesn't strike me as a vital distinction either way. I also differ from Rorty, as with Bleich, in the scope of our claims, as he is taking on the very foundations of Western philosophy, and I am mainly seeking just to supplement text-oriented instructional practices. Another potential difference arises from whether Rorty would agree with me that nearly anybody can potentially effectively approach literature in this way, or if he would follow Bloom's lead in reserving strong misreadings for only a select few, or if perhaps another option is more accurate.[19] I might be justified in feeling somewhat hopeful here because Rorty regards literature as a powerful tool for building solidarity in a liberal society by, for example, raising awareness of the need to alleviate suffering—and it seems to me these aims cannot be achieved without widespread participation.

For Rorty, one way literature can affect language habits is by creating new vocabularies in its readers. Such new vocabularies—a central aspect to Rorty's general philosophy—carry the potential to establish a sense of morality or at least to urge people to think of their own morals, and in this way his literary theory resembles the ethical criticism addressed in the next section. If, like Rorty, we do not believe in a universal "human nature" that accounts for all agency, then it follows that literature—for all its evocative opportunities for making associations and appropriations—can influence our thoughts, language, and behavior. Unlike the previously cited reader-response critics or the following ethical critics, Rorty is not only or primarily thinking about what the reader experiences *while* reading or in the immediate moment of interpreting or—as we have seen—as the author or text dictates. Rather, the usefulness of literary texts for Rorty seems to exist largely after the fact and is mainly political for its effects on readers' social actions. For present purposes, we might think of this action as rhetorical, with an emphasis on the contingency of knowledge.

Janet Horne (1989) provides a clear account of some of Rorty's rhetorical positions in this regard. For him, Horne (1989, 248) writes, "knowledge is discursive, not absolute. What constitutes knowledge is determined by one's community, rather than by correspondence to Truth. Since knowledge is discursive and ethnocentric, it is enhanced by diversity of participation in the conversation. Competing views of knowledge emerge in the form of competing, or alternative vocabularies which gain acceptance in a variety of ways—ways primarily related to their discursive nature." Horne (1989, 249) points to an important consequence of these views: "Clearly, Rorty argues that the hierarchical relationship between 'knowledge' and 'opinion' is based upon the degree of 'intersubjective agreement' that can be obtained, rather than upon accuracy of representation and correspondence to Truth." Knowledge, opinion, and the role of ethos or character in establishing agreement are all central issues for the ethical criticism the next section takes up, which shares with Rorty and me a concern for how texts function as rhetorical influences in human cultures.

IS THIS ANY DIFFERENT FROM ETHICAL CRITICISM?

Yes, rhetor response is different from ethical literary criticism, though they have a good deal in common. In this section I mention the resemblance only in passing, as I think that speaks for itself, and I explain some differences in more length, but I do not dwell on this contrast for long, either. Also, I include a few references that might not ordinarily appear in a survey of this scholarly area. Behind both of these decisions is the fact that my theory does not emerge from and does not seek affiliation with ethical criticism. I neither have nor seek an insider's status. If it is useful to others to pursue further relations (of sameness, difference, or both) than I do here, then I support that endeavor and hope to learn of the outcomes. What my approach and that of ethical critics share is a fundamental interest in understanding the influences of texts on people's lives—as opposed to, for example, the author's intentions or the text's coherence or a variety of cultural implications of texts, all of which a reader can (and many student readers unfortunately do) analyze without having any significant personal investment or reward in the act. Our primary difference is that ethical critics tend to conceive of the reader as a relatively passive recipient of ethical influences from texts, whereas I see the reader as more active, not only in this dynamic but also in making original uses of literary texts (ethical or not), which is a matter these critics do not generally consider. To explain our differences, it will be helpful to clear up a common misconception about the term *ethical* in this context.

As a number of critics in this area have explained, "ethical" in the present usage does not refer to right and wrong, as in the opposite of the popular meaning of *unethical*. Rather, here the term signals relevance to a person's ethos, or character. So ethical literary critics believe that narratives (i.e., stories especially but also other forms of literature) play a considerable role in shaping the kind of people readers become. Marshall Gregory offers many excellent explanations of this effect, including this one:

> To understand the ethical vision of . . . [a story] is imaginatively to ingest the possibility that the narrative actions—and the narrative values—we have just encountered may occur in the real world. In one obvious and important way they *do* exist in the real world. Ingested possibilities that form a part of our potential repertoire of real actions also form a part of our real ethical character. Surely the content of ethical character is precisely equivalent to the number and kind of choices that one perceives possible in the world of action. Consumers of story who imaginatively ingest the worlds of human actions laid out for them in stories are potentially made over in the shape of the ethical vision of the stories that they both love and hate. (Gregory 2009, 37)

I don't disagree with Gregory's point, but I do have to stipulate that the choices for action that readers perceive to be possible—including the literary affordances they make—are at least as much, if not more, a matter of what readers bring to texts than vice versa. I take issue with Gregory's and so many ethical critics' passive characterizations of readers and with this theoretical school's limited view of the text/reader relationship (i.e., *passive* and *limited* relative to my views, not to other theoretical schools, which can be far worse in these ways). Ethical critics tend to treat readers, to return to Gregory's passage above, as "consumers" who "ingest" and are "made over" by texts and textual values that are "laid out for them" and "encountered." The title "*Shaped* by Stories" and subtitle "The Ethical Power of *Narratives*" (my emphases) of Gregory's book demonstrate that this not merely a matter of diction but rather the very nature of the ethical critics' theoretical paradigm. In this scheme, readers are the ones being *shaped*, and *narratives* are the ones with the power, and these are seen as separate entities from each other rather than co-constitutive features of a discursive phenomenon or ecology. As the ethical critic's logic goes: good texts or characters or plots (and similar elements) can have good influences on readers' lives, and bad ones can have bad influences, so ethical criticism trains readers to make the right choices.

Here is Gregory's mentor and one of the most prominent ethical literary critics of the twentieth century, Wayne C. Booth (1988, 178, original emphasis), imagining a hypothetical reader determining whether to accept an invitation to "friendship" by a literary text, addressed here in the second person: "Do you, my would-be friend, wish *me* well, or will you be the only one to profit if I join you?" Robert Coles, an ethical critic in spirit if not in name, similarly describes novels as "buddies" in his accounts of using literature in medical settings for inspirational and therapeutic purposes. "Poets give us images and metaphors," he writes, "and offer the epiphanies doctors and patients alike crave, even if it is in the silent form of a slant of late afternoon light" (Coles 1989, 101). In Booth's and Coles's (and others') formulations, which I admire despite my wish to transcend them, it is the author or the text that offers the terms and values of the transaction decided upon. I appreciate this construction to the extent that it at least grants readers the power to accept or decline, which means they are not entirely passive. But I obviously maintain a much more active vision of the reader's role in putting literary texts to use, wherein the influences shared by texts and readers are not as literal and singularly directed as in the formulations of ethical criticism.

I believe readers can choose to do whatever they wish with texts (or just some textual features; see the introduction), and the local situation will determine the value, if any, of those actions, as need be. Of course, if texts were *real* (i.e., human) friends or buddies, then we could not rightly treat them this way, but then it would follow that they could not rightly "shape" us, either—except in the (rhetorical) way we all shape each other all the time, in which case we've arrived back at my point that people's relations with and through texts are mutual and negotiated. This is a non-issue, though. Contrary to an idea that stems from at least Kant (see Rorty 1992, 106) by way of E. D. Hirsch (1976) and William Irwin (2000), I do not believe texts possess any status of equivalency to actual persons. Nor do they embody the humanity of their authors in any essential way. Though literary texts are not only or necessarily means to ends, I assert that they can be (and are often) treated as means, and I deny that they are ends in themselves—at least once they've reached the hearts, minds, and social contexts of active readers. So while I firmly agree with the ethical critics that texts have considerable power to shape readers, I add that when it is acknowledged that reading is an act of production, not just consumption (see the previous and following chapter sections), then readers can realize that they also possess power to shape their textual experiences and with them to shape the rhetorical situations in which they live. In other words, literary texts do things *and* we can do things with them.

My addendum to the ethical critics might appear to some as just a restatement of a fairly old idea from another twentieth-century critical giant, Kenneth Burke. On some level, Burke's well-known idea of "literature as equipment for living" does correspond to what I am promoting. After all, Burke is interested in the usability, or "active nature," of literature in its proverb-like qualities (Burke 1973, 293–96). Literary texts, for him, "do something" (Burke 1973, 89), including, among other things, strategically naming life's recurrent situations. In this way, literature "singles out a pattern of experience that is sufficiently representative of our social structure, that recurs sufficiently often *mutandis mutatis*,[20] for people to 'need a word for it' and to adopt an attitude toward it [somewhat akin to Holland's 'identity theme']. Each work of art is the addition of a word to an informal dictionary" (Burke 1973, 303).[21] This theory somewhat resembles my descriptions above about the metaphorical function of literary affordances. But on the other hand, Burke's "sociological criticism" turns out to be much more critical than sociological, more concerned with the general and timeless applications of literature to situations made by *authors* than in local and idiosyncratic uses made by *readers*. Burke's method in this case aims "to codify the various strategies which artists have developed with relation to the naming of situations" (Burke 1973, 301). Readers may certainly follow along, but the emphasis in this scheme is notably on *following*. As Burke writes, "If we try to discover what the poem is doing for the poet, we may discover a set of generalizations as to what poems do for everybody" and thereby "make basic discoveries about the *structure* of the work itself" (1973, 73, original emphasis); by treating literature as "proverbs writ large," we can "discover important facts about literary organization" (1973, 296). So whereas Burke returns to the text with his analysis of symbolic action, as do the ethical critics and reader-response theorists with their respective methods, I wish to turn or remain outward in focusing on readers and their situations, which may or may not have anything to do with the original strategies of the author. When Burke (1973, 303) does look outward, he and I agree that readers can apply works of art actively and usefully "to social situations outside of art," but in Burke's scheme these applications would be predetermined by the artist or text and *then* applied as such rather than simply as the reader sees fit, regardless of authorial intention or a text's discrete meaning.

I want to dwell a little longer on an idea that Burke mentions briefly in passing, which, if elaborated, would help clarify how our approaches agree. At the heart of Burke's method in the "Literature as Equipment for Living" section of *The Philosophy of Literary Form* is—to use terminology from above in my chapter—the "common essence" shared by elements of an analogy or metaphor. One way literature is usable, says Burke (1973, 302–3), is by infinitely classifying or grouping texts into analogous life situations "on the basis of some strategic element common to the items grouped." This follows the same logic by which apples might be grouped with bananas in the category of fruit or with balls in the category of round, and so on. Burke (1973, 302–3) even goes as far as to state that it does not matter if making a particular analogy of a literary work would offend good taste. If I understand the spirit in which he meant this, then I agree, except where ill-willed cultural appropriation is concerned. But I choose not to limit Burke's grouping process only to uses of texts that are author-intended (as if we can even be certain about an author's intentions) or that must square somehow with a collectively determined interpretive meaning of the text (as if there were universal agreement about this). Let me offer an example I have used in my teaching.

W. H. Auden's poem "As I Walked out One Evening" has stood out strongly to me in the years since I first read it. I was never taught and have never read any commentary on this poem's meaning, but for the past several years I have been *using* the poem, especially two of its stanzas, in ways that have been only partially conscious to me (in the typical sense). Burke's method of classifying potential uses of the poem, as follows, can be enlightening, but the most significant categories that arise for me in the present case are personal ones, which could not have been intended by Auden and likely would not square with conventional academic treatments of the work. The poem is essentially a list of poignant imagistic reminders of the ephemeral and even possibly false nature of human values, enclosed in a narrow narrative frame. As its fifteen quatrains proceed, love, certainty, beauty, grace, domestic pleasures, innocence, and other values all fall victim to time's inevitable corruption. Prior to the poem's final, framing stanza are the two quatrains that have stuck with me the most. Technically, the charge I feel from them emerges from the conceptual third and fourth lines that follow the descriptive first and second lines in each of these stanzas, chimed in figurative dialogue by personified clocks in an unnamed city where two lovers have hid away to share promises of eternity:

"O look, look in the mirror,
O look in your distress;
Life remains a blessing
Although you cannot bless."
"O stand, stand at the window
As the tears scald and start;
You shall love your crooked neighbor
With your crooked heart."

These remarkable lines would likely stick in many readers' hearts and minds, and they were what might even be called *meaningful* to me, but only in a rather vague way, for years before they started being *useful* to me in a specific way in a social context. That context is the walkup apartment building where my wife, our two-and-a-half-year-old boy, and I live on the fourth floor. Our boy's birth less than three years ago marks the beginning of my period of using the two Auden stanzas above as a literary affordance, when I suddenly realized the health implications of having a neighbor who smokes voraciously. This is my "crooked neighbor." She smokes in her apartment one floor below and down the hall from ours and often while sitting on the stoop of our building, where she sets up for long parts of days with a cushion to sit on, books, magazines, coffee, her phone, and an endless supply of cigarettes. This means my family and I are sometimes subjected to breathing her cigarette smoke. She apparently cannot be compelled to stop smoking in the building, and for various reasons we cannot move out. So this is an abiding situation and a potentially rhetorical one.

I can use Burke's method to place features from Auden's two stanzas into categories that actively "name" functions helpful to the context I have just described. For example, *aspiration* could be one category, considering Auden's allusion to the great commandment from Mark 12:31: "love thy neighbor as thyself." Although I was raised loosely Catholic, I do not consider myself one, but I do try to practice principles from various belief systems, including this one; furthermore, a by-product of having a baby seems to be learning of my remarkably expansive powers of loving. I love my toddler and my wife as myself, actually far more than myself, and I am inspired to try to make that experience a kind of light I can shine on others. So I have been trying hard to approach my crooked neighbor dilemma with a loving attitude. Another reason is that apart from her smoking, my neighbor is a nice person; she's friendly and quick with a compliment that she seems to mean. She's also fairly pitiable—living alone, enjoying no visitors or occupation, and chronically buying from TV shopping channels. Furthermore, she seems to have a number of health problems. But mine would have to be some compromised form of love at best for this person because I often feel she does not deserve it, not when she endangers the health of my family through secondhand cigarette smoke. Her problems cannot become my problems. Or can they? Am I to selectively love my neighbor only for her positive qualities? Is that any kind of love? No, there must be an alternative, and I think I have been building up to it: a crooked expression of neighborly love.

This leads me to another category that might be applied: *linearity*. What does a crooked love look like? I'm imagining it as a crooked time line, like a four-story staircase in two-dimensional profile, a zigzagging trail of resolutions and failures: be kind to this sad person; be angry at her for smoking; feel bad for being kind and for getting angry; feel bad for having felt bad at all because this person deserves scorn for endangering my beautiful little boy's health; but this little boy has taught me more about the value and power of love than anything; feel redeemed for having so strong an intuition of what it's like to live a blessed life in which "you cannot bless"; feel bad because most people would have long ago confronted the neighbor; but as a rhetorician I know that confrontation is usually ineffective or even counterproductive—"most people," after all, are not aware of Rogerian argumentation (Kiefer n.d.), Burke's (1969) argument as collaboration, Corder's (1985) commodious rhetoric of love, Foss and Griffin's (1995) invitational rhetoric,

Glenn's (2004) rhetoric of silence, Ratcliffe's (2005) rhetorical listening, or Lyon's (2013) participatory deliberation.

Does it do me any good to think of my dilemma in terms of crooked loving rhetoric?[22] Yes, I believe it does. Whereas some people might see this indeterminacy in a negative light, I actually take heart from it: a "crooked heart." I may be incapable of blessing, but I am capable of feeling blessed, and that intransitive state of being is a subjectivity I occupy rather than just an action I take, in which case by reflecting as I am here, I may become further in touch with my ethos (a tactile insinuation that anticipates my work on felt sense in chapter 5). My rhetoric may not have found explicit expression to my neighbor yet (though I sense she senses I am working on something, which in turn I think may have her working, too, or am I just projecting?), but rhetoric is not just in the expression, especially where ethos is concerned. I am building steam toward that, and when it comes out, I would like it not to be the blowing of my top but a controlled combustion that might actually propel us somewhere favorable. It may be a crooked line that gets us there, but should I expect any different? There is also the matter of this material's effects on my readers, which I have no way of predicting but which at least comprises another potential ethical dimension of my literary affordance.

Crooked also means criminal, so let's add a category called *criminality*. I don't think my neighbor's smoking in the building is literally illegal, but knowing what is now known about the health detriments of secondhand smoke, I feel we can generally consider smoking to be a figuratively "criminal," antisocial act except when undertaken in areas that are completely isolated or designated specifically for smoking. Putting aside this specific example for a moment, do I really think I can isolate my child from such social ills? Of course not. Every parent likely wrestles with this. I've long ago surmised that the best I can probably do is model for my boy the behavior I would recommend he choose when facing conflicts, give him time and room to develop his own views, and keep our channels of communication open and thriving. We live in a world of abundant, distressing criminal behavior. If we don't want to constantly lament that reality, as Auden's persona cries in looking out the window, then isn't it befitting to take a long, collective look in the mirror, as Auden's persona also does, and be deliberate in shaping the character we wish to see reflected there? Is that what I am doing regarding my crooked neighbor, or am I just stalling because of my distaste for confrontation?[23]

If someone wants to loosely label as *ethical* these sample uses of literature I have just explained because the text plays a role in shaping my character, then I have no significant qualms with that. But if that person should mean by his label that I believe the author intended these effects or that these effects comprise the meaning of the text, then I must object, for I make no such conclusions. I believe literary affordances emerge regardless of whether literature "can be a paradigm of moral activity," as Martha Nussbaum (1985, 516) maintains, or is a significant source of "'how one should live' questions" (1998, 358). In sum, my problem with such ethical criticism is its literalness, which leads to the kind of grand claims that cause understandable backlash against "great books" arguments. Such literalism has also manifested in practices affiliated with what is known today as *fictional bibliotherapy*, where various beneficial effects of reading fiction on readers are being examined in some fascinating studies (Johnson, Huffman, and Jasper 2014; Kaufman and Libby 2012; Kidd and Castano 2013), employed as counseling tools (Markell and Markell 2008; Rapee, Abbott, and Lyneham 2006), and even prescribed as a treatment for depression (Smith, Floyd, Jamison, and Scogin 1997; Jamison and Scogin 1995) or (non-clinically) as antidotes to dozens of other ailments (Berthoud and Elderkin 2014). I do not disparage those views or applications, but I personally prefer a less formulaic accounting of potential uses that may emerge from reading, whereby in Gregory's (2009, 13) terms, "associations stirred by stories" can afford "comparisons between, or associations with, real events and fictional events giv[ing] me a constant set of references that allow me to toggle back and forth between fictional worlds and real life, deepening my understanding of both."

CAN YOU REALLY DO THAT TO A WORK OF LITERATURE?

This is a faulty question, but it has been asked of me and will likely be asked again, so I had better address it anyway. Technically, literary affordances do not do anything *to* texts, only *through* or *in terms of* texts. Toggling between real and fictional worlds, as Gregory says just above, can very well have real consequences, but the work of fiction remains intact no matter what is done through or in terms of it. In other words, the original text is unaffected by the affordances that emerge from it. Of course, I will answer what is meant in the *spirit* of the question at hand, but I wanted to acknowledge this important *in-the-letter* of the question point first. Further, I believe anyone can make literary affordances. I understand why some English instructors and scholars would resist this claim, in which case, of course, they need not teach literary affordance or take it up themselves, or they might modify or constrain the practice somehow that better suits them. But I do hope the instructors would at least consider occasionally sanctioning literary affordance, perhaps as an entry point or supplement to more conventional literary textual activities. For one thing, comparing and contrasting interpretation with affordance can help distinguish and clarify each of these acts and their purposes for students, especially the (many) students who may not share the motivation of literary scholars to "pick apart" texts, as it is often put. Having a familiar context in which to be genuinely engaged in *using* features of a literary work that has been personally significant can be helpful to a student who otherwise sees no good reason to analyze that work. Such an experience may bring to light Mailloux's (1997, 385) important point that "interpretation (establishing meaning) and rhetoric (troping, arguing) are closely connected and mutually defining practices." Chapter 4 says more about these matters.

As for the *spirit* of the question at the heading of this section, I believe that yes, you can do this to literature *if you can*. I will offer more than my own word for it soon, but first let me clarify. I believe that if a literary affordance emerges for you and you wish to use it or write about it and you are able to do so, then you may do so. It should be as simple as that. Of course, there may be any number of reasons why you cannot do so in a given time or place. For example, perhaps no literary affordance has emerged for you, or one has but it seems ineffective for social application (which does not discount personal value), or you have been barred from undertaking the practice of making affordances by some force whose authority you choose (or have no choice but) to respect. Then don't do it. If you are unsure about any of this, then you can always ask, but you may want to be mindful of the subject position and attendant entanglements of your respondents. I can easily imagine a place (in addition to writing classrooms) for the practice of literary affordance within contexts where literary theories are traditionally applied, such as an English class. But I am also realistic in my expectations about this, at least in the early going. After all, my theory's two nearest constellations, reader-response and ethical criticism, are both so marginalized as schools of thought these days that they are sometimes dismissed or omitted altogether in historical surveys of literary theory.

One concern that inevitably arises in the company of reader-oriented theories is what I call the "anything-goes" objection (mentioned in the introduction), which underwrites the question from the heading above that I am in the midst of answering here. *Anything goes* is the worry that if we leave the interpretive meaning or application of literary texts up to unqualified readers to determine for themselves, then some of them will propose incorrect interpretations or outrageous formulations. Such charges have been pressed from the periphery, as in Scholes's (1982, 9) denunciation of "a veritable anarchy of interpretive variation" by readers who think they have "the right to make any meaning that their psychic needs require of a particular text," and defenses have been issued from the inside, such as by Rosenblatt (1995, xix): "Recognition that there can be no absolute, single 'correct' reading of a text has sometimes been seen as accepting any reading of a text. Without positing a single, absolutely correct reading, we can still agree on criteria by which to evaluate the validity of alternative interpretations of a text." I have stated above that my interests are in the *uses* and not in the interpretive *meanings* of literary texts, so this is a non-issue as far as I'm concerned. But I will still mention that it seems to me that anything-goes worries tend to mistakenly emphasize the *anything* part instead of the *goes* part of the matter. One of the things that make the human imagination so wonderful and powerful is that *anything* indeed might occur to it. This strikes me as a gift and a great pedagogical resource, and luckily the occurrence of *anything* to the human imagination seems to be a persistent phenomenon. But witting and unwitting attempts to suppress or marginalize that function do exist, including, unfortunately, in education. So if we take it as a given that anything might occur, then the question really comes down to which *anythings* get to *go* and which do not? That is to say, which ideas count as viable, in this case among readers' responses to a literary text?

Some agree with Fish's answer (which is really an elaboration on Rosenblatt's views) that interpretive communities determine such viability, and where literature is concerned, the leading community should be that of expert literary theorists. But as I have stated, the huge number of people in the world who are not beholden to or interested in the standards of the community of literary scholars (which is anything but unified anyway, so this really means: to a particular sub-community) can determine validity in terms of whatever rhetorical situation it is in which their reading seeks application, if indeed any application beyond the personal dimension is sought. If standards are going to shift as much as this plan assumes they do, then I doubt whether they could be accounted for in advance by any encompassing evaluative criterion and at more than "just" the local level. Call this a cop-out if you like; I call it crossing that bridge if and when we get to it because who knows what it might entail and because a priori rubrics and assignment design do a great deal to influence perception, expectations, and behavior. In other words, I say let's let a reader's *anything* go if it indeed *goes* relative to the context. If it doesn't go (one can try to find out by asking around) and one cares enough about it, then one can revise and try again.

Of course, if someone else disagrees enough with a given affordance, then that person is also free to make a case against it. But simply deciding ahead of time that it just cannot *go* will not always stop it from going anyway and may in fact only increase the other's resolve to make it go (I know it likely would for me). I am not including here legal and ethical boundaries that should be respected. There is also the question of *how far* an affordance goes. Again, this strikes me as something to determine locally, if need be at all. Measuring figurative distances of this kind will always be relative to an abstract point of reference that should not be taken for granted as necessarily clear, settled, true, right, or universal. For example, I providentially stumbled upon an article in a physics journal titled "Looking into Chapman's Homer: The Physics of Judging a Fly Ball" (Brancazio 1985), and I was initially excited to find two great loves of mine, poetry and baseball, combined under a titular affordance of Keats's poem. This literary affordance at least made it as far as getting published in a prestigious journal and scoring puns with "homer" (i.e., slang for home run) and "Chapman" (a physics scholar who theorized about trajectories of hit baseballs). So as far as physicists may be concerned, the affordance may go a long way. But it ultimately went nowhere with me, as I was disappointed to find no actual reference to the Keats poem in the article. I was not the target audience in this author's rhetorical situation.

I do not think texts, authors, or readers are such fragile things that anything-goes concerns are worth worrying much about beyond local contexts, wherein, of course, there may very well be issues to worry about and therefore to study and discuss. But I want to entertain the complaint slightly further because it's not a far leap from worries about misreadings of texts' *meanings* to worries about outrageous—or the better argument would be offensive—*affordances* of texts. This is a shift in charges from misreading to misuse, in which the *goes* in the anything-goes objection might stand in for abuse, theft, or disagreeable indoctrination, for example. In other words, some may worry that I am sanctioning misappropriations of texts for sinister purposes. But I have already said multiple times that I do not condone illegal or culturally disrespectful literary affordances. Beyond this, I say: if someone believes he holds a formula for pedagogically precluding all morally corrupt misuses of literary texts that does not diminish these texts' potential for virtuous rhetorical applications, then come forth with it and let's try it out; I am skeptical but willing to listen. But still I can imagine someone objecting: "Well, at least we should tell our children that they cannot simply do *anything* with a text." I am not willing to say that to a child or anyone else. I *am* willing to state whether a proposed affordance strikes me as ineffective or offensive and to work with the affordance maker on understanding why and on revising accordingly. But that is only *if and when* ineffectiveness or offensiveness is actually encountered, not by means of some universal policy that hopes to predict and preempt problems that may never materialize in the first place. Copyright law and legally sanctioned speech codes are more complicated matters than I can go into here, but I want it to be clear that I oppose illegal or culturally disrespectful literary affordances, and I support preemptive policies where these issues are concerned.

What may likely be at work on a deeper level with concerns about meaning is a somewhat understandable desire to protect literary texts' *aura.* That is, a certain special quality bound up in the interpretive meaning of the great works of aesthetic achievement that supposedly put them in a category above ordinary discourse. "the best which has been thought and said," as Matthew Arnold famously encapsulated the views of an era that included Carlyle, Mill, Pater, Shelley, and Wordsworth. The concern seems to be that letting anyone do anything they wish with works of high art may corrupt those works and their value to our culture, which supposedly seeks to perfect itself in relation to them (to keep with Arnold). The contemporary pedagogical extension of this view prioritizes or singles out *meaning* as the highest or only value in literary study and often implicitly denies authority in this scheme to all but credentialed expert instructors and commentators. I now offer four responses to this issue of the exclusive aura of literary meaning.

First, it seems cynical to me to assume that the unqualified masses would necessarily besmirch the greatness of high art if they were to have unrestricted access (in a broad sense) to it. I note, for example, that the *Mona Lisa* has been appropriated in countless ways over its celebrated lifetime (including in Duchamp's case to the effect of arguably creating another work of high art), and its aura has only seemed to grow brighter and stronger in that same time.[24] *Hamlet* does not seem to have suffered at the hands of, for just one case, its unconventional treatment by Thug Notes (2013); nor has *Pride and Prejudice* lost esteem for being overrun by zombies; and as we speak, flourishing fanfiction communities are bringing together vast numbers of textual respondents in remarkably productive ways (often to the chagrin or disregard of academics).

Second, non-specialists already have a great deal of unrestricted access to the great works of art, so perhaps this issue is already largely moot. Again, consider fanfiction (and see Benjamin and Lessig below in this chapter). Or note that Donald Trump's presidency has caused *1984* to become a bestseller seventy years after its composition, not because English professors have suddenly called for renewed attention to the novel's meaning but because tens of thousands of ordinary people, of their own volition, want to apply it to their everyday experience.

Third, who is to say that making affordances of great literary works would not increase people's appreciation and learning of those works? My experience in teaching this practice has been that students maintain respect for their source text—which, in my courses, they choose themselves—and they often come to grow in their knowledge and appreciation of it in the process. Whether their affordances always draw on so-called *correct* interpretations of source texts is not of primary concern in this context because no interpretation of their meaning is being ventured (or if one is, then a productive discussion can follow any occurrence of seeming inaccuracy, if need be). Because my curricular application of literary affordance is meant to supplement or exist relatively independently of analysis and interpretation, not to replace them, a loss of coverage that might typically be gained through compulsory exposure to unfamiliar texts does not seem worth worrying much about. It is hoped that room can be made for both. But for that matter, E. Shelley Reid (2004, 16) has made a convincing case for what she calls an "uncoverage" model of pedagogy—albeit at the graduate level—which she describes "as practice in a way of encountering the world rather than mastery of skills or facts," basically by digging further into fewer course readings rather than covering more of them in less depth. One of the spontaneous shorthand explanations to have emerged in my work in this area with students is thinking of the act of literary affordance as teaching others how to experience what a text has done for you. So if there is any truth to the familiar phrase *the best way to learn something is to teach it*, then literary affordances can still prompt valuable learning about the texts they use, even though the purpose is not *about* the texts themselves.

Fourth, as Jane P. Tompkins explains, it is only since the twentieth century that specification of textual *meaning* has been the main purpose of literary critical thought. As she notes with irony, "The first requirement of a work of art in the twentieth century is that it should *do* nothing" (Tompkins 1980, 210, original emphasis). That is to say, today "we equate [literary] language not with action but with signification" (Tompkins 1980, 203). By contrast, approaches to literature from antiquity through the Renaissance, Augustan, and Romantic periods were predominantly rhetorical and political. Readers' interest in those times lay mainly in literature's *effects*, not in its meaning, so the text was regarded as "an instrument . . . a force exerted upon the world" (Tompkins 1980, 225). So anyone today who wishes to deemphasize or pause their attention to interpretive meaning for the sake of exploring literary affordances can feel encouraged by the notion that rhetor response theory may not be quite as far afield from the long history of literary critical discourse as it may at first appear to be.

For further support I now turn to a pair of theorists and a pair of their respective subsequent analogues who have had significant influences on my thinking: Walter Benjamin and Michel de Certeau. The analogues are Lawrence Lessig and Henry Jenkins. In his essay "The Work of Art in the Age of Mechanical Reproduction," Benjamin identifies a significant shift in ordinary people's relationship to works of art after the advent of mass reproduction technologies. An original work of high art, whose singularity in space and time endows it with an "aura" that was often associated with ritual, can now be experienced as a duplicate anywhere and anytime. Mass reproduction technologies thus remove the work from the tradition that used to frame its experience, in which the artifact may not have been thought of at all as *art* per se. The result, according to Benjamin, is a tradeoff: although the authenticity of the original is missing and the work's aura is depreciated or lost in the process, "mechanical reproduction emancipates the work of art from its parasitical dependence on ritual" (1968, 224) and "meets the beholder or listener in his own particular situation . . . [and] reactivates the object reproduced" (1968, 221).

As I understand it, this concept of the work being *reactivated* (in the lived context of the audience's situations) aligns perfectly with what I am proposing in my theory of literary affordance. As Benjamin (1968, 225) explains, because it is reproducible, "the work of art becomes a creation with entirely new functions, among which the one we are [until this point typically] conscious of, the artistic function, later may be recognized as incidental." The putting aside of the aura of a literary work potentially democratizes (or socializes) it, bringing new possibilities to this object that once may very well have been alienated from everyday handling by non-specialists. This is the political promise Benjamin sees in the role of art after mechanical reproduction. He argues that "art has left the realm of the 'beautiful semblance' which, so far, has been taken to be the only sphere where art could thrive" (Benjamin 1968, 230), and he proposes that because of this, "the distinction between author and public is about to lose its basic character . . . At any moment the reader is ready to turn into a writer" (Benjamin 1968, 232).

More than seventy years later, the issue of technology's influence on consumption, production, and status of art comes up again, analogically to Benjamin, in Lessig's 2009 book *Remix*. In addition to many other acts that I will not review, Lessig adopts in this book terminology from computer programming to clarify the remixing of artistic content that he demonstrates is now burgeoning, thanks to twenty-first-century technologies. These terms are "Read/Only culture" and "Read/Write culture," the former taken from a label applied to computer files that can only be *read* by users and the latter from files that can be both *read and rewritten* by users. These metaphors represent two very different approaches to texts or art that can be taken or sanctioned by members of the cultures those texts belong to and reflect. One promotes consumption, such as listening to a recorded song, for example. The other promotes production, such as singing (or *remixing*) a song. Lessig (2009, 84–85) supports development of the latter, explaining that this Read/Write kind of culture "extends itself differently" than Read/Only culture: "It touches social life differently. It gives the audience something more. Or better, it asks something more of the audience. It is offered as a draft. It invites a response. In a culture in which it is common, its citizens develop a kind of knowledge that empowers as much as it informs or entertains." Here again, we find language that aligns extremely well with my theory.[25]

In the approach to literature that I am calling rhetor response, the text's aura is similarly (if just provisionally) abandoned, and textual consumption transforms into acts of production through the making and potentially also the expression of literary affordances. These acts have rhetorical lives of their own in some other context(s). In other words, given readers' personal experiences of texts, they are prepared to make use of those experiences for purposes that may be inspired or informed by, but may still or otherwise be "incidental" to, the original "artistic function" of those literary works. As a provisional policy until I can more definitively make up my mind on the matter, I generally do not support affordances that would in any way damage their *original* source texts, which may very well still possess their aura or at least some of it. For example, elsewhere I have worked on making a literary affordance of Geoffrey Chaucer's earliest major poem, *The Book of the Duchess*, but never would I treat one of the few extant manuscripts of this text with anything other than reverence, if I were lucky enough to have access to the physical object. But this is a more complicated and debatable subject area than it may seem.

Consider, for example, the case involving contemporary artist Ai Weiwei, who has variously "appropriated" (Jones 2014) Han dynasty urns by painting on and even smashing them—who, in turn, has had at least two of "his" urns purposely smashed by other people. One instance was by a collector who had purchased the urn he smashed, and the other was by a protestor at a museum. Many critics and institutions are willing to accept and even adulate Ai Weiwei's defacement and destruction of the Han urns as works of high art in their own right. But what about the actions taken by these two others? It's not as simple as dismissing these subsequent destructions as derivative, because they are arguably calling into question Ai Weiwei's arguable calling into question of the very nature of the valuation of art (and many other legitimate related issues). In fact, the opposite may ironically be true, as it could be said that the most daring of these acts was that of the museum protestor, the only one of the three men in question who could not defer to his ownership of the piece he smashed in justifying his creative (or destructive?) literary affordance. As one commentator admittedly failed to settle the question: "So—smashing art is interesting if an acclaimed global artist does it, and even if an art collector does it. But the guy who walks into a museum and smashes it is a vandal" (Jones 2014).

Although I cannot resolve the complications of the Ai Weiwei example either, which perhaps thankfully is a rare case, I am prepared to invite less controversial yet still creative, rhetorical, and even potentially defiant affordances that would bring renewed agency to consumers of literary and artistic content. My greatest inspiration in this regard is Michel de Certeau (1984, 165–66), who rejects as "unacceptable" the stereotype of public readers that he characterizes as "handled" sheep, "grazing on the ration of simulacra the system distributes," which he attributes to the media industry, educators, and other specialists or members of an elite class. In his remarkable book *The Practice of Everyday Life*, which is dedicated to the "anonymous hero" of "the ordinary man," de Certeau reactivates reading and other modes of supposedly passive consumption by reintroducing them as the *productive* everyday practices he takes them to be. The section of this book titled "Reading as Poaching" has had the greatest influence on my rhetor response theory, so for this reason and for the fact that de Certeau's original phrasing (even in translation) is often dazzling, I directly quote him at some length here.

Behind the above stereotype lies an assumption that "the public is moulded by the products imposed on it . . . that 'assimilating' necessarily means 'becoming similar to' what one absorbs, and not 'making something similar' to what one is, making it one's own, appropriating or reappropriating it" (de Certeau 1984, 166). And behind this faulty assumption is the "fiction of the 'treasury' hidden in the work [of art], a sort of strong-box full of meaning," which de Certeau (1984, 171, original emphasis) argues "is obviously not based on the productivity of the reader, but on the *social institution* that overdetermines his relation with the text." De Certeau explains the processes and stakes he sees involved here:

> Reading is as it were overprinted by a relationship of forces (between teachers and pupils, or between producers and consumers) whose instrument it becomes. The use made of the book by privileged readers constitutes it as a secret of which they are the "true" interpreters. It interposes a frontier between the text and its readers that can be crossed only if one has a passport delivered by these official interpreters, who transform their own reading (which is *also* a legitimate one) into an orthodox "literality" that makes other (equally legitimate) readings either heretical (not "in conformity" with the meaning of the text) or insignificant (to be forgotten). From this point of view, "literal" meaning is the index and the result of a social power, that of an elite. By its very nature available to a plural reading, the text becomes a cultural weapon, a private hunting reserve, the pretext for a law that legitimizes as "literal" the interpretation given by *socially* authorized professionals and intellectuals. (de Certeau 1984, 171, original emphases)

Only a very few are pardoned for breaking these laws of literality, as de Certeau (1984, 172) explains: "If the reader's expression of his freedom through the text is tolerated among intellectuals . . . (only someone like Barthes can take this liberty), it is on the other hand denied students (who are scornfully driven or cleverly coaxed back to the meaning 'accepted' by their teachers) or the public (who are carefully told 'what is to be thought' and whose inventions are considered negligible and quickly silenced)."

De Certeau recounts a history of the Western educational apparatus that has reified these arrangements. The Enlightenment was supposed to have transformed and liberated (i.e., enlightened) culture through widespread education, but the system that developed for disseminating knowledge got in the way of its own aims such that the "means of diffusion are now dominating the ideas they diffuse. The medium is replacing the message" (de Certeau 1984, 166). In other words, the educational apparatus (a bureaucracy that has swollen and outsourced considerably in the decades since de Certeau was writing) has supplanted its originating democratic ambitions by putting its procedures rather than its learners at the forefront (see chapter 5 for my take on the specific example case of high-stakes writing tests). Large-scale standardization has isolated producers of culture and eradicated the participatory apprenticeship model, denying consumers creative agency and sustaining a "consumption-as-a-receptacle" ideology that complements the drive for "efficiency of production" (de Certeau 1984, 167). As de Certeau (1984, 167) puts it: "The massive installation of standardized teaching has made the intersubjective relationships of traditional apprenticeship impossible; the 'informing' technicians have thus been changed, through the systemization of enterprises, into bureaucrats cooped up in their specialties and increasingly ignorant of users; productivist logic itself, by isolating producers, has led them to suppose that there is no creativity among consumers; a reciprocal blindness, generated by this system, has ended up making both technicians and producers believe that initiative takes place only in technical laboratories."

Having identified this false but dominant representation of reading and its partial history, de Certeau offers his model of the impertinent reader, the reader as nomadic poacher. In this view, "To read is to wander through an imposed system (that of the text, analogous to the constructed order of a city or of a supermarket)," a process in which the reader "invents in texts something different from what they 'intended.' He detaches them from their (lost or accessory) origin. He combines their fragments and creates something un-known in the space organized by their capacity for allowing an indefinite plurality of meanings" (de Certeau 1984, 169). Such reading takes place by any number of everyday practices (alas, without everyday names), including *bricolage*—described as the use of materials at hand to rearrange previous arrangements—or *tactics* that are "playful, protesting, fugitive," and other games like this, any of which might serve as analogues for literary affordance.

Similarly to how I have drawn attention above to the tacit, perceptual features of literary affordances as embodied source domains of nonliterary conceptual metaphors, de Certeau also encourages a holistic approach to reading. "We should try to rediscover the movements of this reading within the body itself, which seems to stay docile and silent but mines the reading in its own way," a process he likens to "a wild orchestration of the body," in which we are free to move around and "to convert the text through reading and to 'run it' the way one runs traffic lights" (de Certeau 1984, 175–76). As clear as he is in many passages, de Certeau, like any theorist, can also be cryptic, even on highly significant points. The only specific example of an impertinent reading, or in my terms, a literary affordance, that de Certeau (1984, 174) provides is a vague, fleeting one when he mentions that, for instance, "the television viewer reads the passing away of his childhood in the news reports."

Where de Certeau has avoided specificity on this point, Henry Jenkins (1992) offers a book's worth of examples and explanations (though de Certeau might not have endorsed these particular models). As Lessig was my analogue to Benjamin, so is Jenkins to de Certeau. But one difference that diminishes the symmetry of the analogy is that Jenkins explicitly and extensively references de Certeau (even to the extent of titling his book *Textual Poachers*), whereas Lessig makes no mention of Benjamin in his book. The examples of textual poachers that Jenkins provides include fans, bloggers, and gamers, such as writers of fanfiction[26] or devotees of the *Star Trek* television and film series, widely known as *trekkies*. These kinds of fannish readers bring the texts they are devoted to deeply into their own lives in a great variety of ways that can stray far afield from the meanings or intentions of the source texts. Jenkins follows de Certeau in attributing the privileged minority for controlling authority over the majority public through indoctrination of schoolchildren into this ideology by means of the teacher's rewarding and penalizing "red pen." "Often," Jenkins (1992, 26) notes, "education is too preoccupied with protecting its own status . . . at the expense of their students' ability to form alternative interpretations. De Certeau invites us to reconsider the place of popular response, of personal speculations and nonauthorized meanings in the reception of artworks and to overcome professional training that prepares us to reject meanings falling outside our frame of reference and interpretive practice."

Jenkins (1992, 25) also extends this attribution in greater detail to the struggle between commercial agents of the producing class and fans who seek their own appropriations of the texts they love: "Since many segments of the population lack access to the means of cultural production and distribution to the multiplexes, the broadcast airwaves or the chain bookstore shelves, this respect for the 'integrity' of the produced message often has the effect of silencing or marginalizing oppositional voices. The exclusion of those voices at the moment of reception simply mirrors their exclusion at the moment of production: the cultural interests are delegitimized in favor of the commercial interests of authorized authors." The message here, as in de Certeau, is surprisingly positive: that readers or viewers do have agency to appropriate texts for their own interests, despite the considerable forces at work to control the textual economy. "In one sense," Jenkins (1992, 27) explains, "that of economic control over the means of production, these nomadic viewers truly are 'powerless and dependent' in their relationship to the culture industries. Yet, on another level, that of symbolic interpretation and appropriation, de Certeau would suggest they still retain a degree of autonomy." So for those who are willing and able—which may only be some people, part of the time, and in certain circumstances—there is an alternative approach to reading as a productive activity or even as a lifestyle whereby, in Jenkins's (1992, 27) words, "consumers are selective users of a vast media culture whose treasures, though corrupt, hold wealth that can be mined and refined for alternative uses."

INTERCHAPTER 3
The Fringèd Curtains of Thine Eye Advance

As a doctoral student of English at the Graduate Center of the City University of New York, I sometimes played a barroom game with friends in the program in which each of us stated the Shakespeare character we "were" and why. When my turn came, I chose *The Tempest*'s Prospero without a second thought. My explanation at the time was just the tip of an unconscious iceberg of reasons for this association: that Prospero chooses forgiveness after having been wronged by those close to him. I admit there were more dissimilarities than similarities between Prospero and me; for example, he is much older than I was then (and even am now), I was many years away (and a vast maturational distance) from being a father at the time, and I have never been tempted by vengeance against my wrongdoers. In fact, *wrongdoer* is not even an accurate term to employ in the context of the first experience I have in mind for comparison: the divorce of my parents, both of whom took great pains (effectively) to ensure my happiness and well being after the fact of my indirect effect of their decision. But a key commonality fruitfully persisted in co-presence or metaphorical "dialogue" (Seitz 1999, 125–28) with my dissimilarities with Prospero. My parents' divorce and the many years of perpetuating and repeating its effects (i.e., the rest of the iceberg) have constituted the predominant conflict of my life (narrative), and my preference for moving on rather than holding a grudge was enough of a commonality for me to deeply associate myself with Prospero, using elements from his travails as touchstones in reading and (re)writing my own story.

We know from my book's first interchapter that my default and constant approach to loved ones has been to serve their desires above all else. So when I read Prospero's assurance to Miranda, "I have done nothing but in care of thee, / Of thee, my dear one, thee my daughter" (1.2.21–22), and to the audience in the epilogue that the aim of his project has been "to please" (v.i.368), I was hooked by this character for speaking my language. But behind these relatively superficial similarities

DOI: 10.7330/9781607327769.c003b

existed a deeper connection and source of great personal learning for me. What I did not consciously know while playing that grad school game was that more and different kinds of lines by Prospero would emerge as highly significant to the development of my character.

As chapter 3 explains, Norman Holland has theorized that readers recreate their own fears and desires in the literature they read as a kind of Freudian repetition practice seeking resolution of unsettled issues. Though I do not believe it holds true all the time for all readers, Holland's theory does seem to account for many of my most valuable reading experiences, including that of *The Tempest.* For a number of years in graduate school, I was involved in a relationship with someone whose considerable needs I served unflaggingly and unconditionally, frankly, to the detriment of my own studies and even my well-being. At the time, I remained partly willingly ignorant of these serious side effects. Worse, although I knew very well, I refused to admit that the recipient of my efforts did not return the same to me. In truth, her contributions didn't come close. Then again, much of our relationship was false, built more on need than anything else: she seemed to need to repeat an unresolved separation as the one who leaves and I to repeat an unresolved separation as the one who is left. I had no conscious knowledge at the time (nor do I think she knew) that this imbalanced and precarious complementarity was mostly what brought and kept us together, but increasingly as the relationship persisted, a felt sense emerged in me that something extremely disruptive and significant was going to happen. I repeatedly described this feeling to myself and to her as a premonition of a curtain being torn back to reveal something unseen. But where did this imagery of a curtain come from, and why did it feel so perfectly right even though I could not account for it?

By the time the relationship ended, I was aware that we had long since just been playing roles in each other's psychic lives, yet I still half-sincerely and half-performatively (but just for myself) mourned the loss. It's odd to admit to performing for oneself (especially something like this), but if I am to be honest, that's exactly what I was doing. Moreover, this notion of performing became my key to unlocking the curtain premonition mystery and, with it, to explaining my skewed kinship with Prospero. In short, by watching myself mourn the loss of this relationship, I gradually managed to distance myself from the pain it was supposedly causing. I say *supposedly* because at some indistinct point, the pain, too, became more of a prop than a reality. I grew aware of the fact that I was rehearsing familiar lines, so to speak. Soon it seemed as if I were an actor watching a shipwreck that wasn't real but pretending that it were real in order to yield an emotional effect on an audience, which was also me. Then there I was as Prospero telling the Miranda of myself that I was doing it all for thee, for thee, my dear. And then, by providence and yet also by artful manipulation, a (brave?) new world began to emerge in my awareness: a future life lived without the burden of my past. Perhaps for the first time since I was seven years old, I could see and feel that as a reality. I was now my own Prospero opening my own Miranda's eyes to the first sight of a figurative Ferdinand: "The fringèd curtains of thine eye advance / And say what thou seest yond" (which means, *lift the curtains of your eyelids and say what you see*). And later, Prospero lifting his spell over his enemies: "The charm dissolves apace / And as the morning steals upon the night, / Melting darkness, so their rising senses / Begin to chase the ignorant fumes that mantle / Their clearer reason" (5.1.72–76), and again: "the approaching tide / Will shortly fill the reasonable shore / That now lies foul and muddy" (5.1.88–90).

A curtain had gone up on the next act of my life, in which I would be free, restored to myself after a long exile. I will always continue to serve others as my primary (pre)occupation, but now I can do so with far better awareness of who is and is not deserving, of healthy limitations on my efforts, and of the need for genuine reciprocation or appropriate alternative reward. As we shall see in chapter 4, I will also apply this life lesson to my work in writing program administration.

4

INSTITUTIONAL PRACTICE

Who, What, and Why

> Most poor matters
> Point to rich ends. This my mean task
> Would be as heavy to me as odious, but
> The mistress which I serve quickens what's dead
> And makes my labors pleasures
>
> —Ferdinand in Shakespeare's *The Tempest*

Who gets to teach postsecondary writing courses? What can and can't they teach in those courses? What else can they do? Is it wise to prevent or fail to support their use of non-writing expertise in class? Who decides these things? Don't stop reading if you are not a postsecondary writing teacher or writing program administrator (WPA). Many other readers also have a stake in these important questions because nearly every college student takes at least one course in writing, and increasing numbers of students are enrolling in new writing majors and minors. So if these students are not you, then they're your children, your friends, your coworkers, your fellow citizens in a democracy, and so on. College writing courses may be the only or the last organized opportunity for many of these people to investigate what they can do with texts as communicators, and texts of all sorts are among the most pervasive influences on our lives today. In other words, what students learn in writing courses—and perhaps more important, how they are trained to learn—about their textual consumption and production has important consequences for them and for our culture. In fact, this effect is amplified by the growing attention paid to college readiness in secondary and even primary schools these days, as well as in extracurricular preparations families are making toward that end.

DOI: 10.7330/9781607327769.c004

Now let me single out some targeted groups of readers. WPAs, you know that the people who teach these writing courses are your colleagues as well as your constituents (an interesting metonym), and their job performance *and* satisfaction determine the quality of your program. I would like to try to help you support them in these mutually constitutive ways. Graduate English faculty, many of the teachers of these writing courses were, are, and will be your students; and their job placement *and* satisfaction determine your pedagogical legacy. I realize you have your own agenda to rightfully pursue, which may or may not highlight pedagogy, but I still ask for your consideration in preparing or at least inviting your students to adapt whatever you teach them to less specialized purposes, as many of them will certainly face. Non-tenure-track teachers of writing, I am talking mostly about you here. I was among your ranks for over a dozen years, with one foot in writing and the other in literature, wishing to somehow fuse these interests and to produce scholarship, as many of you want to do. I hope to be able to contribute an option that may help you. English graduate students, many of you are or will be teaching writing at some point, if not throughout your career, and I believe my ideas here can improve your performance and satisfaction in doing that. High school English and composition teachers, increasingly you are expected to make your students college-ready writers, often in classes involving literature. That also brings you into the present company; I seek to provide you with productive ideas, including a rhetorical approach to texts that usefully complicates the relationship between fiction and nonfiction. Undergraduates, your presence is welcome, too. You may not realize how much we writing teachers talk about trying to help you, and that is one of my interests here. To all parties, let it be clear that I am not offering instructions so much as invitation, inspiration, and initiation into a discussion. My ideas won't go very far without your continued working with and on them.

I believe there are no definitive correct answers to the questions that open this chapter. They should be negotiated openly and regularly by the groups of people named above and by others in relation to local contexts, which vary widely across programs and institutions. The role of literary texts (again, broadly defined) seems an appropriate topic to include in this discussion any time it may promote the kinds of performance and satisfaction I have mentioned. This chapter explores that possibility as just that: a *possibility*, among others, for application and modification where it may be helpful. Writing is a unique enough discipline to warrant my briefly explaining how its uniqueness affects the questions of who teaches what and how, which might otherwise seem obvious to readers who are not familiar with the following issues.

Unlike most other fields, writing does not have a definitive institutional identity and function across or even within postsecondary institutions, partly because it arguably does not possess (and even more arguably, perhaps should not possess) a stable subject matter. Writing about what? With what emphases? For what purposes? For example, in a first-year writing (FYW) course, do we necessarily teach *academic* writing with emphases on things like argument and genre, which may turn some students off or turn them away from other important acts of writing such as discovery and creative expression? If so and regardless of any potential by-products, then with classes full of students majoring in dozens of different subjects, with widely varying levels of capability, which academic subjects should be argued about, in which ways, and through which genres? It seems unlikely that any single instructor could possess sufficient knowledge to effectively tailor each assignment to so many varying needs and interests. If not that route, then how and who to teach writing as processes of discovery and self-expression (for just one of many other alternatives)? Which processes to favor and not to favor? Discovery and expression of what? According to what standards? Do we and if so how do we connect this "personal" content to students' other coursework and professional ambitions, which may very well be unknown in the first year, when most college students do their required writing coursework? If it is to be a combination of so-called academic and personal kinds of writing, then how to balance and handle that even more diverse workload in a fifteen-week FYW course, which, by the way, some students and faculty in other disciplines are inclined to dismiss or demote as merely a gate-keeping general education requirement? What method works best to equip and encourage lifelong learning about the production and consumption of texts, since we know that merely FYW on its own is insufficient practice? Or maybe no single method works for this; perhaps local circumstances are the biggest determinant of effective writing pedagogy, not the least of which is a given faculty's various subjects of expertise, experience, and engagement.

To complicate this scenario, now add a body of students who may be working jobs or raising kids in addition to going to school, who may be variously under-prepared or largely composed of non-native English speakers, who are not likely (research tells us) to transfer to subsequent contexts much of the learning they acquire in FYW without follow-up support, which in most cases they do not receive, or some combination of these. To further complicate things, now add a writing faculty that is largely part-time, non-tenure-track (NTT), hired on a semester-by-semester basis, underpaid, uninsured, and often busy commuting among multiple institutions to try to cobble together a humble living. Now add that the majority of these instructors are not (sufficiently) trained to be teachers of writing. Though these individuals may be good writers, that doesn't necessarily make them effective teachers of writing. This type of faculty more or less comprises the majority lower tier of a two-tier system that has increasingly bifurcated in recent decades in some college writing programs that have split into independent units from English departments. The higher tier may often consist of only a single or a few tenure-track (TT) writing specialist(s) who serve(s) managerial functions. In many other institutions, writing is still subsumed under English, and all of what I have just described likely comprises the lower level in yet another stratification, with literature on top (though that may be changing in some places).

The relationship between English and writing has been fraught with material and abstract inequities since this relationship's origins in the nineteenth century. That conflicted history has been reviewed many times, and I will not repeat it here in much detail.[1] For present purposes it should suffice to say the following. From the advent of English composition in the late 1800s through the 1970s, writing instruction was considerably marginalized as a service-providing sub-sector—and its instructors derogatively feminized (Holbrook 1991; Miller 1991a, 1991b; Schell 1998)—by its patriarchal counterpart of English studies. To be selective and reductive of a complex history, postsecondary writing instruction was born of and kept in subservience by doing what no one else wanted to do: attending to influxes of students who were designated as requiring remediation—first, a wave of non-aristocratic undergraduates (a novel thing at the time) resulting from a diversifying economy and the Morrill Act's granting of new state universities, then large numbers of recipients of GI Bill educational benefits, and then populations of under-prepared students through open-admissions policies. Historically, the labor-intensive work of teaching these students to write was deemed pre-professional and unscholarly; it has been characterized as gate keeping (Smith 1997), "a tool for surveillance" (Strickland 2001, 461), "self-sacrificial" (Schell 1998, 32), the work of a "martyr" or "caretaker" (Hairston 1985, 276), "drudge work" (Holbrook 1991, 202), and "shit-work" (Scholes 1998, 36). Literary studies, writing's century-long counterpart and frequent institutional bully, benefited most from having the "trivial, skill-teaching nondiscipline" (Downs and Wardle 2007, 553) of composition as "something to define itself against" (Crowley 1998, 2).

The point I want to emphasize is that non-tenure-track faculty (NTTF) in writing have been traditionally seen (and demeaned) as only teachers, not scholars. It's an understatement to say that hard feelings and the desire for change arose from this situation. Thankfully, things have changed for many compositionists since writing studies gradually began separating from English in the 1980s–1990s, largely through the development of its own research agenda. But problematically, today there still remains a majority underclass of NTT writing faculty whose working conditions have not improved (Strickland 2011; Ianetta 2010; Bousquet, Scott, and Parascondola 2004) and who remain on the lower stratum of a lingering theory/practice divide. In writing programs, this population is now, ironically, largely composed of literature specialists who did not find or seek jobs in English.[2] So we can see something of a reversal of fortunes in today's programs, where TT writing specialists conduct scholarship and NTT literature specialists teach. I want to look a little more closely at this modern history and current state of affairs and encourage the various stakeholders in this scheme to work together to improve circumstances for these NTT writing faculty.

For present purposes my scope is limited to adaptation of non-writing expertise to one's writing pedagogy and derivation of scholarship from that.[3] I am not calling for a national reform, though I would certainly promote that if I thought change would happen on such a scale. I have been made skeptical by failed policies such as the laudable but ineffectual Wyoming Resolution.[4] In the case at hand, I think local actions may stand a better chance, for example, if programs were to conduct self-studies and discuss the results together. Literally looking each other in the eyes as colleagues and asking how to avoid repeating past offenses of omission might be an effective start to engaging all faculty, on their own terms, more intellectually in the profession. Susan Miller (1991b, 51) warned long ago, by way of Althusser, that "attempts to overcome what we take to be hierarchical dominance often sustain the hierarchy, the 'means of production,' in which ideologies install us." To avoid this mistake, writing programs can seek to engage all their faculty members as producers, including those with backgrounds in literature. Some additional reviewing of history may be enlightening toward that end.

A definitive moment in the splitting of composition from literature occurred in 1985, when this relationship was irrevocably disrupted by what is often referred to as a *divorce*. At the time I was in the seventh grade and nearing the seventh year of submerging my own parents' divorce in my unconscious.[5] Twenty years later, it would resurface upon my reading an article about the "divorce" between the two fields in which I was immersed. It was Susan H. McLeod's (2006) twenty-year retrospective on Maxine Hairston's (1985) Conference on College

Composition and Communication (CCCC) chair's address, in which Hairston famously initiated the proceedings for separating composition from English. When McLeod's reflection came out in 2006, I was in my seventh year as a full-time doctoral student of English at one university and in my seventh year as a full-time NTT writing instructor at another university. My hiring was one of the consequences of the splitting of my writing program from English just a few years earlier.[6] There was no way I could read McLeod's *College Composition and Communication* (*CCC*) article without experiencing an uncanny double sense of personal connection to her divorce analogy, as well as a dawning intuition that I would continue to work in this subject area. There I was again learning of a divorce that I was implicated in and again with wishes not for a reunion but for a workable reconciliation. The literature/composition divorce functioned as something of a surrogate for me to work on in place of personal issues stemming from my parents' separation, which I was often reluctant to address directly. I was singing a familiar tune in an easier key.

As chair of the 1985 CCCC in Minneapolis, Hairston delivered an opening address that brought her audience to their feet with cheers and brought rhetoric and composition to a turning point in its compliance with English's subjugation. Hairston characterized the relationship between these two disciplines with domestic analogies, calling on compositionists to rally together in breaking emotional, psychological, and intellectual bonds with their "elitist" "adversaries" in literary studies. She noted that this "leaving [of] the house in which we grew up" (Hairston 1985, 282) is "going to be difficult and painful precisely because the enemy is intimate, a member of the family" (Hairston 1985, 277). Dialogue was not an option because English had repeatedly refused to listen, and it had been composition's compulsive mistake to try to cooperate: "We keep trying to find ways to join contemporary literary theory with composition theory. Such a goal makes sense in many ways, but people who are trying to achieve it seem to be on a one-way street—they are eager to find ways by which we can use literary theory in the teaching of writing, but I hear no one talking about using what we know about writing processes to help us teach literature" (Hairston 1985, 274).

In separate articles in *CCC* twenty years later, McLeod (2006, 525) and Joseph Harris (2006a) reflected on Hairston's "declaration of independence" speech, at which they were both present. Hairston's familial characterizations are indirect, but it's fairly clear that her central metaphor is a child who must "cut the cord" and leave the parental home despite "still crav[ing] love" (Hairston 1985, 274). Yet in looking back,

McLeod (2006, 526) introduces the term *divorce* to this context, which seems to have stuck as part of subsequent discourse: "It was the domestic metaphor Hairston implied in her talk that struck me most then—compositionists as the undervalued wife who must decide, finally, to leave home." McLeod describes the severely dysfunctional English department she belonged to in 1985, which badly discriminated against the all-female composition faculty, known as the "housewives." She notes that in the 1990s all of the breakup stories of composition programs and English departments resembled descriptions of failed marriages: "We (literature and composition) grew apart, our interests were different, we did all the hard work and they didn't appreciate us" (McLeod 2006, 527).

Later in her article McLeod (2006, 529) acknowledges the grown-child-leaving-home analogy, though she attributes this to Sherry Little and Shirley Rose, seeming to ignore or forget that Hairston herself insinuated this image. Perhaps McLeod may have been predisposed to associate this content more with divorce than with coming of age, given her professional history, the same as I am inclined to do, given both my personal and professional history with divorce. In fact, what has influenced me (and this book) the most from this discourse is the following aside by McLeod (2006, 527, my emphases): "Although the relationship with English is now one of distant cordiality, *we still do have shared custody of the TAs*, and occasional flare-ups occur over that issue. And like many wives who left home, the Writing Program finds itself in a much less prosperous financial state trying to go it alone. Nevertheless, from my point of view, the split was for the best; *we are so different from our English colleagues in terms of our research and focus that a reconciliation would not be possible.*" I will return to these notions of shared custody and reconciliation two paragraphs below, somewhat in the spirit of Joseph Harris's pragmatic approach to this subject area, explained in the next paragraph.

In his reflection piece "Déjà Vu All over Again," Harris (2006a, 536) rejects the zero-sum terms of the independence debate, arguing that the discussion has "gone stale." He contends that what matters is not where composition is housed but what can be done right now to achieve the highest-quality teaching and learning of undergraduate writing. Harris specifically cites the under-preparation of NTTF as the primary challenge to this objective, noting that a few more tenure lines and more research in writing studies (i.e., the typical aims of disciplinary independence) are not going to solve the problem. Whether it be a standalone department, an equitable place within English, or anywhere writing finds itself located, Harris feels the argument about independence is missing the point by dwelling on disciplinarity instead of on staffing and pedagogy. For support he points out the "eagerness of many current composition theorists to distance themselves from the service mission of the first-year course," an irony that triggers the "déjà vu" of his title (Harris 2006a, 540). Harris (2006a, 540) provides statistics showing that the majority of basic and first-year writing courses are taught by part-time faculty, whom he assumes to be poorly qualified and poorly supported, concluding: "It is irresponsible to argue that we need a discipline in order to improve the teaching of first-year writing when the data suggest almost the reverse—that we have now built a discipline and yet are worse off in terms of staffing than we were before we began." Many writing programs had achieved independence by the time Harris wrote this, but mere absorption of a new discipline into the academy—what Gerald Graff (2007) refers to as the "field coverage" model—strikes Harris as "business as usual" unless it results in better teaching (conditions). Wherever undergraduate writing can best be taught, he contends, is where writing belongs, and that has to be determined locally, case by case (Harris 2006a, 541).

I would like to add and comment on additional points by Harris and Hairston to extend and apply this discussion to today, ten more years later. Harris (2006a, 536) writes: "What we most need now are strong classroom teachers of writing, and plenty of them. I thus believe that we need to invite faculty from other fields to join us in the actual work of teaching writing. And I don't see that this teaching needs to be sponsored by any particular program of research. On the contrary, I think we can make the best case for writing as a central aspect of liberal study by imagining its teaching as a multidisciplinary project." I agree but wish to add that faculty from other fields have already joined "us" in teaching writing, and many, if not most, of them (I'm inclined to call *them* "us," too) are from English. This includes not only the teaching assistants (TAs) of whom McLeod says writing shares custody with English but also NTT faculty with master's degrees and increasingly with PhDs in literary studies. Many of these full- and part-time members of writing programs, whose degrees are not in writing, conduct scholarship or wish to do so. Others are tenured or tenure-track and hold administrative positions in writing programs. Some have been editors of journals and leaders of professional organizations in writing. Even Hairston (1985, 274) concedes that trying "to join contemporary literary theory with composition theory . . . makes sense in many ways," and she anticipates that once writing is independent and thriving, then separation may need not be the field's only relation to English (1985, 280). Hairston (1985, 282) imagines that at such a point "perhaps we can once more engage in a mutually satisfying dialogue with a group for whose traditions we once felt an affinity."

I ask, then, are the interests of writing studies today really "so different" from the interests of at least the literature-trained members of the field's own writing programs "that a reconciliation would not be possible" (at the local level), as McLeod diagnosed the situation to be? I don't think so. In many cases there should be enough commonalities to outweigh or counterbalance the differences: a shared student body and curriculum, for starters. I suppose it depends on how one looks at the situation and defines *reconciliation*. When discourse remains at the disciplinary level, the strokes can be too broad to paint an accurate picture of program-level realities. As an alternative to accepting generalizations, members of writing programs (or even English departments and beyond) might try to think of themselves in Kenneth Burke's (1969, 20–21) terms as *consubstantial* with each other, that is, as sharing in mutual actions (e.g., professional development, supporting student writing) but still separate in other ways (e.g., being of diverse disciplinary backgrounds). As I explain further below, I believe that writing faculty should acquire some training in writing pedagogy theory if they don't already have it upon being hired, but that should not and need not impede them from also bringing knowledge, skills, and motivation they otherwise possess to bear on their work as writing instructors and scholars. I can only speculate, as this notion would be difficult to validate, but it seems at least feasible that allowing writing faculty to adapt their capabilities with literary texts, for example, to suit some aspects of their teaching—in exchange for training in and application of orthodox writing pedagogies—could yield results as good as if they were solely retrained in orthodoxy (whatever that may be, if such a thing exists).

In the same year as Hairston's declaration of independence, another prominent figure, Robert Scholes, published an alternative proposition for an integrated literature and composition curriculum centered on *textuality*. Given the history I have just recounted, we already know that this plan from Scholes's (1985) book *Textual Power* did not take root; nor did his more detailed elaboration of it in *The Rise and Fall of English* (1998). In fact, Scholes (2011, xiv) humbly admits as much in *English after the Fall*, his most recent iteration of a career-long argument for integrating English studies.[7] Textuality engages individuals in the "production, consumption, and history of texts" and can be thought of as the "study [of] textual power and pleasure wherever they exist," including nonprint media and sacred and profane sources (Scholes 2011, xviii). In the mid-1980s it was never likely that many literary scholars, then near the apex of their high theory frenzy (and near the nadir of applications to practice), would have warmed to the idea of restructuring the discipline around textuality, with its premium on teaching. As for reaching compositionists, Scholes's ethos and kairos may have missed the mark despite his offering them something of an olive branch. After all, Scholes was a literature scholar and semiotician at Brown University (who went on to become president of the MLA in 2004), whose books were published by Yale University Press. That's not an ideal profile for wooing masses of low-status compositionists freshly mobilized for divorcing from belletrism. Furthermore, Scholes's examples often appear to be much closer to literary criticism than to textual production (the blurry boundary between the two in his view notwithstanding). It also probably did not help that John Clifford's (1987) fairly critical review of *Textual Power* was likely some compositionists' first and perhaps only point of contact with the book. One of Clifford's critiques is that Scholes repeats arguments already made by others, including Terry Eagleton (1983, 698), who also sought to deconstruct the "literature and non-literature" dichotomy.[8] But again, I surmise—because of Eagleton's (1983) focus on other readers, as inferred from his book's title, *Literary Theory*, and perhaps also for his Marxism—that compositionists did not rally behind this opportunity to reinterpret rather than reject the lit/comp relationship either. Hairston's feminist insider rhetoric rang much truer, and so separation it would be for English and writing.

My purpose in taking this detour has not been to entertain a fantasy: *what if writing and English had reconciled instead of divorcing?* Although I feel allegiance to both disciplines, I see no benefit in longing for what could have been. The point is to learn to come to terms with moving on as effectively as possible. The same is true of the divorce between my own parents. They did what was necessary for their own good, which took courage, and thankfully both have fared much better for themselves for that. My brothers and I adapted in our own ways, improving on our tactics over time. As we know from the first of my interchapters, my adaptation (or natural disposition or maybe there's no difference) took the form of an eagerness to please and to forge strong bonds, whatever the circumstances may be. Pursuit of these aims came easily and happily to me, as did favorable results. Deferring to the other's desire and fostering connections turns out to be not only my preoccupation in life but also my life's occupation, more or less. Teaching writing from a relatively content-neutral standpoint has allowed me to serve others with my linguistic skills without having to assert much will of my own on students, mostly just curricular standards and whatever a given devil's advocate may have to say. But now I am on a detour from my detour. The point I am building to is that my inclination to please and to connect has led me to offering literary affordance as an agreeable compromise to the next generation of the lit/comp family: WPAs, English graduate faculty, NTTF, and so on. I accept that we are both separate and together. I prefer to dwell on the togetherness in support of the greater good.[9]

So although they divorced, writing and English still share custody of their progeny, as McLeod puts it. These are teachers and graduate students who do not necessarily possess their forbears' resistance to integration. In fact, as we have seen, some of this next generation has long-term simultaneous stakes in both literary and writing studies. Choosing between the two does not have to be the only option for NTT writing faculty. But not everyone would agree. Some have argued for a writing-only pedagogy, expecting faculty either to have or to develop expertise in the requisite content. As I have said, I hope my book will reach a wide audience, including educators in a number of fields and across institutional levels and types, as well as various public stakeholders; but here I would specifically ask for the consideration of my primary target readership of WPAs, graduate English faculty, and NTT writing teachers with backgrounds in literature. I call on WPAs especially for their possession of the most potential influence in this context. My aim is to invite and encourage these parties to work together with more awareness of their shared and conflicting interests—even if it would be the first time it were explicitly triangulated as such—in an intermittent effort to improve the teaching, learning, and application of rhetorical power. This includes that which may be derived from working with literary texts. Toward this end, I offer a supplement to current discussions of expertise in writing studies that pertain more directly than one might think to graduate English education and labor issues, in addition to writing pedagogy.

It's not hard to make a theoretical case for staffing a postsecondary writing program or department with only writing specialists. One argument goes something like this: *in order to teach writing, one must be an expert in writing. After all, only biologists teach biology and only sociologists teach sociology, so why would writing employ individuals with backgrounds in other fields to do its teaching?* But in reality, for economic and other kinds of reasons that are mostly beyond their control, WPAs usually cannot be so selective in hiring; in many cases the majority of their instructors will include specialists in a wide variety of areas other than writing, with literary studies often the most common of these. Nor (arguably) is it certain that having a homogeneously writing-trained faculty would be more desirable than having a faculty with diverse backgrounds and some shared fundamental knowledge about writing studies research. A significant complicating factor here is that literature (or biology, sociology, and so on) scholars may very well be expert writers in their field, but that does not mean they have expertise in *teaching* writing to students who are non-English majors, a category that fits most students in required FYW courses. Furthermore, there are neither enough willing and able disciplinary-writing specialists nor sufficient organizational capabilities to arrange high-intensity, low-paying FYW courses according to students' areas of major, which is a disputed method anyway. What is more, many students do not know their majors or will change them early in college, and it would not be feasible for individual teachers to effectively arrange FYW courses around the various disciplines of each of their enrolled students, even if all of these students' majors were known and fixed. So a quandary arises, which has become increasingly important beyond pedagogical reasons now that the disciplinary independence of writing studies is burgeoning: writing *about what*? (There's that pesky "about" preposition again, so ambiguous and abstract.)

Historically, college writing has been taught *about* a great variety of things: literature, themes, rhetorical modes, students' own thoughts and feelings, cultural studies issues, popular culture, the teacher's personal or professional interests, whatever is in the textbook the teacher was required to use, various combinations of these, and so on. A recent, compelling alternative option is writing about writing (WAW), introduced in 2007 by Doug Downs and Elizabeth Wardle. In this approach, FYW students learn and write about the content knowledge of writing studies, marked in large part by what is increasingly identified as the field's "threshold concepts." Threshold concepts can be thought of as ideas whose comprehension is necessary for one's participation in a given community (e.g., a scholarly discipline). Kathleen Blake Yancey (2015, xix) helpfully explains that a threshold concept is not a "canonical statement" but an "articulation of shared beliefs providing multiple ways of helping us name what we [i.e., in writing studies] know and how we can use what we know in the service of writing. That use value . . . takes various forms." So an FYW course with a WAW approach would introduce students to the field much in the same way Biology 101 and Sociology 101 do for their students and fields. That is, as an introduction to the discipline's key concepts and other features, *not*—as FYW is often mistaken to be—as a supposedly once-and-for-all depositing of all the information and skills students ever need to succeed as writers henceforth.

Threshold concepts seem clearly very important for writing studies to develop and teach, but I still must ask: who gets to designate, delimit, and deliver them? How far beyond the field may "we" go to "use what we know" before we are afield of "*shared* beliefs"? How "various" can the "forms" of "use value" be? Can one, for example, use material from outside the field in service of the field's objectives? If so, then how about material from the field from which writing studies is most trying to distinguish itself: English? I ask because what some of us *use* and *know* as teachers of writing draws on backgrounds in fields other than writing, most often including literary studies. I highly respect and admire the members of the veritable who's-who list of contributors to the groundbreaking collection on threshold concepts in writing studies, *Naming What We Know* (Adler-Kassner and Wardle, 2015), and I suspect they would say the ideas in the book are open to discussion, and the questions and issues I have raised should be taken up in national and local settings.[10] If so, then I agree. But because *national discussion* is a nebulous thing in which huge numbers of writing instructors do not participate (in the literal sense of *discussion*), all the more important it seems to me to generate utmost openness and engagement in *local* dialogue. So if, for example, a given writing program is largely composed of NTTF with expertise in literature or other non-writing subjects, as we know many programs are, then it seems worth discussing—at least in the given setting—how the non-writing expertise of such instructors can be brought into "the service of writing," genuinely, usefully, and conscientiously, in addition to whatever writing studies training these individuals may hopefully receive. Attempting to entirely replace the former with the latter strikes me as prone to breed resentment, if not also to fail.

Regardless of whether a given writing program adopts a WAW curriculum or preaches threshold concepts in writing studies, the above questions and those I opened this chapter with still require answering: who gets to teach college writing, what can and can't they teach, what else can they do, is it wise not to support their use of non-writing expertise, and who decides these things? WAW, a writing-only curricular theory, has been invoked in support of a writing-only faculty, which is one of the points at which I depart from the movement. To me, an important threshold concept for the field has to be that texts (of all kinds) do things and readers can do things with them, as producers, not just as consumers. That's not a particularly controversial idea, but I also believe this idea can be effectively taught in writing classes with knowledge, experience, and materials from areas other than writing studies, including literary studies. I generally support the idea of training a writing faculty in writing studies content and methods, but not if that comes at the expense of or does not leave considerable space for trainees' prior expertise, on which much of their motivation, ethos, and even worldview likely depends. Ann M. Penrose (2012, 116) offers a useful warning about the spirit and circumstances in which professional development often occurs: "Under the conditions of contingent employment, 'professional development' can easily be interpreted as a euphemism for brainwashing or remediation, deepening the skepticism with which such activities are often viewed . . . Under this interpretation, professional development activities are intended to regulate and regularize and thus present a clear challenge to an experienced faculty member's autonomy and professional identity . . . It's no wonder that professional development 'opportunities' may be perceived as coercive rather than supportive . . . the 'malevolent force' of the profession resides not in its influence over non-members but [in] its power over those within. The community's professional right to self-determination is seen as a hegemonic exercise."

Years after insinuating in their initial case for WAW that writing instructional expertise should be required of writing instructors (Downs and Wardle 2007, 575–76), Wardle and Downs (2013, original emphasis) tempered their insistence with a more inclusive concession that I can agree with: that faculty "who work with texts and are familiar with genres and conventions in a variety of disciplines, professions, and civic pursuits bring an abundance of expertise to the table as writing teachers, but they can do so more effectively if they are directly familiar with some of the research *about writing*." Along these lines, in 2015 Elizabeth Wardle and J. Blake Scott published in *WPA: Writing Program Administration* what could become a landmark essay, as Downs and Wardle's 2007 article became. Wardle and Scott return to the question of faculty expertise with a subtler argument for professionalizing faculty while writing programs are adding new majors and minors and expanding their disciplinary independence, course offerings, and budgets. Making a case study of their own impressive WPA experiences and noting recent concurrent national increases in the number of upper-division writing curricula and percentage of NTTF, the authors seek to define and to help develop expertise in "all aspects of program delivery including teaching, curriculum planning, advising, and coordinating" (Wardle and Scott 2015, 72). To their credit, Wardle and Scott genuinely want NTTF to participate in theses activities, and they admit to NTTF's considerable professional alienation. They also acknowledge NTTF's potential prior expertise "in other areas" that might be "leveraged" for work in writing programs (Wardle and Scott 2015, 72–77). But the authors' inclusiveness comes with a pair of limitations that I would like to constructively critique, despite my sympathy for their main argument that writing teachers should have some training in writing studies scholarship. My contribution here offers a supplement, not a rebuttal, to that claim.

First, Wardle and Scott's explanations of how to leverage NTTF's prior expertise in subjects other than writing seem a bit too narrow and convenient. They only quickly and vaguely mention examples of NTTF in their writing and rhetoric department who have effectively drawn on prior experience in health and medicine, social change (Wardle and Scott 2015, 76), library science, publishing, or professional writing (Wardle and Scott 2015, 81–82); however, no explanation is offered of how the authors go about "valuing the kinds of expertise NTTF have already developed" (Wardle and Scott 2015, 91) in the more common and more conflicted area of literature. I worry that their contingent faculty with backgrounds in literature disproportionately comprised the group of instructors who Wardle and Scott (2015, 86) say (a little too casually for my taste) eventually "found teaching positions elsewhere, cycling out" of the department after these "long-time, part-time composition teachers resisted the claim that what they had been teaching might be in conflict with disciplinary knowledge about writing." I can understand why Wardle and Scott, in the short space of a journal article that is only partially about this matter, might want to avoid the trickier business of how to work with faculty inclined toward literature. But WPAs in general who are going to try to leverage their faculties' prior expertise in other domains, as Wardle and Scott (and I) believe they should do, would arguably benefit most from being given strategies and examples pertaining to individuals with literary backgrounds, which high percentages of NTTF in many writing programs are likely to employ. I propose that welcoming and adapting these colleagues' expertise to writing program work may be easier and more fruitful if the involved parties can learn to make and teach rhetorical affordances of literary texts.

Second is the related matter of an oversight Wardle and Scott commit when listing aspects of writing program life into which they wish to bring inexpert NTTF. They make no mention of contingents' scholarly production except to note in passing as they conclude that "instructors who don't have research assignments . . . might develop research projects if given the opportunity" (Wardle and Scott 2015, 74). The authors instead focus on a number of pedagogical and administrative contexts in which to examine and develop NTTF expertise, such as curriculum development and student advisement. The omission of scholarly production here strikes me as somewhat inconsistent with a case for professionalizing faculty who are supposed to be considered *more than just teachers*, especially given the credit brought to teaching-based scholarship by Ernest Boyer and others, which is highlighted in Steve Lamos's (2011, 55, 91) article that Wardle and Scott reference twice. Writing studies is fortunate not to maintain (much of) a bias against scholarship that emerges from teaching, learning, and administering, presumably in part because we believe this scholarship benefits the teaching, learning, and administering of writing, which we greatly value.

Although there are considerable material challenges to conducting scholarship off the tenure track, there are also good reasons for some to seek and others to help them overcome those challenges. So a discussion of faculty inclusion and development that fails to take up these considerations strikes me as at least incomplete. I do not regard this omission on Wardle and Scott's part to be necessarily dismissive; it may just be a by-product of their having to prioritize other objectives. Furthermore, the authors are hardly alone in excluding scholarly production from their call for professionalizing NTTF. That oversight has been all too common in work done in this area, especially of the report variety (e.g., Council for Higher Education Accreditation 2014; Kezar and Maxey 2015; MLA Office of Research 2014), with the exception of occasional passing references (Arnold 2011, 423–24; Penrose 2012, 117–18) and the familiar reductive nod to scholarly conference attendance. But as Lynée Lewis Gaillet and Letizia Guglielmo (2014) argue capably throughout their book on contingent faculty scholarship, there may very well be widespread desire and good potential among NTT writing faculty to conduct and publish research, and that should not continue to be generally overlooked.

Toward this and other ends, I am inviting my readers to consider opening up or abandoning conventions when needed to serve alternative purposes—an issue at the heart of tension in the present case about who and what belongs or does not belong in our programs, publications, and disciplinary identity. One of Wardle and Scott's purposes is to integrate (or conventionalize) into their evolving department a group of instructors who are already among its members or who were hired without expertise in writing studies, which suggests that these individuals need to evolve in order to remain, or at least advance, in the department. As Faye Halpern (2015, 647) notes of the contemporary WPA's dilemma concerning expertise, "'outsiders' can include, ironically, those within the field itself."[11] Drawing on sociocultural theorists, Wardle and Scott identify several key functions of welcoming such outsiders into relevant domains and levels of expertise, including, among other acts, "engaging and interacting" (2015, 77), "social connection" and "conversing" (2015,

78), and "the transfer of expertise from one domain into another" (2015, 81). I propose that how, when, and why to undertake these acts should vary according to local circumstances, so I am certainly not offering a universal strategy here. But I do think our WPAs, publications, and disciplinary identity *also* ought to evolve to better integrate faculty from across ranks and specializations. In other words, I am suggesting there be a give and take on both the program/administration's and the faculty's respective sides. Given the notably social nature of Wardle and Scott's strategies quoted just above, a good starting point toward such transactiveness might simply be the professional equivalent of asking instructors that standard icebreaker "so, what do you do," followed perhaps with "what do you wish you could do?" These gestures—metaphors for more substantial modes of engagement such as listening, brainstorming, and collaborating—carry important ethical and rhetorical implications, maybe most notably the effect of welcoming the other's difference into a shared, valued, explicitly open context.

In a 2015 *College Composition and Communication* article, Halpern exhibits a daringly strong commitment to her writing faculty's difference as such, even to the point of denying her own expertise as their WPA to make space for each individual's pedagogy to take its unique course. Halpern's essay provides an excellent counterpoint to Wardle and Scott's, published only a few months later, and these two together with Jenny Rice's *College English* article on a different aspect of the same subject, also published in late 2015, suggest that expertise is a burgeoning subject of current disciplinary discourse. If ever there were a need to demonstrate the influence of local circumstances on writing program development, a quintessential example exists in the contrast between Wardle and Scott's and Halpern's cases of administering newly independent writing units. Whereas Wardle and Scott were able to hire dozens of full-time writing faculty (tenure-track and otherwise) and to train them in exchange for stipends, raises, and other rewards in their department at a large public university, Halpern was forced to try to recruit (read: *coax*) faculty from across the disciplines to teach writing courses, presumably on a part-time basis, in her program at a small liberal arts college. As we have seen, Wardle and Scott's mandate is for each faculty member to adapt her or his pedagogy to the program's WAW curriculum, a curriculum that represents a metonymic extension of Wardle's and Scott's own expertise as the founders and orchestrators of this new system. Halpern's administrative style takes exactly the opposite form; she deliberately withdraws the presence of her expertise and invites her faculty to discover and develop their own writing pedagogies in their own ways and time, despite their lack of knowledge in writing studies.

Halpern developed this method of disavowing her expertise as a response to earlier, failed efforts to win over colleagues by highlighting her extensive knowledge of the field. With those previous experiences, she found that neither promises of training nor provision of supporting materials could sufficiently woo faculty to her program—just as, she admits, offers of workshops and textbooks would certainly not tempt her to teach intro to microbiology (Halpern 2015, 645). Halpern calls her revised approach "strategic disingenuousness," after a tactic by that name employed by nineteenth-century American sentimental women authors, who were dismissed by contemporaneous men of letters for being supposedly rhetorically inexpert. Halpern's "sentimental solution" positions the WPA as at most a facilitator rather than a dispenser of professional development, whereby the admittedly risky assumption is maintained that non-expert faculty will eventually develop the ability to effectively teach FYW through their own effort and experience, accompanied by a kind of standing invitation to solve emergent problems collaboratively with the WPA.

Halpern's (2015, 658) method requires that WPAs put aside the fact that they know better than their inexpert faculty who may very well "fly in the face of the best practices advocated by professionals in rhet/comp." In this way, "WPAs will not alienate the outside faculty on whom they often depend by making them feel like outsiders to a discipline" (Halpern 2015, 653). Reference to an apt insight by Barbara Walvoord helps Halpern's readers imagine the impact of this approach on not just new faculty in a writing program but also seasoned teachers who may not have stayed up-to-date on writing studies research: "Given faculty autonomy, it is hard to change teaching by external directives" (cited in Halpern 2015, 653). Although the sentimental solution is admittedly "radically inefficient" because it regularly "reinvents at least part of the wheel," Halpern (2015, 657–58) believes that is a reasonable price to pay for generating a consequent "buy-in to writing pedagogy that cannot be elicited through even (or especially) the most intellectual-sounding theorizing at the WPA's command."

Although Jenny Rice's article on expertise and writing pertains to students, her theory still overlaps usefully with the present discussion, for which I would like to pose a tentative substitution of the students Rice is talking about with the faculty I am talking about. Rice (2015, 119) strays from the familiar dichotomy between expertise (possession) and non-expertise (lack) by introducing the idea of *para-expertise*: "the experiential, embodied, and tacit knowledge that does not translate into the vocabulary or skills of disciplinary expertise." She wants this para-expertise to be "seen alongside (touching the side of) different forms of expertise," helping the student (or in my case, the teacher) solve problems in alliance with others (Rice 2015, 119). What makes the tacit knowledge "para-" is a knower's inability to pose corresponding problems in an appropriate bordering lexicon, hence the need for alliance. Rice (2015, 131) believes "para-expertise may be a more rhetorically useful term than 'nonexpertise' in some contexts," the benefit being "that we may reimagine ways of increasing the rhetorical efficacy of those who lack expert ethos . . . In thinking of para-expertise as one part of what we might call 'strategic expert alliances,' our goal shifts away from any attempt to transform the nonexpert into an expert. Instead, we shift attention to how para-expertises can lead to problem-posing."

This pragmatic, situational focus strikes me as worthy of applying, when possible, to the issues raised by Wardle and Scott and Halpern, revealing something of a middle way between their relatively extreme methods. It seems a shame to dispense with or to block a teacher's prior, possibly tacit expertise if that teacher has developed or could be collaborated with to develop effective ways of using her para-expertise (and all its attendant personal investment and ethos) toward relevant ends. It also seems impractical or worse in some professional circumstances, as Halpern (2015, 658–60) admits, to leave para-experts to their own resources when the alternative of willful, fruitful collaboration is available. I am more inclined to try forging strategic alliances—among individuals as well as disciplines—in applying colleagues' para-expertise to problems if and as problems emerge, drawing on a local faculty's existing fluencies and modes of engagement and bringing that into a mutually evolving shared set of beliefs and practices. In the case of writing teachers working with literary texts, this would entail the articulation (meaning both clarification and joining) of methods and outcomes as a natural part of program assessment procedures applied across a department.

In her introduction to *Naming What We Know*, Yancey remarks with pleasure and perhaps some relief and pride that writing has finally definitively separated from English, where, she notes, previous generations of writing scholars did their doctoral work but not the majority of the next-generation contributors to the collection, who hold rhet/comp PhDs. She writes: "The assumption underlying *Naming*, of course, is that the field *is* now established, and it thus would be a useful enterprise to consider together what it is that we do know" (Yancey 2015, xxv–xxvi, original emphasis). To an extent I agree and am happy to join in celebrating. But I also cannot help but get tangled in metonymic assumptions behind the ideas of "field," "we," and "know." They who tend to speak for (i.e., publish about, negotiate on behalf of) writing studies may have professionally purged themselves of literary influences or avoided them in the first place. They may also have rhet-comp PhDs, and they may serve as program administrators. But these traits describe only a minority of the field's faculty membership. What many of the rest of us "know" intellectually and institutionally may still involve aspects of literature, English, or both. So to what extent are *they* "we," or is this *we* all together (altogether) established *as separate from English*?

I realize that WAW, threshold concepts, and works like *Naming What We Know* aspire to an ideal integrated state, and despite how it may appear, I do not raise these complications to impede that process. As I have said, I merely want to emphasize the necessity of local adaptations and to propose and model one of any number of potential approaches to practicing intellectual and pedagogical inclusivity with our colleagues who have literary inclinations. Some remarkable work is being done by leaders in the field today, like that reflected in *Naming What We Know*, which will have repercussions on curriculum design and thereby on teaching and assessment and thereby on hiring/reappointment, promotion, and professional development. I want to be sure that the inevitably many faculty members and would-be members of the field who are not its leaders have a fair chance to get and do jobs in writing that incorporate their strengths and preferences, whatever they may be. This does not mean abiding a free-for-all curriculum or the kind of writing *about* literature (i.e., conventional interpretation) that better suits an English than a writing course designation, but it does mean working with the considerable number of writing faculty in our programs to adapt their literary interests for mutually beneficial purposes.

Yes, the abstract collective that is the field of writing studies may at last have its own material, but the material circumstances of individuals' employment in the field are anything but level in relation to that content. I want to prevent the addition of content generator/content receiver to the list of regrettable high/low binaries that strain disciplinary and departmental cohesiveness, including tenure track/non-tenure track, scholar/teacher, and administrator/employee. Another persistent dichotomy is writing/literature, reversed here from its more familiar ordering to reflect an updated sense of writing's recent rise relative to English's fall in some places and in some people's estimations. In a moment of metacognition while wrapping up her introduction to *Naming What We Know*, Yancey (2015, xxvi, original emphasis) narrates: "It occurred to me . . . that the literary context so prominent in so many accounts of our history and even in accounts of our pedagogy" is "no longer our default context—or, and at least as important, our default *content.*" The default *has* thankfully changed, yet I believe writing cannot so easily turn the page on English. After all, writing's independence is hardly complete or universal: nationally, many, if not most, writing programs are still housed in English departments, and where independence does exist, it certainly has not been a boon to legions of struggling NTTF in writing, many of whom, again, have literary backgrounds. Furthermore, I submit that literature *is* "composed knowledge," which is the phrase *Naming* editors Adler-Kassner and Wardle identify over and over again as the foundational "common theme" of writing studies (Adler-Kassner and Wardle 2015).

In response to a critique of her 2007 article with Downs, Wardle (2008, 180) seems to leave an opening in WAW theory for what I have been calling for; she states: "I encourage teachers from a variety of backgrounds to design curricula in ways that draw on their own strengths." To me, it follows from this reasonable suggestion that a writing teacher with expertise in literature could productively use literary texts (again, broadly defined as in my introduction) with students to examine what such literarily composed knowledge does (e.g., for them individually, for others historically) and what readers could do with such texts in rhetorical situations. Let me briefly try to dispel controversy over some of my usage in the previous sentence. The words *literature* and *literary* would raise no eyebrows if they were replaced with *rhetoric* and *nonfiction.* But for the particular purposes I have in mind, these distinctions are relatively unimportant. What is important is understanding textual power (of various kinds) and how to use it. I am talking about making affordances *not interpretations* of literature, and I do not recommend that this be the only approach one takes to an FYW course. Literary affordances might make for a good assignment at that level, perhaps a unit of study or a course at the advanced undergraduate level, and a subject of research at the graduate level and beyond.

If a focus on the use value rather than the interpretive meaning of literary texts seems amiss to you, then I direct you to chapter 3 of this book, which I hope should prevent or mitigate that impression. If that doesn't work, then I ask you to at least consider this bit of testimony from Penrose (2012, 117, original emphases), especially if you have any authority over curriculum, professional development, or graduate students: "Studying teacher mentors, [Katharine] Burn highlights the importance of 'an identity which depends not merely on *existing* knowledge, but on the capacity to generate *new* professional knowledge; an identity which includes a role as learner, not merely one as an "expert" teacher' ([2007,] 460). The 'learner' role is a participatory role, implying an interactive social network as opposed to a loose collection of isolated experts. Both of these elements, continued learning and collegiality, routinely appear as essential components of professionalism in this research base."

In such a spirit of openness to new knowledge and genuine collaboration with colleagues of different expertise—not the "coercive" type of faculty engagement Penrose critiques further above—I offer the following literary affordances in support of my case for inclusive writing program administration, professional development, and pedagogy. Halpern, while her article is still fresh in our minds, makes a number of similar literary affordances of Harriet Beecher Stowe novel characters as models of the sentimental solution for WPAs to use with inexpert writing faculty. These models include Rachel Halliday from *Uncle Tom's Cabin*, "who, like all the most effective sentimental speakers," says Halpern, "persuades through her essence and not her words" (2015, 652), and Mary from *The Minister's Wooing*, who "transforms everyone around her, not through engaging them in a course of rigorous disciplinary training but through exposing them to her own essence . . . not because of the way she has put her words together but because of her innate qualities . . . because the hearers have qualities within themselves that the sentimental orator can call forth" (2015, 652). Though Halpern does not identify her rhetorical technique by the name *literary affordance*, she is indeed making use of a form of that tactic. I do so, too, in the following formulations, which conceive of WPAs, graduate English faculty, and NTT writing faculty with literature backgrounds through the lens of key characters and events in Shakespeare's *The Tempest*. Occasionally, to facilitate understanding of the one thing in terms of the other, I employ this figure to clarify equivalencies: (≈).

We can perceive, conceive of, and even be WPAs *as Prospero*, the protagonist of *The Tempest*. I am not claiming that everyone should do any or all of these acts, only that those who are so inclined may derive certain benefits from immersion in this extended conceptual metaphor. Doing so affords WPAs some justification in feeling resentment for offenses, past or present, committed against them or their kind by literary scholars and others. WPAs and those they represent have been, and in some cases still are, exiled from the status they deserve in the academy (as Prospero was from his dukedom), and relevant parties must become aware and accepting of this fact. But as Prospero does, WPAs should also take deliberate action to move on productively without harboring permanent grudges, which is more than just a personal issue. The affordance

I am proposing also acknowledges a kairotic moment and rhetorical tactic for WPAs. Much as the plot of *The Tempest* takes place over the course of arguably the most important period in Prospero's life, many WPAs today have opportunities to advance their programs and their own careers to unprecedented degrees. But the model of Prospero provides a framework for considering how to work toward such advancement while embracing difference within one's program or department, even difference of the most seemingly threatening kind. Prospero learns to forgive his transgressors and merge his powers with theirs toward a collective good that especially favors his issue (meaning both his daughter and his interests). Some WPAs today are uniquely poised to do the same.

The play is set on a remote, nearly uninhabited island, where exiled Prospero governs and educates his daughter, Miranda. He had previously been duke of Milan, ousted twelve years prior by his brother in collaboration with Alonso, the king of Naples. According to the present affordance, Prospero's overthrow by his close sibling can signify rhetoric's nineteenth-century displacement by literary studies from the center to the margins of the postsecondary curriculum, causing compositionists to struggle for a century to overcome misrepresentation as mere remediators. Miranda signifies the contemporary state of writing studies, for having grown mature in such exile and for inheriting Prospero's knowledge and power, as writing programs perform and perpetuate their WPAs' influence. In the play she meets and marries Alonso's son, Ferdinand (≈a literature scholar), who has been stranded on the island (≈hired to a writing program) after a shipwreck. Ferdinand's merger with Miranda in this setting makes him accountable to Prospero, as an NTT writing teacher with a literature background is accountable to a WPA. Although Prospero has legitimate cause to resent or reject this descendent of his ouster, he opts instead to embrace Ferdinand (≈accept his difference) after testing his intentions with Miranda (≈providing training in writing pedagogy), recognizing that Ferdinand will also retain allegiance to Naples (≈literature).

Prospero's acceptance (some would say deliberate recruitment) of the boy into his family models how WPAs can productively accept and adjust to the inevitability of hiring NTTF with literary backgrounds. Prospero's blessing is as savvy as it is compassionate, ensuring that future generations of his issue will be better off for the merger: "Fair encounter / Of two most rare affections! Heavens rain grace / On that which breeds between 'em" (3.1.75–76). WPAs may want to similarly renounce the field's lingering resentments and resistances and promote mutual benefit by helping the NTT literature scholars they oversee pursue opportunities for hybrid teaching and scholarship, possibly by means of literary affordances. In exchange for training in writing studies (or not), WPAs can sanction and support their faculties' conscientious partial use of literary texts in class, including by offering resources or even just encouragement for them to derive scholarship from and infuse that into their teaching. Programs might try to offer promotion opportunities, increased job security, stipends, travel funds, and other forms of support to NTTF who reciprocally make significant contributions to their students, colleagues, program, institution, and field(s). These and other such efforts can go a long way toward bringing together and bringing out the best in a faculty with diverse qualifications.

Increasingly, compelling evidence from areas as distinct as cognitive science and contemplative studies suggests (what phenomenology has contended all along) that thinking, perceiving, and being are deeply entangled with, even constitutive of, each other. If so, then that makes the following recommendation regarding WPAs' *performance* all the more exciting, but this need not be the case for it to still give WPAs potential pause. Of course, WPAs can simply tell their NNTF with literary backgrounds that they need to be retrained to teach writing or else find employment elsewhere. Or WPAs can provide training *and* invite these colleagues to brainstorm with them ways to bring literary textual expertise into the work these NTTF were hired to do. That seems fair, considering it was no secret what these individuals had specialized in prior to their hiring. So I recommend that WPAs who aspire to such inclusivity visualize themselves as performing these lines from Prospero (to Ferdinand upon granting him permission to marry Miranda after undergoing trials of his character):

> If I have too austerely punish'd you,
> Your compensation makes amends, for I
> Have given you here a third of mine own life,
> Or that for which I live; who once again
> I tender to thy hand: all thy vexations
> Were but my trials of thy love and thou
> Hast strangely[12] stood the test here, afore Heaven,
> I ratify this my rich gift. (4.1.1–8)

I also invite NTT writing faculty with literature backgrounds to turn to *The Tempest*'s Ferdinand for inspiration and fortitude in achieving clarity and purpose in the face of professional adversity. Naive or not, Ferdinand does remain collected (but hardly stoical) throughout the play, despite the constant belief that he has lost his way and lost his father in the tempest (1.2.391, 406, 431, 433–37, 488–89; 2.1.60–61). He neither allows these heavy losses to prevent his benefiting from unexpected experiences with Miranda (≈teaching writing) nor begrudges Prospero's trials of his character (≈training in writing instruction). In my literary affordance, Ferdinand's actions reflect an attitude that some NTT writing faculty with literature backgrounds may benefit from adopting. As disappointing and trying as their professional circumstances may be to them, these NTTF are bound to their tasks at least for the time being and must determine to clear their minds and decide upon their inclination toward or against seeking tenure. That decision, which for many individuals is not as easy or fixed as one may think, has a considerable influence on one's performance, as I will explain here.

With apologies for being reductive of a fundamentally diverse population, I want to provisionally draw on Douglas C. Maynard and Todd Allen Joseph's (2008) classifications of "involuntary" and "voluntary" contingency to distinguish NTTF who, respectively, prefer to switch over to the tenure track from those who do not prefer to switch.[13] For one recent indication of how tenure inclination breaks down, a recent landmark study of contingent faculty (across all disciplines and colleges) at George Mason University found that nearly a third (32%) of all respondents and more than half (52%) of those under age forty said it was important or extremely important to them to be hired to a TT position (Allison, Lynn, and Hoverman 2014, 27–28). Thirty-six percent of these respondents have doctorates (Allison, Lynn, and Hoverman 2014, 14), and by far the biggest motivating factor in their work is "passion for [their] subject area" (Allison, Lynn, and Hoverman 2014, 20).[14]

I recommend that involuntary NTT English scholars apply and adapt their likely greatest strengths—training, creativity, and critical thinking—to their adverse circumstances. In the present case, this may include merging research and pedagogy, literature and writing, and collegiality and authorship. Whereas an obvious reason for involuntary NTTF to conduct scholarship is to improve their chances of attaining TT employment (at least where publishing is a primary criterion in hiring), the reasons for their voluntary NTT colleagues to do so are less apparent but no less valid. These scholars may be more inclined to pioneer new directions in hybrid literary/writing scholarship because they are not necessarily beholden to the conventional publishing constraints of the tenuring process. They may more readily choose, for example, to innovate in their subject matter, medium, genre, rhetoric, style, length, individual authorship, status and venue of publication, and so on—which means nothing either way about the potential quality of this work. So NTT writing teachers with literary backgrounds (and others) may want to reconsider Ferdinand's lines quoted in this chapter's epigraph and ask themselves which mistress they serve and how they can figuratively point their "poor matters . . . to rich ends." Literary affordances and other rhetorical innovations may be viable options for those who seek to overlap research with pedagogy, and perhaps a modicum of Ferdinand's enthusiasm will transfer to those who try, figuratively making their "labors pleasures."

Graduate English faculty play an instrumental (if seemingly indirect) role in this context.[15] I call on them to assess how many of their graduates go on to teach writing, partially or wholly, and to consider the following invitation if the tally turns out to be more than just a rare few. Taking responsibility to help these students connect what they are taught with what they go on to do does not have to entail radical changes to a graduate English professor's pedagogy (Khost, Lohe, and Sweetman 2015), and that is not solely the charge of a TA practicum or the students themselves, if what they go on to do includes teaching writing. I invite graduate English faculty to consider emulating the actions of *The Tempest*'s Gonzalo and, by extension, of Thomas More (a British knight *and* Catholic saint), whom I contend Gonzalo partially symbolizes. This character performs an astute and righteous deed beyond the normal purview of his duties, after having played an unintended part in banishing Prospero from Milan. Listed in the *dramatis personae* as "an honest old councilor" and repeatedly praised by Prospero, Gonzalo is charged by Alonso (in backstory) to cast Prospero and Miranda out to sea to perish, but the "noble Neapolitan" secretly furnishes their boat with provisions and, importantly, with Prospero's cherished magical books. Dedicated to the service of Alonso's Naples (≈literature) by his position (≈graduate English professor), Gonzalo's charity reveals his regret for institutional divisiveness and his awareness of its ill effects on good people.

In my affordance of the play, Gonzalo and Prospero's mutual affinity represents an ideal state of collaboration between English and writing faculty. In a somewhat similar vein, it has been proposed that Shakespeare was expressing qualified solidarity with Thomas More for his *Utopia.*[16] Utopianism is obvious in Gonzalo's tale of the ideal commonwealth (2.1), and though we know Shakespeare had Montaigne and other sources in mind, More also appears to be a rhetorical target for his praise and critique. Some readers may decode double meanings in such lines spoken to and about Gonzalo as "Prithee, no [Thomas] more. Thou dost talk nothing [i.e., no-place, *utopia*] to me" (2.1.175)[17] and

"What impossible matter will [Gonzalo] make easy next? . . . bring forth *more islands*" (2.1.91–96, my emphasis, as More's Utopia is an island). This Morean figure's provision of books to Prospero is what allows the father and daughter to survive and to eventually recuperate their power upon returning to civilization, as if Shakespeare were insinuating that although fantasies about ideal states of being (or even real but isolated ones) have some merit, they ultimately require social integration to achieve fuller value.[18]

Graduate English faculty may be able to dwell in a purely literary utopia, but most of their students will not be able to do so, needing to integrate their expertise with other contexts and values. For this reason, I encourage graduate English faculty to make their "provision[s] of books" to students—partially and where there is interest—in ways that allow rhetorical and compositional application (e.g., affordance making). In other words, because only a small percentage of English graduate students complete their studies and earn TT jobs teaching literature and the rest will take other paths, their mentors would do well to embody Gonzalo's insinuated moral of the story, that life's difficulties can help us find our way: "Ferdinand . . . found a wife / Where he himself was lost; Prospero his dukedom / In a poor isle; and all of us ourselves / When no man was his own" (5.1.210–13). Since we know that significant numbers of graduates of English master's and doctoral programs go on to teach writing, it seems reasonable to propose that their graduate instructors (of *all* specializations) should help them to at least anticipate seeking means of synthesizing literariness and rhetoricity.

So far I have made affordances of *The Tempest* that are more *apparent* than *subtle*: WPAs should consider being forgiving and strategic like Prospero; NTTF, industrious and collaborative like Ferdinand; and graduate English faculty, foresighted and compassionate like Gonzalo. Not that their apparent quality makes them any less potentially effective, but once they are pointed out these traits are fairly obvious aspects of their corresponding characters, and it does not require a great stretch of the reader's imagination to consider applying them to real-life rhetorical situations, at least not once the suggestion has been made to do so. But now—both to strengthen my case and to illustrate the distinction—I wish to propose a subtler affordance by reconsidering and repurposing Miranda, the main character in the play who seems to get the least amount of critical attention. When scholars do mention her, they tend to perceive Miranda as passive, objectified, innocent, emotional, or victimized, often in juxtaposition with a male character. For example, she may be a political pawn of Prospero's, a faithful fool for Ferdinand, or a coveted conquest in Caliban's anti-colonialist resistance. Most often and famously, Miranda is remembered for her "brave new world" declaration—perhaps thanks to Huxley's title-making affordance of the line[19]—which most readers seem to unquestioningly equate with naïveté. Near the end of the play, for the first time (excluding Ferdinand) since she was about three years old, Miranda encounters other people (i.e., Prospero's usurpers), and she exclaims "O, wonder! / How many goodly creatures are there here! / How beauteous mankind is! O brave[20] new world / That has such people in't" (5.1.182–83). I want to establish an alternative possibility: that we can treat Miranda as anything but naive here and elsewhere in the play. In doing so I will be making an affordance of the text that can help WPAs better understand and enact the kind of strategic disingenuousness Halpern has called for and the kind of openness to literary expertise for which I have called. First, some scholarly context.

Two prominent figures in writing studies have made a literary affordance by coining the term "Miranda Effect" to connote a kind of professional naïveté, whereby a would-be scholarly work falls short of standards by "describ[ing] a teacher's classroom experience, experience which appears to be significant to the teacher only because it is new—new to her or to him" but which "offers little to a larger professional audience" (Salvatori and Donahue 2010, 3). One can imagine a scholar stumbling upon an idea with a neophyte's enthusiasm, not knowing that it is already well-established to experts, similarly to how Miranda seemingly mistakes the band of corrupt aristocrats for something wonderful simply because they are new to her. The problem with "citation difficulties" of this variety, say Mariolina Salvatori and Patricia Donahue (2010, 2–3), is that they "elide the responsibilities of shared inquiry [and] undermine scholarship for the sake of self-expression," thus confirming biases against better, rigorous scholarship of teaching and learning, which deny this work "the academic status it deserves." Salvatori and Donahue make a passing concession that the kind of "unscholarly" work they critique "may be of personal interest—to the individual teacher and his/her colleagues," and the authors claim they do not wish to take that experience for granted. They also make it clear, however, that as journal editors they have rejected increasing numbers of submissions that demonstrate the Miranda Effect, and they have been disappointed to find it "even in published pieces" (Salvatori and Donahue 2010, 2–3), including an anonymous primary example, "Essay X," which had recently appeared in "one of the leading journals in English studies" (Salvatori and Donahue 2010, 1).

Salvatori and Donahue rebuke academic writers like the author of Essay X for insufficiently citing previous research in favor of relaying personal anecdotes, and as part of their case the authors name another citation difficulty "autochthonous," after Hesiod's *Theogony* (thus making another literary affordance), in which full-grown men emerge from the ground without origin. Autochthonous citation difficulties are "incomplete [citation] genealogies which go far, but not far enough" (Salvatori and Donahue 2010, 3). I grant the point to a degree, but I would hope that such critiques could be offered in more of an inclusive and productive manner. After all, standards for judging what passes and doesn't pass do not appear to be fixed, clear, or unanimously decided. To remain with Salvatori and Donahue's complaint, for example, how much anecdotal content is permissible in a given scholarly article? Would 22 percent be reasonable? That's the amount of anecdotal sentences I count in Salvatori and Donahue's article (not including the abstract), in which they non-ironically state "we will offer exempla based on what we have read or experienced firsthand," and "we provide an example that is partially made up" (Salvatori and Donahue 2010, 3). I have nothing against firsthand and made-up evidence. I just hope the field will make room for varying degrees of this kind of evidence, based on local circumstances and acknowledging the learning curve individuals experience at different stages in their career, as affected by editorial feedback, peer review, and article submission rejection, among other factors. The capaciousness I am calling for does not have to mean that anything goes, as I discuss in chapter 3, but if something genuinely *goes* for some of us, then perhaps the rest can try to respect it on those terms (if it doesn't go at all, then assistance or advice can be provided). Otherwise, we are too prone to attacks based on each other's inevitably shifting interpretations of standards, such as my following point would be if I meant it to be an attack instead of a good-natured case in point of what I wish scholars in our emerging discipline would *not* do as we enact our self-determination.

The backdrop to Salvatori and Donahue's concern is composition's struggle for disciplinary independence by way of a legitimate scholarly agenda, the main challenge here being that scholarship about teaching and learning is dubious if not disrespected in the eyes of other disciplines. So all the more reason, the authors suggest, to be "vigilant" and do "due diligence" in "digging" into an existing "research trajectory" on a given topic of scholarly production (Salvatori and Donahue 2010, 2–3). Salvatori and Donahue (2010, 3) hold up non-pedagogical researchers as a standard: "responsible scholars," that is, "who would never write about Shakespeare or Hesiod without first reviewing the critical literature." I am confident that Salvatori and Donahue do know their Shakespeare (and I'd be willing to listen to them even if they didn't), but if one were to judge only by their article, one would have no evidence of their having reviewed the critical literature on *The Tempest,* despite their significant references to Miranda. In fact, digging into the research trajectory on Miranda turns up a few publications that variously challenge the conventional notion of her as a naive neophyte, which Salvatori and Donahue simply take for granted (e.g., Leininger 2001; Sebek 2001; Slights 2001; Thompson 1998). For the rest of this chapter, I wish to make an alternative affordance of the Miranda character, an affordance that applies to the context of writing programs and pedagogy. It is my hope that we can make room enough in our discourse for Salvatori and Donahue's and my and anyone else's uses of any given subject, even rediscoveries and narrations of old news, which may be naive but which also come charged with an organic engagement that differs valuably from learning by external directive. None of us will ever have the last word, and it is not always possible or advisable for one to wait until one has figured everything out before offering contributions in good faith. I prefer to celebrate the abundance of uses we can make of rich textual content, and I invite readers to do so, too.

In reading many dozens of scholarly interpretations and viewing a number of staged and filmed performances of *The Tempest,* I have been continually surprised by the near uniformity of approaches to Miranda, as described above. That's not because the text doesn't bear out the "naive" reading—of course it does—but because I can clearly see a viable alternative. Instead of being an innocent and passive cog in the political machinations of the men in the play (though she is constrained by cultural forces they represent, as they are by each other in different ways), Miranda seems to me to be (able to be [treated as]) a savvy rhetor who employs what Halpern calls strategic disingenuousness to effectively pursue her own objectives. Regardless of whether Shakespeare *intended* this possibility or if the play *means* as much, I believe the Miranda character can *afford* this approach, not only to model a particular course of action for WPAs, as Halpern would have it, but also to inspire marginalized parties of all kinds to poach from texts as may benefit them, even despite contrary boundary markers that have existed for hundreds of years, as in the present case. Let's reconsider Miranda from a rhetorical perspective, focusing on what we know she knows when she speaks and acts—the point being to help us use this material to better understand how WPAs can potentially make conflicted professional circumstances more favorable for themselves and their program.

Miranda is a fifteen-year-old who has been stranded on a deserted island for the last twelve years with only her father and a would-be rapist man/monster, Caliban. It might be safe to assume that she would be interested in leaving the island if even just a pretty good opportunity to do so came along, let alone the outstanding one that does come along at the outset of the play. She has been very well educated by Prospero, who is supposedly unparalleled in his erudition in the liberal arts (1.2.73–74); in fact, he says she has learned better than do royal pupils abroad, who are distracted and whose tutors are inferior (1.2.171–74). When Miranda appears onstage, her very first act is rhetorical: urging her father to allay the tempest he has magically conjured and to spare the passengers of a ship wrecked in it. Regardless of whether it was his intention to do so otherwise, Miranda gets the outcome for which she has petitioned.[21] Then Prospero informs Miranda of the following, in this order: (1) the people from the ship are all safe and unharmed, (2) he protected them for her benefit, (3) she happens to be the princess and sole heir of Milan, (4) Prospero was ousted from this dukedom by his brother and the king of Naples, (5) these men were on the ship and are now ashore on the island, and (6) Prospero thinks now is an opportunity to change Miranda's and his fortunes. Throughout this dialogue, Prospero repeatedly thinks Miranda is not paying attention (1.2.37–38, 78, 87, 106), but as Jessica Slights (2001, 368) rightly points out, "her responses to his tale indicate quite the opposite. Miranda appears not only alert, but also attuned to the political nuances of Prospero's description of their past as she punctuates her father's narrative with perceptive questions." Rather than distracted, Miranda appears to me to be intensely focused, probably on planning her potential moves in the scheme of which she is learning. After all, this highly educated and articulate young woman has just found out that the arrival of the royal castaways marks her chance to return home as a princess, so it seems likely that she would anticipate how she can improve the odds of that happening: how to speak, how to act, and so forth.

Then the following happens: Miranda meets Ferdinand, with whom she seems to share a genuine mutual attraction. She finds out that he was one of the men on the wrecked ship. He is obviously not old enough to have been one of the perpetrators in Prospero's exiling, and her father describes him to her as a "goodly person" (1.2.417), so he's clear of conspiratorial charges. Ferdinand says his father was the king of Naples and has been drowned in the shipwreck, making Ferdinand the successor to the throne. He says he wants to make Miranda the queen of Naples (i.e., his wife). Later in the play, Ferdinand has passed Prospero's trials and sworn his upright intentions with Miranda. He has also informed her that he is single and dedicated to her, and he repeats that he is a prince, possibly a king. At this point, I propose, Miranda begins a series of rhetorical moves so effective that she has convinced Ferdinand and Alonso, possibly even Prospero, and seemingly most readers over the past 400 years that she is little more than a love-struck ingenue, all while getting (arguably) exactly what she wants. Some lovers in Miranda's position might be content at this point to simply know that Ferdinand adores them, but Miranda seeks further confirmation. "Do you love me?" she asks (3.1.67). He makes an elaborate—Slights (2001, 369) says evasive—affirmation. Then Miranda ups the stakes: "I am your wife, if you will marry me" (3.1.83), to which Ferdinand again assents somewhat vaguely. So Miranda follows up about as directly as possible: "My husband then" (3.1.87), finally securing clear verbal nuptial commitment from Ferdinand. They take each other's hands and exchange informal matrimonial gestures. Later in the play Prospero performs an elaborate symbolic wedding ceremony for the two, with plans explicitly established to conduct formally binding procedures upon returning to Naples.

Late in the play's final act, Ferdinand is happily reunited with his father and the royal entourage, whom he had thought to have drowned, and then Miranda delivers her "brave new world" lines. Given the knowledge Miranda possesses, which I have just outlined above, I cannot help but perceive her as being rhetorical in greeting this party with such cheerfulness and flattery: "O, wonder! / How many goodly creatures are there here! / How beauteous mankind is! O brave new world / That has such people in't" (5.1.182–83). How else should she act? Not ignorantly, since Miranda has known from the beginning of the play who these people are (and what they did to her father and her). Also, before Miranda speaks, Alonso reconfirms his identity as Ferdinand's father and king of Naples in embracing his son here near the end of the play. I further contend that feigning ignorance would gain her no advantage. Miranda also knows that if things work out with her new father-in-law, not only will she join his court, but she will also co-inherit his throne. A failure to win Alonso's blessing, however, might annul her prior pseudo-marriage to Ferdinand, who seems to acknowledge as much: "She's mine. / I chose her when I could not ask my father / For his advice, nor thought I had one" (5.1.189–91). No one could blame Miranda if she were to harbor resentment against these villains, but expressing such a feeling to them would yield the opposite of the outcome she is seeking, even if that outcome is nothing more than Ferdinand's companionship regardless of his station. Mere politeness or coyness might be appropriate options, but choosing them would hardly distinguish Miranda above the many doubtless sophisticated suitors vying for Ferdinand's hand. After all, Ferdinand has informed her that she is up against stiff competition from many virtuous ladies for the obviously highly diplomatic position of his wife: "Full many a lady / I have eyed with best regard and many a time / The harmony of their tongues hath into bondage / Brought my too diligent ear: for several virtues / Have I liked several women" (3.1.39–42).[22]

So I propose that Miranda's brave new world speech can quite justifiably be seen not as naive but as suitably and effectively diplomatic, a savvy response to her complicated rhetorical situation.[23] Whether intended or not, the first impression Miranda makes with her "brave new world" comment does achieve, or at least does not interfere with, the fulfillment of her desired outcome, for only a dozen lines later in the play Alonso declares himself to be her second father and even asks her forgiveness (5.1.196–97). Two disclaimers seem necessary before I can conclude. These anticipate charges that could understandably be brought against my case: (1) that my reading is cynical for ignoring signs of Miranda's being genuinely in love, and (2) that my reading is a literary interpretation, which I have previously stated I am not advocating for inclusion in writing pedagogy. First, nothing about my rhetorical view of Miranda denies the possibility of her being genuinely in love. She could be smitten with Ferdinand *and* still press him to marry her (that's hardly an uncommon occurrence), and Miranda would not be the first or the last young lover to put on a good face for a future in-law upon their first meeting. I see no contradictions here, but even if there were, many of the great Shakespearean roles possess or are even defined by their contradictory characteristics: Hamlet, Hal, and certainly Prospero, for example. So why should Miranda not be entitled to the same subtlety, except that readers may not be expecting it and therefore do not see it?

Second, you may be thinking that this passage about *The Tempest* reads like an interpretation, and I admit that it does. However, for one thing, I have stated above that interpretation and affordance making are not mutually exclusive of each other. For another thing, a key difference exists, which distinguishes my affordance (i.e., usage) from an interpretation (i.e., claim about meaning). That is, for my purposes it does not matter whether I am right or wrong about Miranda. Either way, she has helped me to conceive and express ideas that happen to be unrelated to the play: that in some circumstances it may be advantageous for WPAs to believe or appear to believe in the wondrous possibilities their inexpert writing teachers bring to their program and that literary texts can be helpfully appropriated for unintended and unconventional purposes.

Unlike an interpretation, an affordance need not be correct, only useful. So to the extent that I have interpreted *The Tempest* in my process of appropriating it, I lay no claim to a truer or better reading of the play than anybody else's. By contrast, many interpreters insinuate or state outright that their analyses have grasped the meaning or the truth of the text. For example, take Slights (2001, 364), whose argument for Miranda's "independent and embedded" agency is the closest I have been able to find to my view. Slights (2001, 359, my emphasis) presents her work as an "antidote" to weaker interpretations: "I contend that past and present readings of *The Tempest* alike have *misread* the play by emphasizing the nature of Prospero's relationship with the island of his exile without considering the alternative models of selfhood, moral agency, and community life posited by the magician's daughter." For someone writing strictly to an audience of other literary scholars, as Slights is, this may be a fine case to make. But I am not writing to such an audience, at least not primarily or exclusively, and I do not believe students in FYW and even other (non-English literature) writing courses should write primarily or exclusively to such an audience either. I have merely selectively drawn attention to a well-known work of literature to help me demonstrate that and how strategic disingenuousness works. We might call this the Miranda *Affect*.

I have encouraged WPAs, graduate English faculty, and NTT writing teachers with literature backgrounds to become more aware of their role in institutional practices complicating these NTTFs' work, especially as scholars, and to consider an alternative pedagogical option for these individuals and potentially others. I hope such awareness will prompt these groups to accept partial responsibility for adapting (to) the conditions in which NTT writing faculty labor. In turn, this acceptance might motivate action toward corresponding curricular innovation and professional development. I do not pretend that literary affordances represent an outright solution to the issues I have raised, but I do believe this tactic, among other actions, can begin to improve these overlooked aspects of today's evolving postsecondary writing programs and writing curricula more generally.

INTERCHAPTER 4
Irresolvable Indeterminacy

When I began to teach rhetor response theory, I did what many instructors do: try to translate my own experiences for students to adopt and modify. Fortunately, I knew better than to try to make students have the same experiences I have had or to use the same texts I have used, which would be needless and probably counterproductive. Rather, pedagogical uses I have made of my own affordances serve only to demonstrate, including for rehearsing a practice that helps students work with their own texts and contexts, whatever those may be. I call this practice, in which one investigates a significant past literary affordance one has made and which doubles as a written genre in itself, *autotextography*. It's an innovation on the social-scientific method and genre known as autoethnography. I do not have sufficient space here to expound, but chapter 6 says more about, and each of my interchapters in this book is a product of, autotextography. The aim of this practice is to understand social or cultural experience through the explicit lens of personal experience that is somehow mediated by literary textual material. This entails both evocative description (Ellis 1997) and systematic collection and analysis of information (Chang 2008) about significant literary textual effects on one's life. The better one understands such effects, the more likely one may be to make applications of these or other affordances in subsequent rhetorical situations.

So to initiate in my students such inquiry into significant effects literary texts play on their lives, I devised an assignment in which each student anonymously brings to class a personal top-five list of movies, briefly summarized. Books, songs, and other kinds of texts can also be used, but I find that film tends to work best for starters. As a class or in small groups we identify patterns in these lists (by theme, conflict, character, genre, race, class, gender, and so forth), and we venture tentative guesses about each anonymous viewer's subjectivity and what she or he may be looking for in and from the chosen films. Privately, each anonymous subject of discussion can compare these comments against

DOI: 10.7330/9781607327769.c004b

her or his own sense of her or his textual experiences. To rehearse (or, if time is short, to stand in for) this process, I offer my own top-five list as a starting point—narrowed to only recent or familiar English-language films. The first time I introduced this list, I was astonished by the patterns I found after the fact, and upon returning to it in subsequent presentations, I continue to gain valuable insights into my uses of cinematic texts and my reading and rhetorical habits more generally. My list is *Casablanca, Annie Hall, Eternal Sunshine of the Spotless Mind, Lost in Translation,* and *The Royal Tenenbaums.*

SPOILER ALERT: the following material reveals elements of the plots of these films. For your own sake, I beg you not to read the rest of this interchapter until you have seen these movies. Much of their power and enjoyment revolves around a sense of suspense, which my following commentary may confound if you read it before watching the films.

It turns out that I have used these films—especially during the crucial developmental period mentioned in interchapter 3—as rich sources of incidental reference points and vocabulary for self-analytical and behavioral purposes. I call the organizing theme of these affordances *irresolvable indeterminacy*, since the conflict in my life that resonates in these films centers around a loss of certainty or connection, always by way of a separated relationship, after which the implicated characters have no choice but to learn to live on. My interest specifically lies in losses resulting from circumstances other than death, because separation by death both fails to correspond to my own experience, thankfully, and strikes me as an easy out for filmmakers of fictional unfulfilled romances. Furthermore, it's not separation itself that fascinates me but living/moving on afterward, which has been my own primary challenge since age seven.

Although many would agree that the first three of my top-five films are great cinematic works, this supposedly objective greatness (or its lack in the other two) has nothing to do with my uses of these films, and there are many elements in each work that my affordances completely disregard (and even some elements of which I outright disapprove). My identity themes found here focus on separation, unfulfillment, and indeterminacy, in the context of which these films have functioned broadly as company for my figurative misery to love. More specifically and significantly, however, I have derived models and vocabulary from these films for surviving irresolvable conflict. With the exception of *The Royal Tenenbaums* (the only picture on the list *not* to win the Academy Award for best screenplay, though it was nominated for that honor), the key moment for my affordance occurs during the final sequence of each film.

Respectively, Rick and Ilsa agree they will always have Paris, Alvy admits to figuratively needing his brother's eggs, Joel and Clementine mutter "okay" to each other, Bob and Charlotte share an inaudible whisper, and Richie and Margot concede they're "just gunna have to be secretly in love with each other and leave it at that." These partial reconciliations with the indeterminacy of separation reach right to the core of my being, and I have used them for more than just company and ethical influence—though they also serve these purposes for me. The conflicted, living memory of Paris, the absurd need for illogical eggs, the understated relief of a flaw-laden "okay," the perfect, excruciating aporia of an unheard whisper, and the somehow delicious prospect of being secretly in love are all now strategies in my rhetorical toolkit. I say *rhetorical*, not "just" *ethical*, because I find myself actively negotiating some aspect of separateness and togetherness in most of life's situations. That is to say, the boundaries between things often strike me as conceptually permeable in ways that require coming to terms with, personally and socially.

What does any of this mean to *you*? Maybe not much or maybe something I cannot anticipate. Or perhaps you can learn from these ideas and experience greater enjoyment or satisfaction from your own applications of them. At least you have another model for how autotextographic inquiry uncovers past and potentially inspires future literary affordances.

5

AFFORDANCE, AUDIENCE, AND ARGUMENT

Closing the book, I find I have left my head / inside.
—Mary Oliver, "An Afternoon in the Stacks"

This chapter makes affordances of the Orpheus myth to demonstrate my theory in general and to provide an example of one (of infinite possible) context(s) in which literary affordance can play the role of an alternative to conventional interpretive practice. Along the way, I offer a conceptual basis and strategy for teaching an expanded application of felt sense theory, one of the aims of which is to avoid a standardized approach to written argumentation that adopts an unnecessarily limited notion of audience and fails to acknowledge important aspects of the rhetorical situation. As a symptom of this danger, I single out—as a representative example—the Common Core State Standards (CCSS), which have significantly influenced primary and secondary school curricula and thereby shape students' composing habits prior to college, potentially determining postsecondary placement practices (Smith 2015).

My complaint about CCSS-aligned high-stakes tests (and other evaluations like them) is that they risk training students over many years to adopt a reductive and potentially unethical attitude toward audiences by privileging a monologic, agonistic brand of argumentation.[1] This chapter encourages teachers to take counteractive measures, especially postsecondary first-year writing instructors whose students have been brought up on CCSS tests. To enhance my application of felt sense theory, I make a literary affordance of the myth of Orpheus. I contend that Orpheus could have avoided the failure of his one-track argumentative mode by means of a rhetorical/ethical application of felt sense. I do not pretend to be able to solve the deeply embedded problems of overtesting and the removal of curriculum and assessment from teachers' hands in American public education. But I do believe the counteractive

DOI: 10.7330/9781607327769.c005

pedagogical measures I am proposing can help and are not difficult for teachers to implement.[2]

Let it be clear that I am not criticizing fact-based argumentation per se in this chapter; rather, I am lamenting the exclusion of other modes of argument from the most consequential educational writing situations in young people's lives, as well as the uncritical, lifelong habituation of agonistic argument as a default approach to audiences through these high-stakes tests.

After examining problems of audience in the treatment of argument by the Common Core's writing standards, this chapter engages theories of audience from rhetoric and composition scholarship, reviews the concept of felt sense, introduces my proposal for its rhetorical applications, and, by way of my Orpheus affordance, offers a pedagogical model for reconceiving audience more ethically in written argumentation.

SOME PROBLEMS WITH HIGH-STAKES WRITING TESTS

Although some have praised the CCSS for increasing the importance of writing (Applebee 2013) and argument (Marzano 2012) in K–12 education, many more have objected to the high-stakes tests associated with the standards, the latter group including a large and growing national "opt-out" movement. One reason for objection is the dubious treatment of audience by the writing prompts of CCSS-style tests, which have been administered—along with multiple interim benchmark assessments—from third grade through twelfth grade in dozens of states. Writing is one of the central foci of these tests, and argumentative writing occupies a "special place" within them (NGA Center for Best Practices and CCSSO 2010, 24). Some attention is given to informational/explanatory and narrative forms of writing, but the standards explicitly state that they "put particular emphasis on students' ability to write sound arguments," especially in later years (NGA Center for Best Practices and CCSSO 2010, 24). According to the CCSS, "Argument is a reasoned, logical way of demonstrating that the writer's position, belief, or conclusion is valid. In English language arts, students make claims about the worth or meaning of a literary work or works. They defend their interpretations or judgments with evidence from the text(s) they are writing about" (NGA Center for Best Practices and CCSSO 2010, 23). Students are required to "make claims," "argue," and "defend" them, with the purposes being "to change the reader's point of view, to bring about some action on the reader's part, or to ask the reader to accept the writer's explanation or evaluation of a concept, issue, or problem" (NGA Center for Best Practices and CCSSO 2010, 23).

But who is this ubiquitous "reader" supposedly receiving millions of students' arguments year after year, and is there any reason for students to engage this audience in discourse other than being required to do so? The Common Core standards repeat several times that one must give "careful consideration" to the "audience" and write in a way that is "appropriate" to them (Common Core State Standards Initiative 2010, 41, 63). Appropriateness to audience applies to the grade 6–12 standards for both writing generally and writing literacy in history/social studies, science, and technical subjects more specifically (Common Core State Standards Initiative 2010, 43, 66). Yet the reader is never identified, let alone made real or interesting to student writers. Nor is a context provided for addressing this cipher, other than perhaps the condition of test taking itself. Under these circumstances, how can one be expected to change anyone's mind, motivate action, or win acceptance other than by treating the reader as a straw man, which can hardly be considered an "appropriate" rhetorical gesture toward one's audience? So as students are continually tested on this model under timed high-pressure circumstances, they become accustomed to targeting passive recipients with evidence in defense of arguments that receive no response other than test scores rendered incontrovertibly by an anonymous authority. Seen in this light, the rhetorical situation posed by high-stakes writing tests might aptly be characterized as Kafkaesque.

Let us consider specific language from my home state of New York's CCSS-aligned ELA (English Language Arts) Regents Exam, two thirds of which consists of writing argumentatively. In a sample test provided online by the state, part one of the exam entails multiple choice reading comprehension questions about literary texts. Part two, "Writing from Sources," prompts students as such: "Closely read each of the five texts provided . . . and write an evidence-based argument on the topic below" (New York State Education Department 2013, 21). Part three, "Text Analysis Writing," asks the following of students, which will register to many writing teachers as a form of argument: "Closely read the text provided . . . and write a well-developed, text-based response . . . In your response, identify a central idea in the text and analyze how the author's use of one writing strategy (literary element or literary technique or rhetorical device) develops this central idea. Use strong and thorough evidence from the text to support your analysis" (New York State Education Department 2013, 36).

As indicated, the standards underpinning these test prompts make big claims about the importance of engaging audiences in significant ways, but the language of the tests themselves belies those intentions by substituting monologic, agonistic routines for genuine communicative exigency, which often begins with invitation rather than compulsion.[3] While serving as president of the Modern Language Association, Gerald Graff (2008, 3) criticized this kind of assignment or prompt for asking students to "say smart things about [literary] works in a vacuum" without "address[ing] the kind of questions that real readers would ask, like 'Does anyone say otherwise?' or 'So what?'" For a more direct critique of the significant influence played on the CCSS by the context-deficient legacy of New Critical reading practices, see Ellen C. Carillo's (2016) excellent article "Reimagining the Role of the Reader in the Common Core State Standards."

I suspect few people want to write such texts as described above and under such circumstances, and perhaps even fewer genuinely want to read them. Yet this writing and reading proliferates in Common Core–style tests, regardless of the inauthentic relationship to readers these tests force on writers. So unwanted and inauthentic writing may often be the result, lending support to the familiar slogan: "standardized tests produce standardized students." A less catchy but more befitting revision might be: "standardized writing tests (re)produce unethical rhetorical situations." I say *unethical* rather than unrealistic, empty, or unsound because I believe a constant regime of monologic, agonistic writing not only subjects students to go through continual, anxious motions but also conditions them to disregard the vital roles of introspection and social interaction in academic communication. At the least, students learn to regard writing in this context as somehow exempt from the attention to others and to oneself that one naturally pays in other contexts. This includes listening, responding, and speaking with an authentic voice (Monahan 2013).

A few disclaimers and clarification of terms are in order. I want to note that I have nothing against conventional argumentation per se; it is a valid and significant rhetorical form under authentic circumstances. My objection here is limited to the near exclusion of other modes of argument and discourse in high-stakes writing tests and especially to the lifelong habituation to agonistic argument as an uncritical default approach to audiences that students are subjected to by these tests. I also acknowledge how conflicted the concept of *authenticity* is—or realness or unrealness (Bitzer 1968, 11) or genuineness (Petraglia 1995, 19)—especially where human subjectivity is concerned. In fact, authenticity and audience in this context may be largely indeterminate phenomena whose insinuation of essentialness or singularity contradicts their constructedness and plurality in rhetorical situations. However, writers may be more likely to determine (or construct or both) at least a better working "*sense* of audience" if their experiences of motive, purpose, and responsiveness emerge from willful engagement in discourse with responsive others (Park 1986, 487, emphasis added). So in speaking of audience I really mean to suggest something closer to interrelationality or transactiveness.[4] *Audience* can suffice here as shorthand for the mercurial nexus of purposes, motives, and negotiations that circulate in discourse. In speaking of *unethical* or *inauthentic* situations, then, I mean something closer to compulsory engagement in writing contexts in which there exists no interrelationality with others or no desire to engage in such. Under these circumstances, students enjoy little or no opportunity, let alone motivation, to dwell on audience and the related issues they may otherwise try to untangle, such as why they write in the first place, how the implication of readers affects their performance, or what these issues do to influence one other.

Furthermore, *argument* in CCSS-style contexts really means a particular brand of argument, which carries certain assumptions about and stances toward audience that seem natural or indisputable. This is argument seeking to change readers through fact-based reasoning that ignores other means of persuasion.[5] As the CCSS state, "logical argument," the kind required by these tests, "convinces the audience because of the perceived merit and reasonableness of the claims and proofs offered *rather than either the emotions the writing evokes in the audience or the character or credentials of the writer*. The Standards place special emphasis on writing logical arguments as a particularly important form of college- and career-ready writing" (NGA Center for Best Practices and CCSSO 2010, 24, emphasis added). Constant rehearsal of this kind of arguing may very well teach students that the audience's "emotions" and the writer's "character or credentials" have no "perceived merit" (NGA, CCSSO, and Achieve 2008, 24).[6]

Catherine E. Lamb (1991, 13–21) describes as "monologic" the kind of argument critiqued above, and one of her respondents refers to it as "agonistic" (Farrar 1991, 493), as have others for various reasons (e.g., Long 1980, 222; Lynch, George, and Cooper 1997, 63; Ong 1975, 18). Such an approach to discourse foregrounds competition for control and dominance through logocentrism. As the Common Core State Standards Initiative's (CCSSI's) favored mode, this brand of argument comprises the bedrock of what the standards hail as "the foundation for *any* creative and purposeful expression in language" (Common Core State Standards Initiative [CCSSI] 2010, 3, emphasis added). But obviously, such a skewed emphasis hardly accounts for the many different kinds of rhetorical encounters with others to be experienced in school, the workplace, and life generally. As Russell C. Long (1980, 223–24) points out, in "almost every writing 'mode' . . . we find repeated examples of workable prose which are not developed upon the assumption of an adversary relationship with the reader." Even within the area of argumentation alone, there are many other methods and motives than just logically convincing an opponent of one's own point of view. As listed in chapter 3, these alternatives include Rogerian argument (Kiefer n.d.), argument as collaboration (Burke 1969), commodious rhetoric of love (Corder 1985), invitational rhetoric (Foss and Griffin 1995), rhetoric of silence (Glenn 2004), rhetorical listening (Ratcliffe 2005), and participatory deliberation (Lyon 2013).

Ryan Hays (2015), an institutional administrator, sees a need to counterbalance what I'm calling the monologic, agonistic mode. He worries that first-year college students lack experience in listening and dialogue across differences because of the ease of living today in "silos" or "bubbles." Hays (2015) proposes that "we first have to engage the minds we would change: our own as well as others.' " To take part in such "real debate" is "to find a sense in which we're in it together," or else, "if an 'us vs. them' dynamic prevails, everybody loses. In this way, dialogue is equally pledge as practice: it urges us to uphold a sense of community above all" (Hays 2015). A pledge to community, however, does not match—in fact, it somewhat opposes—the Common Core's underlying ideology: "competitiveness and prosperity in the age of globalization" (NGA, CCSSO, and Achieve 2008, 5) and "workforce training" (CCSSI 2010, 4, 60).

The tests affiliated with the CCSS and other such exams manage to maintain a widespread public misperception that they are paramount measures of some singular notion of *performance*, a fact that makes the writing practices and the stakes involved in these tests seem self-evident and even justified in causing children and teens considerable anxiety. By yoking high-stakes tests inextricably to students' advancement through school and thereby to the successes that presumably follow, our culture affirms for its young people that the kind of writing done for these exams is the most important kind. What does and does not count in this context becomes apparent to students as quickly as the tasks determining these values become rote and resented. Writing thus seems to students not to entail engaging with authentic, responsive interlocutors because of a shared sense of exigency but rather, sweating out a quick defense of a decontextualized literary interpretation that will be evaluated by an unknown reader who may turn out to be a machine (see Human Readers 2013).

A similar teleology affects new primary and secondary school teachers these days, whose job security may have more to do with high-stakes test scores than with whether students can improve their abilities to conduct frequent low-stakes writing, engage in peer review, treat genre markers as indicators of social activity, conduct independent research, transfer their writing knowledge to digital environments, communicate ethically and across differences, or just enjoy writing meaningful texts. These are all practices that will ready students for college composition that are not effectively engaged by standardized tests, though the Common Core Standards' introductory language acknowledges a few of them (CCSSI 2010, 7). Nor do high-stakes writing tests engage students in the eight "habits of mind" professional organizations in composition studies nationally endorse in the *Framework for Success in Postsecondary Writing*: creativity, responsibility, engagement, metacognition, persistence, curiosity, openness, and flexibility (Council of Writing Program Administrators, National Council of Teachers of English, and National Writing Project 2011). It is not hard to understand, then, why a 2014 Gallup Poll found that 72 percent of the 854 US public school teachers surveyed did not support standardized tests as measures of student performance, and 89 percent objected to linking CCSS-aligned scores to teacher evaluations (Gallup 2014).

Along with readiness for college, career readiness is the other grand principle the CCSS and its high-stakes tests strive to uphold. But just as the values of actual college writing instructors are misrepresented by such tests, it seems the needs of employers of college graduates may not be well represented either. According to a 2014 study sponsored by the Association of American Colleges and Universities (2015) that regularly surveys 400 organizations hiring new college graduates, the postsecondary learning outcomes rated as most important to employers are, in order, effective oral communication, working effectively with others in teams, effective written communication, ethical judgment and decision making, and critical thinking and analytical reasoning (Hart Research Associates 2015, 4). By putting so much stock in standardized exams that mischaracterize written communication and ignore collaboration and ethical decision making, our test-obsessed culture seems not to prepare college students very well for entry into the professional world.[7] After all, how effectively can one communicate, either orally or in writing, without establishing an authentic relationship with one's interlocutors or paying close attention to them? How can one work well with team members and treat people ethically if one has been conditioned to address others primarily as anonymous sounding boards for monologues that lack emotions and credible ethos?

The problem I have identified here will not be overcome easily; that effort will require advocacy at the political, public, and institutional levels. But teachers' greatest influence is still arguably exerted in their classrooms.[8] For this reason, one of the many potential pedagogical steps we can take to counteract the systemic mistreatment of audience by high-stakes writing tests is to introduce students to the basics of audience theory and encourage them to employ felt sense as an ethical rhetorical gesture, which is what the next sections of this chapter address. These steps may or may not help students on high-stakes tests, but they should help students break out of test-based routines once they reach college.

AUDIENCE THEORY

Formal theories of audience go back at least to Aristotle's (1984) *Rhetoric* and have sustained a consistent area of scholarly inquiry for thousands of years. The subject has generated enough attention to make impossible a comprehensive review of the literature produced in composition studies even since the 1980s. In fact, audience may be one of the most disputed concepts in the field, partly because the subject overlaps with the concerns of a number of schools of thought—each with its own agenda and point of view, including, recently, social constructionism, genre theory, and activity theory—to say nothing of wider applications in linguistics and philosophy that sometimes find their way into writing studies scholarship.

What will suffice for present purposes is a quick tour through some major trends concerning audience in more recent composition and rhetoric theory. My position is that students brought up on constant high-stakes writing tests ought to learn about and accept the complexities and significance of audience theory so they can mindfully engage in their own holistic musing on and transacting with audiences. First of all, teachers can make students aware of the audience for which they have been unwittingly trained. The ones who read their tests, students may be shocked to learn, are often temporary hires with no teaching experience, recruited on Craigslist for twelve dollars an hour to score a per-day quota of Common Core–aligned tests that must meet a designated distribution of outcomes on a six-point scale (DiMaggio 2010; Farley 2009; Ravitch 2015; Rich 2015). Students will see that this situation does not reflect the rich variety of dynamic relationships that writers and audiences share in other contexts, including in the activities of *college* and *career.*

When writers write, they usually address audiences who are not present or not interactive with them in the given moment. In fact, even the physical or responsive *presence* of a reader far from guarantees a writer accurate awareness of that reader's responses to a text. The absence of immediate or accurate information about the reader has caused a great number of enlightened minds to speculate—collectively and inconclusively—about whether the rhetorical audience is singular or multiple in person or perspective; real or not real, or to what degree, or how to determine realness; active or passive in the making of meaning, and if active, then collaborative or antagonistic, or to what degree; outside or inside the text; and, to introduce a key set of terms, addressed or invoked. In 1984 Lisa Ede and Andrea A. Lunsford introduced the field to their addressed/invoked framework, which accounts for competing sides of an ongoing debate about whether the audience exists independently or is constructed by the writer in a rhetorical situation.

Aristotle is the champion of the audience-addressed school of thought, with his ample classifications of types and states of human beings, to which rhetors should refer in making identifications and issuing corresponding strategies toward a desired effect. As the theory is popularly received today, if a given readership appears inclined toward logical reasoning, for instance, then one does well to appeal to them with logical evidence. Or if the occasion calls for sympathy or outrage, then one does well to appeal to their emotions, and so on. A good deal of writing instruction has conceived audience along these lines, and like-minded scholars have followed Aristotle's lead in providing their own taxonomies in support of the audience-addressed view. For example, Ruth Mitchell and Mary Taylor (1979, 250) offer their "audience-response model" for application to "all writing for all audiences," represented as a cyclical process of writing, feedback, and response in which audience functions to "challenge" writing into this circulation of give and take. Mitchell and Taylor's (1979, 250–51) model promises to classify a text "according to its effects, not according to its conformity to extrinsic standards." Shortly after that model appeared, Fred R. Pfister and Joanne F. Petrick (1980, 216) published their "heuristic model," a checklist for writers offered as "a comprehensive probe of [the audience's] basic social, educational, and ethical identities" meant to help writers grasp the influence of readers' relationships to them and to the subject of their composition. If one belongs to the audience-addressed camp, one considers (consciously or not) the reader to be determinate enough for the tailoring of a persuasive text that will yield intended effects.

Another school of thought considers the rhetorical audience to be an unreachable entity whose readers writers invoke by strategically leaving them textual cues to follow or assigning them roles to perform in such a way as to yield intended effects. The best-known representative of the audience-invoked point of view may be Walter J.S.J. Ong, whose 1975 article declares all audiences to be fictions created by writers out of an inability to know or interact with the absent reader. In this way, the writer is different from a speaker: "He is writing. No one is listening. There is no feedback. Where does he find his 'audience'? He has to make his readers up, fictionalize them" (Ong 1975, 11). One of Ong's examples analyzes the opening sentence of Hemingway's *A Farewell to Arms*, in which the author invites readers to play the role of "companion-in-arms" by means of specific usage of definite articles and demonstrative pronouns: "In the late summer of *that* year we lived in a house in a village that looked across *the* river and . . . *the* mountains" (emphases added). The reader presumably knows which year, river, and mountains these are and that what matters about them is not their facticity but the feelings they "recall" through the sense of already having been there with the author as his "boon companion" (Ong 1975, 12–13). Twenty-five years earlier, Walker Gibson (1950), an admitted influence on Ong, proposed the similar idea of the "mock" reader, a fictionalized version of oneself who plays roles posed by texts in order to experience them in certain ways. Both theorists suggest that readers will generally play along with roles assigned to them, as long as the writer has convincingly constructed them.

It is not difficult to imagine exceptions to both the addressed and the invoked approaches to audience. For example, respectively, there are occasions when a writer is incapable of determining very much or anything about an audience to whom she must nevertheless write, such as in composing a statement for the famously inaccessible US Citizenship and Immigration Services or in emailing a complaint to a major corporation's headquarters. Also, it is not uncommon for a reader to resist or reject the role assigned him by a writer. For example, some readers would not wish to play the part of Hemingway's bosom buddy. Scholars have noted that assignments such as *make an argument and support it with evidence* often ask students to write to no one in particular or to no one authentic, given that the teacher as default reader is quite unlike nearly any other audience. A teacher is paid to be a "watchdog" (Reiff 1996, 418) and a critic of a given composition (Long 1980; Miller 1984). Jasper P. Neel (1984, 94–95) claims that most writing done in response to such assignments (or, I would add, to high-stakes tests) does not effectively engage readers, making these texts, figuratively, "nearly impossible to read." Joseph Petraglia (1995, 21) criticizes writing of this kind as "pseudo"-realistic and "unauthentic" because no genuine reader is engaged—and no one is actually persuaded by the argument.

Alternatives to the addressed or invoked binary were soon developed. Ede and Lunsford (1984) argue that writers perform *both* of these actions: addressing what they know of real audiences outside of the text and invoking roles for imagined ones within it while establishing themselves as readers of their own texts during revision. In addition, readers play an active role in this "creative, dynamic" scheme, "whereby writers create readers and readers create writers" (Ede and Lunsford 1984, 169). Ede and Lunsford (1984, 169) conclude, "In the meeting of these two lies meaning, lies communication." James E. Porter (1992, 114) proposes a variously collaborative or communal writer/reader relationship, in which constructions of these "blurred" roles are subsumed by the discourse community of which each is a part. Mary Jo Reiff synthesizes a number of other theorists (cf. Park 1986; Rafoth 1988, Selzer 1992) in deconstructing the addressed/invoked binary and, along the way, critiquing Ede and Lunsford (Reiff 1996, 421) and Porter (Reiff 1996, 411), whose pat solutions to the binary seek too much to "stabilize" or "subdue" the audience rather than "enlarge and complicate our understanding of this concept" and "encourage students to see that writing often entails a negotiation among various and multiple readers" (1996, 422). Reiff (1996, 414–21) cites compelling examples of detailed, heterogeneous constructions of audience in workplace writing. This collective discussion contradicts the vague, homogeneous approach to audience taken by CCSS-style writing tests in supposed alignment with students' prospective academic and career needs.

So it seems that after millennia of theorizing on the subject, scholars still cannot definitively identify the nature and role of audience in rhetoric, let alone agree on how writers can most effectively engage readers. If, as the aggregate of modern audience theory suggests, readers are multiple, changeable, heterogeneous, constructed, participatory, or in any number of other ways unstable or unknowable to some degree, then a rhetoric tailor-made to audiences seems impossible to muster or manage. I suggest, then, that writers would be well served to develop their abilities at guesswork, trial and error, and seeking out and responding to feedback. They should also practice engaging with difference in significant ways, opening themselves up to possibilities of connection, and accepting their participation in an ongoing mystery. In other words, I want young writers to be aware of and to accept the audience's indeterminacy and—when a genuine desire occurs in them—to do their best to engage with readers anyway, no matter how little may be known about them. A key takeaway from audience theory is that although audiences may be variously indeterminate, writers can and sometimes do intuit and develop mutual relationships with them where connections emerge. As Arabella Lyon (2013, 53) defines what she calls *recognition*, these are "acts where two people understand a connection between them—not a connection of dominance, identification, or projection, all of which deny difference, but simply one of a shared communicative act." This relationality is where an expansion of the concept of felt sense can be of use.

FELT SENSE

Felt sense is a term psychologist and philosopher Eugene Gendlin coined to refer to a bodily awareness of meaning that comes prior to language—and I would add, or is otherwise incidental to language. As the theory goes, some knowledge exists within one's body in the form of feelings and sensations apart from one's conscious and linguistic understanding of it. A felt sense might originate in impressions of the internal or external and past, present, or future. It is not an emotion but an embodied perception of one's interaction with the world. This perception is initially something unclear or vague that exceeds one's descriptions but which can eventually emerge and be known explicitly. Since the 1960s, Gendlin has developed and taught a process by which he has clients concentrate deliberately on their felt sense. In this process, called *focusing*, a person pays close sustained attention to the pre-lingual, inchoate sense of a feeling. Words are tested to see if they match the felt sense, until the person arrives at a tangible internal shift in which language emerges that feels right. Gendlin (1978, 32) takes care to specify that "felt sense is not a mental experience but a physical one. *Physical.* A bodily awareness of a situation or person or event." Some examples I have used to explain this concept include the feeling of a blocked word or name on the tip of your tongue or a lingering sensation that you have forgotten something until the unknown content finally emerges or knowing that you have used an incorrect word but not being able to explain why it isn't the right choice. How does one know—on one's own, without resources—that an imprecise word has been chosen among a number of synonyms, for example? "It's just a feeling," one typically says in such an instance in which one doubtless possesses the knowledge in question and yet cannot fully account for that knowledge.

Relatively little rhetoric/composition scholarship focuses specifically on the concept of felt sense, though the subject is tangentially connected to a somewhat broader body of work (e.g., Cunningham 2010; Doherty 1995; Mancuso 2006). The phrase *felt sense* has become familiar enough for casual referencing among composition scholars, which is not uncommon since the field's affective turn. Most work on felt sense pertaining to written communication is attributable to Sondra Perl's writing on the subject, and nearly all of it is primarily pedagogical in nature. Beginning in the 1980s, Perl (1980) began to adapt Gendlin's theory and eventually developed her Guidelines for Composing exercise, which she disseminated in 1989 (Elbow and Belanoff 1989) and 1994 (Perl 1994) and expanded in 2004 (Perl 2004), including an audio-recorded version. In addition, in 1995 Steve Sherwood explained applications of felt sense in the writing center; in 1996 Linda Miller Cleary investigated felt sense's influence on the roles of gender, purpose, and audience in student writers; in 2001 Randall Popken theorized connections between felt sense and students' genre acquisition processes; in 2002 Robbie Clifton Pinter explored links between felt sense and listening; and in 2003 M. Elizabeth Sargent described her teaching of felt sense in relation to invention and metacognition.

Perl's Guidelines for Composing consist of a series of questions focusing on felt sense, meant to help writers mainly during the invention process of composing, such as generating ideas, developing a subject matter, or getting in touch with the feelings at the edge of one's thought. In summarizing the estimated stages of the guidelines exercise, Perl (2004, 4–5) notes that first, "felt sense occurs—is located—in our bodies," after which we can "dispel" this sensation's murkiness by paying close attention, and then the process will culminate in words "that will help us express" the developing feeling and put us "on the right track." Perl and others speak of a relieving "aha" moment when one's felt sense emerges in the form of language (i.e., the culminating "right track"). Early in his career, Gendlin (1962, 74) explains the idea of arriving at a so-called *that* in beginning to address a problem through felt sense; this inchoate idea is something to attend to, an identifiable point of reference, or "a grip on" one's felt meaning that allows one to begin focusing. Later, the idea of "that" becomes symbolized graphically as "....," which indicates what Perl (2004, 50–51) describes as "a space that is open but not blank," which contains "all that awaits implicitly before words come."

As concerns one's felt sense *of the audience,* however, I speculate that this "aha" experience might not be achievable in any culminating or permanent sense if the audience is and is respected as indeterminate in nature, as noted above. That is, if posed by the genuine (i.e., irreducible, un-subsumed) otherness of an audience, the open space in one's felt sense graphically represented by "that" or "....." may need to remain *indefinitely* open. Yet language must continue to come forth into the space of (or be posed by) the audience if verbal communication is not to cease. Clay Walker (2015, 9) has theorized an ecological agency emerging from similar conditions, which he imagines as "feedback and feedforward loops between ourselves and the world in which we act . . . emphasiz[ing] potentiality or unpredictability over intentionality."

So I assert that *sustaining* ongoing contact with one's felt sense would be an advisable practice to engage in for learners of rhetoric who seek to maintain abiding, non-appropriative relationships with their audiences. That is to say: not considering one's "grip" on words the culmination of a discrete intention but rather just one of innumerable related points within ongoing discourse. Indeed, Gendlin's and Perl's theorizations of felt sense call for recursive attention to one's developing feelings and continual revisions of the corresponding language for those feelings. But the idea of recursiveness seems not to get its due in pedagogical applications of felt sense theory. Compositionists have tended to apply felt sense primarily as a method for eliciting conscious knowledge out of unconscious embodied experience or, in other words, for deriving language from feeling and then moving on, for example, by employing felt meaning to generate topics for writing and then writing about them. The intention in such cases is to eventually arrive at—or *to shift attention to*—language per se. That's the outcome as well as the point at which writing takes over and the focus on feeling subsides. There is much to be admired about this application of felt sense, and many individuals have benefited from it, especially students and teachers.[9] But I wish to expand on this usual application of felt sense.

My approach is neither as scientific nor as philosophical as Gendlin's is, and it also varies somewhat from most pedagogical uses of felt sense. Perhaps it can be called rhetorical, which neither discounts it from pedagogical classification nor positions it very far from the philosophical. In short, I see no reason to limit the process and function of focusing so that one experiences a feeling, then focuses on it, then arrives at language, and then moves on. The relationship between feeling and language may also operate in the reverse order or by a different arrangement or by means other than linear sequencing altogether. For instance, in focusing on felt sense, the experience of feelings and emergent language may coexist in balance or emphases may oscillate between them or their nature may change in process, thereby prompting a different but related direction. In other words, felt meanings and the language generated from/for them by focusing do not necessarily correspond to an orderly process of evocation, and in some cases there may be considerable back and forth before arriving at a resolution.[10] For that matter, in at least some circumstances, no amount of emergent language will settle the matter of audience indeterminacy with finality.

Few felt sense practitioners would probably admit to seeking such an orderly process of focusing on feeling as that just described. In fact, a noted early description of felt sense by Perl (1980, 365) characterizes the phenomenon as prone to "break apart, shift, unravel, and become something else."[11] Yet for all its potential chaos, felt sense still seems to be celebrated by writing teachers mainly as a stepping stone toward achieving a more orderly subsequent state, namely, some form of sensible verbal expression. In other words, focusing on felt sense is often seen as a temporary condition, a means to an end, something one does first rather than maintains throughout writing. Peter Elbow calls felt sense "a kind of blueprint for a precise meaning" (cited in Perl 2004, ix), which suggests that felt sense is different from the meaning itself (i.e., the structure the blueprint plans out). Sargent (2003, 57) calls felt sense one of the "tools" in her student "writers' tool bag," which suggests that felt sense is different from the thing that is built with the tool. Sherwood (1995, 12) calls felt sense a "faculty" used "to cultivate and finetune [a student's] ear," which suggests that felt sense is different from the mind's ear itself.[12] Anecdotal accounts of classroom usage of the Guidelines for Composing suggest that achieving functional written language is indeed the desired end product of this process that begins in one's feelings. This seems to confirm the notion of a presumed sequence as described above: feel first and write second. Note, for example, the directional emphasis on order in Sargent's subtitle: "Felt Sense in the Composition Classroom: *Getting the Butterflies to Fly in Formation*" (2003, emphasis added). This is clever and alliterative, and readers know what she means to suggest by the metaphor, but we should still note that butterflies do not fly in formation. This fact partly accounts for the beauty of actual butterflies and for Sargent's appeal to figurative ones. If people convert their figurative butterflies into something orderly, logical, or definitive, then these converted feelings lose the status of butterflies, just as actual butterflies lose much of their appeal when they are pinned and mounted. Luckily, feelings during writing do not have to be pinned down.

I mean to suggest that the great value achieved by attending to one's felt sense in the context of rhetorical situations exists in both the written product of this process *and* in the experienced feelings themselves. In other words, the language produced by dwelling on felt sense is only one of the uses of engaging in the practice. Other benefits include gaining a deeper sense of one's feelings for their own sake and for their relevance to a communicative context, as well as for perhaps developing a corresponding non-verbal capability through ongoing practice. This last point can be thought of as a fluency in embodied rhetoric. Such a capability would be especially desirable where the indeterminate audience is concerned since the aporia of audience is arguably irresolvable, yet communicators need to engage with/in/across it anyway. So other people are always in some respect *other* (i.e., different), and no amount or quality of language can fully fill this gap (i.e., make them same). But if one still continues to communicate with these others, then one may wish to develop a workable sense of audience relationality. So, ironically perhaps, one finds the other *within* oneself or, better, senses the breaking down of such geographies into a state of engaged openness. It would seem advisable to generate an explicit awareness and acceptance of the fact of indeterminacy, which involves both verbal and embodied fluency.

To rephrase the point again, at least insofar as audience indeterminacy is concerned, remaining alert to one's felt sense over the full course of a rhetorical encounter seems preferable to merely attending to one's feelings at first and then downplaying or disregarding them once language has begun to flow from them. The nature of audiences and of one's perception of them will often shift during communication, even while addressing hypothetical readers. Therefore, one's feelings and corresponding language will also shift. So writers should remember that dwelling on felt sense can help them achieve both verbal and embodied knowledge and that the value of felt experience lies not only in how it helps them find a right topic or word to begin their composing but also in experiencing through the body a continual sense of something beyond conventional awareness. This is an experience that is somewhat separate from language, even if it eventually or partly yields to language. Both Gendlin and Perl acknowledge this aspect of felt experience in terms of the "edge" of meaning, where something inside and unknown may come into articulation. Gendlin refers to this coming to words from the edge of meaning as "carrying forward." I wish to add to this concept the idea that where indeterminacies of audience are concerned, one can constantly return to one's feelings so that the *direction* of one's "carrying" may be "forward" only in terms of endless circular revolutions.[13]

To emphasize the specifically simultaneous and ongoing nature of this dual felt and verbal phenomenon, I replace Gendlin's term *focusing*, which perhaps highlights the endpoint of the process in cognition, with the term *dwelling*, which hopes to insinuate the sustained return to physicality I have just described above.[14] These are nearly identical notions, except for the matter of emphasis. *Dwelling* suggests a spatiality that seems appropriate for emphasizing continued feeling, an indefinite thing. This is distinguished from *focusing*, which seems to bring about a final point in reasoning: once something comes into focus, one stops dwelling; one has focused. The difference might be likened to that between the imperfect and preterit tenses. Both of these experiences and their respective descriptors are necessary, to be sure, but the indefinite experience of feeling deserves its due compared with the greater attention paid to rational verbal outcomes of felt sense exercises. My interest here is in keeping the focus on feeling as well as on "languageing" (Perl 2004, 60) so as to draw attention to the recursive rhetorical relationship prompted by audience indeterminacy.

Toward this end, the phrase *come to terms with* will be instrumental in making my example case from the myth of Orpheus in the next part of my discussion. This phrase conveniently maintains a concurrent dual interpretation, as just specified above: one literal, "come to terms," as in *to arrive at language* presumably after an interim or process, and one figurative, "come to terms," as in *to accept*. The former of these interpretations suggests the verbal product of dwelling on felt sense; that is, conceiving words after working through an experience of speechlessness. The latter interpretation suggests the physical products and processes of dwelling, which correspond to the notion of embodied fluency. The following section uses the well-known mythical/literary text to provide a compelling example of a communicator who struggles to come to terms (in both senses) with audience indeterminacy. This character's circumstances arise from having been displaced from conventional, routinized assumptions about rhetoric and audience, specifically by experiencing stifling uncertainty about his auditor's receptiveness, state of being, and presence. This literary affordance demonstrates the complications of choosing suitable approaches to audience and should inspire contemporary rhetors to seek awareness and acceptance of audience indeterminacy and not fall back on rote behaviors by dwelling in their felt sense.

ORPHEUS AND AUDIENCE INDETERMINACY

In the hope of demonstrating what I have discussed about applying felt sense to audience indeterminacy, I employ a generative and heuristic literary affordance of the myth of Orpheus that regards this character as a rhetorical agent. Orpheus's method of engaging his audiences favors certainty over ambiguity, sameness over difference, singularity over plurality, and competition over collaboration. His method is similar to the standard argumentative essay assignments common in high-stakes writing tests, and his mythical experience sheds light on why writers should explore broader and richer approaches to rhetorical situations.

The Orpheus myth provides an apt conceit for presenting my case, since this character is well-known to be a persuasive genius who nevertheless fails to come to terms with his most famous expressive challenge. I propose that we instruct writers to be mindful not to repeat Orpheus's regrettable over-reliance on certainty, sameness, singularity, and competition but to dwell on our felt sense as a preferable or supplemental means of accessing more diverse and appropriate rhetorical approaches. As did this tragic mythical figure in his moment of utmost crisis, contemporary writers may find themselves engaged with audiences who are partly or mostly indeterminate to them, with considerable stakes on the line. So it can help students to remember what Orpheus failed to grasp: that not every communicative occasion calls for the same approach, despite the false consistency suggested by standard high-stakes argumentative essay prompts. Instead, a greater awareness of one's felt sense in rhetorical situations might help to negotiate the audience indeterminacy that is inherent to them.

My literary affordance treats Orpheus's tale as incidentally reflective and instructive of the condition of a writer whose intentions are mainly or only predicated on monologic, agonistic argument. In the myth, whenever his rhetorical task is certain, same, singular, and competitive in nature, Orpheus's persuasive powers remain dominant. But when the context for rhetorical engagement suddenly becomes uncertain, different, pluralistic, and collaborative in nature, then the great poet's language tragically fails him. This distinction offers opportunities for exploration and instruction on the nature of audience, the significance of felt sense, and the corresponding aims of (teaching) composition. Writers should be aware to avoid defaulting to such single-minded argumentative rhetoric as Orpheus constantly employs.

The most common version of the myth goes as follows. After the untimely death of his young wife, Eurydice, Orpheus employs his remarkable argumentative powers to rescue her from the afterlife. He charms his way into the underworld and convinces the gods to release her from death, but they set a condition on this unprecedented deal: Orpheus cannot look backward during the couple's ascension from the underworld. Nearing the surface, in a moment of panic, Orpheus doubts Eurydice's presence and famously turns around, only to see his wife fade away into the darkness below forever. Afterward, Orpheus's rhetoric fails to convince anymore. He wanders around mourning for seven months, able neither to argue his way back into the underworld for another rescue attempt nor to negotiate a confrontation that leads to his own death.

Orpheus is an accomplished argumentative rhetor whose tactics seem to work because he always succeeds in convincing audiences (e.g., even inanimate objects in nature, as well as the various guardians of the underworld). But this is true only as long as the situation calls for monologic, agonistic rhetoric (i.e., changing the guardians' minds, controlling rocks and trees). The quality of these outcomes is measured in terms of appropriative intentions: they are meritorious achievements only because *Orpheus gets what he wants.* But convincing others of one's intentions is hardly the only reason to engage in rhetorical exchanges; nor does success in this aim often occur in the non-mythical world. Inevitably, Orpheus encounters a situation that confounds his usual intention and method, just as students will encounter rhetorical contexts that call for other kinds of writing than the argumentative essay and other reasons to communicate than passing a test. Such situations call for different and deeper awareness of the nature of the communicative act. Orpheus's challenging encounter is primarily characterized by doubt, plurality, and audience indeterminacy, all of which render ineffectual the mythical character's singular intentionality and competitive tactics. We certainly do not want the same to be true of real-world writers for the sake of insufficient engagement in authentic rhetorical situations.

The most important part of the Orpheus myth to the present reading is what Helen Sword (1989) calls "the turn," the moment when Orpheus looks back without a word and loses his wife forever, left to mourn his now-double loss of her. It can be said that in this unprecedented moment of speechlessness Orpheus has lost his senses, or his *sense of audience.* He never asks his wife if she is there behind him during the ascension; nor does he express his feelings of doubt to her. It does not occur to him to collaborate as such. In fact, Orpheus does not ask a single question of anyone throughout the entire story. One key effect of an interrogative rhetoric is to include others in the discourse as legitimate participants in the making of meaning instead of merely as passive recipients of one's arguments. In so doing, the other might be engaged as truly other rather than as merely an instrument for gratifying one's own self-oriented worldview.

One can infer (or project) a possessiveness in Orpheus's regard for his wife, as in Virgil's telling: "He looked back toward *his own* dear Eurydice." Then Eurydice, already fading away into the shadows, laments "alas not *yours to have*" (Anderson 1982, 29–30, emphases added). There is nothing unusual about a couple referring to each other in such terms as one's *own* or *yours* to have (e.g., marriage vows that specify "to have and to hold"). But if taken for its rhetorical implications and coupled with Orpheus's denial of Eurydice's alterity and agency, the turn demonstrates at least an appropriative rather than a collaborative emphasis in the exchange between the spouses. A collaborative approach might have included an exchange of dialogue and the terms *our* and *ours* instead. W. S. Anderson (1982, 30) also notes these pronouns: "Orpheus tried to make Eurydice 'his' rashly and prematurely; therefore, she has ceased to be 'his' forever." Overly eager to claim his victory, he fails to comprehend (and to claim) what he would have won had he taken a more appropriate rhetorical stance. That is, a relationship, which is better understood in terms of interaction than of acquisition. Even if Eurydice's life had been restored, Orpheus would still not have *possessed* her; he would only have earned opportunities to collaborate with her as a spouse, largely through verbal communication.

Orpheus's rhetorical error at the point of the turn denies Eurydice any chance to play an equal—or for that matter, *any*—role in achieving her resurrection. In terms of ethics, Orpheus has reduced his wife's significance to merely a negative role opposite himself, ironically, even as he seeks to rescue her from death. The turn represents the mistake of denying (or ignoring) an audience's agency in a rhetorical situation—a misapprehension of otherness as well as an overemphasis on self and sameness. We can and should learn from this example and expect better from students and ourselves. Orpheus is not wrong to feel anxious during the ascension, just as writers are not wrong to feel insecure about appealing to their audiences. But Orpheus lacks the rhetorical flexibility to explore these feelings with his wife rather than resort to his monologic, agonistic routine. He is so intent on conquering opponents that he misconstrues his own feelings as adversaries, as if he were losing a battle to his doubts. But in fact, these feelings are an opportunity to build community because Eurydice must also have been feeling anxious. The point of the husband's endeavor was to come together with his wife, so his rhetorical stance should have been open, engaging, and interrogative. In other words, dialogue with Eurydice rather than his wavering assumption that he had won his argument with the gods would have been the appropriate means of communicating in this case.

We can treat the moment of the turn as a missed opportunity for Orpheus to have dwelled on his felt sense in *coming to terms with* an indeterminate audience that included Eurydice as well as the gods. In his moment of panic, this hero may have been more heroic to have paused, breathed, and become aware of his feelings—allowing them to exist, dwelling at their limits, letting language emerge naturally from that source, and returning intermittently to this practice. If Orpheus had only dwelled as such on what was bothering him, on his felt sense of that moment and his intuitions, then he would likely have discovered a solution to the crisis that did not include the need to look at his wife. Even with her dying breaths, Eurydice manages to speak to Orpheus: "alas not yours to have." Bringing her back again is something he never manages to do, despite his ability to sing of his wife's loss for seven straight months after her death. While it may be fitting to be eulogized in death, Eurydice would likely attest that it is better to be spoken to in life. But to a rhetor such as Orpheus, who has learned to objectify audiences in order to win monologic arguments, this difference does not register.

All audiences, visible or not, are un-possessable, unknowable to some degree or one way or another. Someone as accomplished with language as Orpheus was should have been aware of this, yet his panic at the turn reveals the opposite of awareness. Dwelling on his felt sense could have eased the husband's worrying considerably or reminded him to ask Eurydice a question or yielded a number of creative expressive alternatives to turning around. But he had not developed a sense of his feelings (let alone that of others') when confronting audiences whose interests also matter in an exchange's outcome. Eurydice does not require convincing at the point of the turn; nor is she apparently mute. Indeed, as an allied interlocutor, she could have assured him of her presence and even corroborated the difficult conditions of their ascension (or pointed out their temporary status), had Orpheus informed her of his feelings. Unfortunately, he did not.

APPLICATIONS

Students brought up on CCSS-style high-stakes writing tests may be in danger of misconstruing audiences as passive recipients of monologic, agonistic arguments in academic contexts and the workplace. This conditioning may convince learners to narrowly regard the power and purpose of rhetoric only in terms of attaining preconceived outcomes of one's own, reflecting an ethic that minimizes or dismisses the inherent differences among people. Student writers must learn that other people cannot be *gotten*, per se, through discourse. Audiences are not theirs to have or make same. Though a reader's attention can be engaged, there are many different modes and reasons for doing this, all of which involve active participation on the part of the reader, who necessarily occupies a different point of view than the writer's. Preparation for this inevitability ought to be a central part of rhetorical education, which must entail more than just training in a single form of argument. As Ede and Lunsford (2001, 363) suggest, it is often preferable to cooperate with the differences one faces in communicating than it is to combat them by arguing for sameness.

This lesson can be effectively taught by referencing Orpheus's tragic oversight, to help students learn and remember to dwell on their felt sense in accepting audience indeterminacy. If Orpheus's true goal was to help restore Eurydice to her own being rather than as a condition of his being—which is to say, if he could have attended to the collaborative rather than the appropriative dimension of his rhetorical engagement with her—then the uneasiness Orpheus felt at the moment of the turn would not necessarily have been unusual or unbearable to him. For if he had ever before dwelled in the felt sense of his wife's otherness, then the experience at the point of the turn would not have been especially foreign to him. He would already have been familiar with the uncanniness of engaging others who are accepted as truly other. Orpheus can be forgiven for his good intention to save his wife, but we must learn from his error that on a rhetorical level, our interlocutors cannot and need not be saved from their difference. His wife's first death is unavoidable; she is mortal. Eurydice's second death is attributable to her husband's folly. It represents his refusal to accept and engage her difference.

I acknowledge that students usually come through the high-stakes testing obstacle course without necessarily becoming insensitive and competitive in all acts of expression. But many of these students do seem to hold low expectations of their written rhetorical encounters in academic writing and to possess little regard for audiences in that context. High-stakes tests are certainly not the only cause of this problem, but as the most unified, consistent, and prominent measures of writing quality that are presented to students in our culture, these exams likely play a significant role. One way to estimate this impact would be to employ and compare an alternative mode of pre-college writing assessment whereby, for example, students reflect on a body of compositions they chose to do, identifying the effects this work had on others as well as the strategies they used to accomplish those effects. Such a method would probably call for students to communicate with others about their portfolio and analyze the feedback, which would make for a kind of autoethnography of their lived rhetorical situations with a socially constructed and dynamic point of view. Such self-assessment should help students become increasingly aware of the wide diversity of audiences, purposes, and tactics they would encounter in other disciplines, in the workplace, and in their lives generally.

POSTSCRIPT

Because of my reluctance to potentially taxonomize what should be a unique, personal, and somewhat spontaneous practice, I hesitate to provide specific instructions for evoking students' felt sense of the rhetorical audience; however, my own felt sense of this chapter's readers (at least the favorable ones) suggests that they may have some desire for guidance along these lines. So to encourage teachers and writers to forge their own paths toward felt sense of indeterminate audiences and without my claiming that the following questions are exhaustive, below are adaptations and additions I have made to some of the Guidelines for Composing created by my mentor Sondra Perl (2004, 36–42). These questions can follow on Perl's (2004, 34–35) introductory instructions and focusing techniques in the same way the originals do.

Who is on your mind? Is there a person or a collective audience you've been thinking about lately? Who else are you thinking about? Are there memories or future projections of audiences that strike you as interesting or compelling? Who else are you overlooking, not just specific people but types of readers, moods they may be in, expectations or biases they may have? Ask yourself: "which one of these readers or audience types draws my attention right now? Which one could I engage through my writing for now, knowing that they are not actually my audience, or if they are that there is so much of their experience of my topic about which I will not know?" What things do you know about the situation in which you are engaging your audience? How do you know? What things do you not know? Ask yourself: "what is the nature of my energy associated with my sense of an audience?" When you imagine yourself engaging that audience, where do you locate that energy? Is it in your hands, in your head or heart or stomach; floating in front of you; a combination; or somewhere else? However you describe it, wherever you may locate that connecting energy, be aware that you will not know the whole of your audience's impressions. Go to the place where you sense the edge of this reality and dwell there, sitting calmly, breathing naturally. How does that make you feel? What would it mean for you to accept the incompleteness of your sense of audience? What would it take for you to do that? To whom can you appeal, or where can you go to ask for feedback, knowing that this will be a partial, temporary, and not necessarily representative collaboration with your audience? Why would someone want to read your composition? Why wouldn't they? How does that affect you? What can you do about that? What is likely to change? Ask yourself: "how is my mind affecting my sense of audience? How is my body affecting it? How about my spirit? My environment?"

INTERCHAPTER 5
No Vampires

Among the groups that are likely to decline my book's invitations (or do worse) is the Writing about Writing camp. It may be hard to tell from the present work, but I admire the advocates of that movement and actually go a long way with them. Above all, this includes the great Linda Adler-Kassner, despite the fact that I have to disagree respectfully with one of her ideas here. My saying "I have to" is literal, as in there not being any other choice. That's because Adler-Kassner has staked a claim on—by putting a stake in—an issue that I cannot help but take personally, the shorthand for which is "no vampires."

In her keynote address at the 2012 conference of the Council of Writing Program Administrators, Adler-Kassner uses vampires as a metonym for any theme around which writing instructors might design courses (wrongly in her view) other than writing itself. As a rule, no course like Writing about Vampires should be permitted, argues Adler-Kassner (2012, 132): "Writing classes, especially first year classes, must absolutely and always be grounded in Writing Studies, must always [be] about the study of writing. They should not . . . engage students in writing about vampires—nor about political issues, nor about recent controversies, nor about other things that are not about writing." My aim is not to issue a direct counterargument—as others have done (Friedman 2013; Scott 2013)—but to illustrate why I feel any "no _____" policy seriously risks disenfranchising some teachers and students. In my case, *vampires* specifically trigger concern, but any forbidden subject could easily do the same for other people.

As in chapter 3, the preposition *about* causes the trouble for me again here. I, too, am skeptical of writing courses that are primarily or exclusively *about* vampires and so forth; however, I can see value in working with students who deeply connect with vampirism (e.g.,) to write *through* or *in terms of* vampires as *part* of their coursework. At least in first-year writing (FYW), no single course theme, neither vampires nor writing itself, seems engaging enough to me to focus on with all students all

DOI: 10.7330/9781607327769.c005b

semester, and as chapter 4 notes, many FYW instructors are not knowledgeable enough about writing studies scholarship to make that their course theme anyway. Some teachers, myself included, prefer to minimize a course's common content and support each student's writing about/through/in terms of whatever concerns *him or her* (within constraints). That may have to do with professional, academic, or personal contexts and modes of discourse. It might even be something that cuts (or bleeds?) across all of these, such as in my case, vampires.

At an early age, the vampire figure became so deeply linked to my psychic development (with nothing to do with entertainment) as to have become a central rhetorical trope in my life. This trope became a key to better understanding important aspects of discourse—and once I started teaching, this key became a metonym for equivalent potential tropes in my students, which I would seek to engage. Hence the irony conjured in me by Adler-Kassner's denunciation of vampirism while demanding a content-based pedagogy at the same time as I was coming to terms, partly *through* vampirism, with the fact that I thrive on a relatively content-vacant pedagogy. Each of this book's interchapters helps explain why I downplay content delivery in favor of helping my writing students with their own issues. In short, I have approached other people all my life by putting their concerns first; I'm good at that, even a natural, you might say. Content delivery, by contrast, can often be difficult and unappealing for me.

That may be partly because some of the content of my actual person was forcefully taken from me when, at four years old, my tonsils were removed. I acknowledge the privilege of my physical well-being today, and I'm certainly not comparing my minor childhood surgical procedure and its precursor maladies to the considerable health and disability challenges others experience every day. Rather, I wish to explore how my experiences of and associations with throat wounds—significant only relative to my own life—came to influence my subsequent textual and rhetorical experiences, as what we can call a *vampire trope.* Although I have never taught and do not plan to teach writing *about* vampires, I do inevitably teach (as I implicitly do everything else in life) somewhat *in terms of* this trope, and therefore my students do indirectly learn *through* it. I wish to preserve a place in writing curricula for such a pedagogy of giving oneself over instead of handing over a content (to put it reductively for stylistic purposes).

Tonsil surgery opened me up, like a text, to being taken apart by pieces. This instilled in me a semi-conscious lexicon of pain and subjugation but also an embodied sensitivity to the stakes of social give and take and the benefits of giving oneself over. Exposed and vulnerable as I was (made to be) through that procedure, I became aware of the same states to which my own being subjected others, namely at first, my parents. Their own suffering for my pain was palpable back then and has been famously chronicled in family lore, for example, upon my being wheeled away at the hospital in a crib by an enormous nurse, reaching out between the bars and screaming "don't let him take me! Don't let him take me!" There we were—indeed, here everyone is—vulnerable to each other simply by virtue of our mutual being, to which we bring to bear (and in which we forge) our rhetorical dispositions, histories, habits, and tropes.[1]

For a period of time when I was a boy, my vampire trope came to me in the form of a recurring nightmare. My recovery from tonsil surgery was typical, including temporary throat pain, and the story as it is usually told ends there. But my psychic entanglements with this episode—nearly unspoken till now—would repeat in the form of a menacing dreamed vampire. He would intermittently appear at the window at the foot of my bed (remarkably, I'm realizing only now: the window facing our neighbors, the *Paines*). Sometimes he remained at the windowpane with a piercing stare; other times he would enter the room, wheel me into the hallway on a gurney, and lean in to bite my neck. As my brother with whom I shared that room can attest, I would wrap a small blanket around my neck before going to sleep in those days. I still have that blanket, preserved in good condition, but because of these associations, I could not bring myself to give it to my son as his baby blanket. So it remains an odd artifact in a drawer, like a piece of radioactive moon rock too precious to discard but too dangerous to handle.

After a while these dreams subsided, and I would not think of them except on a few occasions. One has already been mentioned: upon reading Adler-Kassner's "no vampires" dictum. "Easy for her to say," I thought to myself at the time, "but vampires can't be banished so easily." Another occasion was the first extended period I ever spent entirely alone, when my college roommate went home for a long weekend and I stayed in, kept the blinds closed, and read Bram Stoker's *Dracula* for the first time (in those lovely days before cell phones and the internet). I was hypnotized by the book's themes of giving over—of body, blood, and soul—and also by the sensuality darkened by violation and infidelity. I admit that I secretly wanted the three sisters to feed on Jonathan; after all, readers get to witness Lucy's and Mina's respectively consummated and partially consummated violations, so why not Jonathan's? I was also confused. How could I be anything but repulsed by these actions and by figures resembling the terrorizer of my childhood dreams? I wondered if the spell Mina was under might have *enabled* some as well as *suppressed* other aspects of her character or at least what her character might represent, regardless of Stoker's intentions. Only weeks after reading the book, I watched Francis Ford Coppola's compelling film adaptation (something of a creative affordance in itself), which greatly complicated and multiplied such issues. I did not pursue these questions as academic investigations into the meaning of the novel, which I was not reading for class anyway. Rather, these were psychic revolutions turning in closer and closer concentric spirals toward an unresolved issue inside (and, of course, outside) of me. Years later I would enter the center ring and discover the unexpected powers of emptying out.

When my brother—the one I shared my childhood room with—got married and had his first son, he bought the house we grew up in from my mother and stepfather. He and his family lived there for some years before eventually selling the place. I helped him with the packing up and moving out, and on the very last night in that house which had always been "Home" to me, I slept in our old room. Something remarkable happened that night, which I recount here without embellishment. After thirty-plus years since he had last lurked in my dreams, my vampire reappeared, looking the same as before. This time, however, he entered the house through the front door and was ascending the staircase to the second floor, where I was. In my dream I arose quickly from the bed (where I was actually sleeping), ran to the top of the staircase in the hallway, and leaped feet-first at the vampire, knocking him hard back down the stairs. I screamed threats and profanities at him and punched him repeatedly, with increasing force and confidence. After each blow, he fell and retreated farther back out of the house, across the driveway, and eventually into the street, where I left him lying defeated. I do not remember returning to the house in my dream, and only an hour or two later in real life, my brother and I shut the door of our childhood home behind us for the last time ever. Prior to that morning, I had expected that moment to become a standpoint from which I would always look backward with sadness. Instead, it became exactly the opposite.

6
TEACHING AUTOTEXTOGRAPHY AND LITERARY AFFORDANCE

You must write, and read, as if your life depended upon it. That is not generally taught in school.

—Adrienne Rich, *What Is Found There*

I like this quotation from Adrienne Rich for what it suggests about the high stakes of reading and writing education. But we should remember (and I think Rich would agree) that people probably cannot be *told* what their life depends on, let alone in just a semester's time. Figurative life dependencies develop more organically and gradually than that. So in a writing or English class, I imagine Rich's kind of life-dependent textuality being effectively "taught" more through inviting than informing, listening than lecturing, and guiding than grading. I agree with Rich (and take inspiration from others such as Paul Ricoeur, Jerome Bruner, Walter Fisher, Mark Turner, and Jonathan Gottschall) that our lives depend on—or are even indistinguishable from—the narratives of our lives, both those that are written and those that are read. But these vital narratives are not just any texts, of course; they are the ones that do significant things to/for us and with/through which we can do significant things. It pays to practice exploring and expressing these dynamics, and literary affordance can help toward that end.

In support of this approach, I share in this chapter some corresponding teaching tactics. It might go without saying, but I will say anyway, that much of what follows is work in progress that makes sense for me in my lived contexts and which may very well require adjusting to make sense to others in their own contexts. This is partly why, as I specify in the introduction and chapter 3, I refer to literary affordance as an *approach* instead of a *method*: I neither possess nor believe there should be a definitive procedure for undertaking this act. Most of my effective moves in teaching literary affordance amount to the setting of stages

DOI: 10.7330/9781607327769.c006

for experimental—and later, revisionary—performances. These moves include (1) establishing permission and inspiration, (2) practicing precursor exercises, namely autotextography, (3) studying sample texts by professionals and students, and (4) distinguishing literary affordance from interpretation. Below I offer chapter sections organized around each of these four moves, but first I will answer the question *why study and practice literary affordance?*

WHY STUDY AND PRACTICE LITERARY AFFORDANCE?

I have to admit that I was tempted to not even raise this question, let alone respond to it. That's partly because I feel I have been providing direct and indirect answers intermittently throughout the book to this point. But also and more important, because much of the power and pleasure I believe can be derived from literary affordance—once one has a working sense of what it is—has to do with discovering and refining one's own means of practicing it, including one's reasons to do so. My rhetoric throughout this book has been deliberately mostly invitational in nature, and I take that metaphor fairly seriously and literally. So let's start there (just to be clear: *without* sarcasm): you might study and practice literary affordance because you have been invited to do so (if you're reading this), and that prospect may somehow seem attractive to you. In other words, I am not trying to sell you this approach; I'm offering it.

You're Invited

Let's imagine that I'm throwing a literary affordance party over here, and I have told you what that means and entails to me, as well as who would most likely be participating in it, how other people and I have gone about party activities so far, that regardless of whether you know it, you've probably already done some of the things typically done at parties like this (but they can likely still be developed, and new ideas are always welcome), and that *you are invited to attend*—come as you are and no protocols required, except to please be culturally respectful in your affordance making. (We can talk about what that means if you're uncertain, which I would welcome because I'm not entirely certain of the boundaries myself, especially perhaps where affordances with creative emphases are concerned.) And no hard feelings if you don't come; I know you're busy. Or maybe this just doesn't float your boat; that's fine, too. No explanation necessary. I can't help thinking now of this lovely invitational stanza: "Come to the orchard in Spring. / There is light and wine, and sweethearts, / in the pomegranate flowers," but also of the author, Rumi's, subsequent reminder, "If you do not come, these do not matter. / If you do come, these do not matter" (Barks 2004, 37).[1]

Having already done those things just listed above, I would like to believe that you, dear reader, could decide for yourself by this point whether and why to attend or not attend the literary affordance party, even if your reason for choosing "only" takes the form of "just" a felt sense at this time. And guess what? Felt sense is already at the party! She's been mingling all around but especially in chapter 5, where the basement door to the marginalia has been left open and Sarah Ruhl's (2006, 1.25) Eurydice has now entered, in search of "interesting arguments,"[2] and Geoffrey Sirc (2005) and Maurice Blanchot are playing (their) cards (wrong) at a table, in profile, like Cezanne's painting,[3] and I am reciting a Lawrence poem from a darkish corner, which mostly exists in my undergraduate junior year:

> Life is for kissing and for horrid strife.
> Life is for the angels and the Sunderers.
> Life is for the daimons and the demons,
> those that put honey on our lips, and those that put salt.
> But life is not
> for the dead vanity of knowing better, nor the blank
> cold comfort of superiority, nor silly
> conceit of being immune. (Lawrence 1994, 596)

I am tempted to leave my answer at just that. But this is probably too informal or abstract an invitation for some of my would-be readers, in which case I will offer some more explicit responses to what is after all, I suppose, a reasonable question they may be asking: *why study and practice literary affordance?*

Teaching and Learning

Literary affordance is a good way to teach and learn about rhetoric, literature, oneself, others, and especially rhetorical applications of literature among selves and others, particularly for those who may not otherwise have much investment in this subject area. The benefit derives in part from the organic motivation to be potentially unlocked through inductive inquiry into these entangled personal (e.g., psychological), social (discourse-community), and textual (authorial, textual, political) dynamics. As I see it, the primary issue here is not whether to make literary affordances (as the main section heading's question insinuates) but rather to understand that they occur organically regardless of our conscious intentions, at least initially. Once conscious awareness of this embodied reality is achieved—I recommend autotextography for this—then related matters can be pursued. These may include how your literary affordances work, how to derive more power and pleasure from them, whether and how to classify and assess them, and whether to pursue further rhetorical applications of them. Giving names to organically occurring literary affordances can be an important early part of the process, but that's not nearly the whole of it. Once you have identified (in cases of unintentional affordances) or created (in intentional ones) a particular literary affordance, then it may be wise, if not also instructive or even enlightening, to analyze the optimal conditions for its most effective expression, if indeed you are going to express the affordance publicly.

This brings us back to the "anything-goes" concern addressed in the introduction and chapter 3, which as I see it is largely a question of rhetorical effectiveness. A literary affordance maker (and her or his audience) can benefit from the maker's anticipating and testing where the "anything" of a given affordance may in fact "go"; what the conditions are for its effective *going*; what may or may not be transferable from the present situation to different contexts (and which ones); and why any of this is significant, to whom it's significant, and how much it is significant. It seems clear that this approach at least offers a means of doing things with literary texts that is different than interpretation, in method and especially in aim. These "things" may often be more personally significant to their doers than "only" an interpretation would be, especially if these people—like most people in the world—are not literature specialists. If so, then literary affordance may attract the interest of many more readers and rhetors than would interpretation alone while also potentially serving as an engaging gateway into, or some other supplement to, more squarely interpretative practices. That's because once a person has examined what a given text has done for herself or himself and once she or he has done something desirable with or through a text, then this person may be more inclined to consider the text's meaning (or will at least be more immersed in it for other potential applications).

This generative function complements another pedagogical advantage to be pursued through literary affordance. To earnestly put aside the issue of a text's interpretive meaning, even if just provisionally, can be an effective invitational move in relocating (at least some of) the agency in literary textual study from the hands of the grading expert and into students' hands. Again, we can do this by asking our students:

what has your chosen text done for you, what might you do with it, and what are the various rhetorical conditions that would be advantageous or necessary for you to do so? This does not (or should not) mean merely settling for casual *identification* or expressions of texts' *relatability*.[4] Rather, we may branch out from such a vague starting point, if need be, into a much fuller investigation of the relational condition in question. There seem to be occasions on which many of us dedicate more attention (consciously or not) to fictional texts than to the real circumstances of our life such that the line between the two blurs or becomes less stable or significant (Adrienne Rich says as much in the context of the quotation that serves as this chapter's epigraph). Something about our relationship to certain literary features holds us in a special way, which I suspect is partly a result of the dialogic nature of the nearness and distance of these textual features to our lives—the wakeful dreaminess of living through texts that change us upon crossing back through the rabbit hole or mirror surface or wardrobe wall (or take your pick of other literary portals that apply). See the "Why Literature?" section in chapter 3 for more on this. Taking this experience seriously may be the least we can do for students in trying to provide alternatives to the passive, receptive posture that many reading assignments (especially the high-stakes ones) put them into. If given the chance (and the responsibility)—I know from firsthand experience—our students can derive significant and satisfying means of taking advantage of their embodied knowledge of what has worked for them and may be put to work by them.

The making of affordances from literary material is hardly limited to operations on the personal and individual level. Some theorists go as far as to suggest that the capacity for collective imagination—that is, participation in social and rhetorical experiences of *fictional concepts*—is one of the defining characteristics of the human species and even a source of our dominance as such. This is the fascinating position advanced by historian Yuval Noah Harari (2015) in his theory of the evolution of our species. Harari argues that Sapiens have thrived primarily because of our unique capacity to cooperate in large numbers in complex ways, which is often a function of collective belief in complete fictions. These fictions include things such as corporations, legal codes, political structures, nations, and religions, each of which is an abstract concept without a concrete foundation. Take the example of corporations. Harari (2015, 30) points out that "we have grown so used to them that we forget they exist only in our imagination." A corporation is not its offices, staff, products, or any similar entity. Take away any or all of these things and other components, and the corporation is still a corporation (Harari

2015, 28–29). The best we can say is that a corporation (as well as the other examples listed above and much more) is a collective willingness to believe in a declaration made by an authority, or in other words, a fictional story.[5] According to Harari, this ability to collectively believe in stories "gives Sapiens immense power because it enables millions of strangers to cooperate and work towards common goals. Just try to imagine," he adds, "how difficult it would have been to create states, or churches, or legal systems if we could speak only about things that really exist, such as rivers, trees and lions" (Harari 2015, 31). This reminds me of a description of Wayne C. Booth's literary criticism (which we can extend to that of others like him) as an inquiry into "how human readers respond to human subjects presented by human authors within an imagined world that represents . . . anterior reality" (Schwarz 2001, 7). Indeed, some features of certain literary texts affect some of us in ways that have similar powers to shape and affect our sense of reality.

Sample Cases

Let me provide two examples from two different undergraduate courses, in two different years, that I regularly teach, which in six total semesters (ca. 300 students) have enrolled so few humanities majors that I can count them on a single hand. I mention this to remind readers that I am not advancing my theory for use only in specialized settings for those who may already be inclined to work deeply with fictional material (though, of course, such individuals are also invited to practice rhetor response). Both of the students I will mention here were scientists headed for medical professions, and the considerable similarities in their experiences suggest a possible trend worthy of further future investigation. One of my aims in both courses—knowing they would be populated by non-specialists—was to awaken (or to remind) and inspire students to greater awareness of the (rhetorical) value of literary textuality in their lives by understanding the significant effects such texts have had on them, which they might repurpose as assets in unrelated future contexts involving other people. In other words: to learn to make intentional literary affordances after having discovered past unintentional ones through the processes of autotextography. I provide the assignment prompts in subsequent sections of this chapter. In these two sample cases the students variously struggled at first, as some will inevitably do, with the unconventional treatment of literary material for which the assignment called. In each case, however, after some mentoring, the outcomes of their efforts were fairly remarkable.

The Dermatologist

This student emailed me after drawing a blank in trying to identify a literary text that has done something significant for him. I responded by asking him to answer a series of questions:

- What is your major, and why (in detail) have you chosen that?
- What do you hope to do after graduation (including but not limited to your job)? Why?
- What are your favorite fictional novels, plays, poems, movies, TV shows, and/or other texts (pick as many as you can/like)? Make separate lists of answers to the following questions for each text you're potentially interested in working with.
- Name some key themes in these texts that especially appeal to you.
- Who are your favorite characters in these texts? Why?
- What are some favorite or especially notable scenes in them? Why?
- What are some favorite or especially notable images in them? Why?
- What have these texts (or their themes, characters, scenes, and/or images) *done* for you in your life beyond entertainment (e.g., taught you a lesson, helped you to understand or cope with something, provided you with a helpful key word or vocabulary, moved your emotions strongly, kept you company when you needed it)? Note: that's not quite the same as what the texts say and *mean*, though there might be overlap with that.
- What are some issues in your life, major, or other important contexts to you that are in urgent need of improving, solving, or some new product to make better?
- Who are people in these areas who are capable of enacting such improvements, solutions, or product making?

The student said he was pre-med with the intention of becoming a dermatologist because of a fascination with the skin. His top literary text was a novel about a character who suffers facial disfigurement by fire in connection with a self-destructive response to heartbreak. I followed up by asking the student why he had a fascination with the skin, why he chose a scene depicting the main character's facial disfigurement as the most notable detail in the text, and for more information about various socially constructed values he had listed in connection, generally, with people's physical appearance, subjectivity, and happiness.

It turns out that the student had suffered from eczema and consequent alienation while growing up. Yet he was unaware (at least consciously) of the fact that he shared in the experience of significant social conflict of skin-based origins with his favorite novel's main character. Nor, surprisingly, did he connect any of this with his desire to become a dermatologist until I pointed out this likelihood to him. But after a few more email exchanges, it ultimately became a difference—not a similarity—between this student and the novel's protagonist that became most instructive to him and potentially beneficial to his future patients. Their similarities with each other, however, became the backdrop against which the difference emerged in relief. Once he saw why the novel had captured his interest so profoundly, it wasn't hard for him to see how he could make rhetorical use of it in his profession.

This student said that as he grew up, he eventually learned to cease retreating inwardly because of his condition and to privilege empathy for others instead of obsessive self-consciousness, unlike the novel's protagonist. This vivid and embodied point of ethical contrast, said the student in communication with me, will have a powerful influence on his future "holistic" bedside manner as a practicing dermatologist. The following is an excerpt from an email I sent him following this theorization of the literary affordance he had made of the novel. My prompts were intended to turn our discussion from the personal effects of the student's past affordance to the rhetorical promise of its future application to others.

> Your [literary affordance] could . . . seek to make this experience somewhat replicable for your readers; that is to say, you could try to "teach" your readers how to learn the lesson you have learned, to feel the passion you feel, to commit to the ideals you aspire to as a prospective dermatologist, in part as a result of your chosen novel. What do these lessons, passions, and ideals consist of? Determining to help patients become who they are instead of someone else (unlike [the protagonist]), not to let themselves (figuratively) burn in a self-created, self-consuming fire of doubt and insecurity. In other words, you can use [the protagonist's] story as an allegory for your commitment to a *holistic* dermatological practice, where patients' skin is part of their complete being, not a mere disembodied recipient of medical treatment. You wrote of skin playing a major role in [creating subjectivity] and it seems you are committed to bringing out the real person in your patients as opposed to some projection of who they may think society wants them to be. The difference will entail getting to know the "story" that your patients are writing of their lives (again, figuratively), and helping them to make it an honest story instead of a fictional creation of someone else.
>
> I realize some of this may sound a bit "out there," but bear with me. I want you to really focus your attention on imagining yourself years down the line in your office with a patient suffering from a skin-based lack of confidence. Close your eyes and picture that: see the street the office is on. See the front door. See the waiting room and reception desk. See your office. See the diplomas on the wall and the plants next to the windows (or whatever you like). See that patient and try to sense his or her feelings. Sense it in his/her body language, his/her eyes, his/her voice. Now

> ask yourself how you are going to connect with his or her humanity. Long before the prescription pad comes out, and before you explain your diagnosis, how are you going to connect with this patient (just one of many hundreds you will treat) on an *individual* basis? How will you empathize with his/her suffering, the figurative fire that is burning them up, making them feel ashamed, alone, unloved? Burnt, ashamed, and unloved, like [the protagonist].
>
> Isn't [the protagonist] a completely appropriate figure to help you train for this moment, and maybe even try to train others for it? Wasn't [the protagonist] there for you as a boy or young man, when you were feeling the same way that your patient is now feeling in your office? Doesn't the vividness of the novel's narration inspire you to draw on it for inspiration? Doesn't [the protagonist]—as an *actual* part of your own character—provide you with a point of reference that you can refer to both implicitly in your own reflections and explicitly (i.e., to patients and colleagues) in your explanations of what drives you as a dermatologist?

The Radiologist

Although this student had a backstory that resembles the previous one, a childhood malady that shaped her professional aspirations, her challenge with the assignment was something of an inverse to that above. She knew exactly which passage from which text deeply affected her, as well as why. In fact, this text was literally tattooed on her. But she could not see how she could repurpose to anyone else's benefit her experience of this passage, which happened to be the final sentence of *The Great Gatsby*: "So we beat on, boats against the current, borne back ceaselessly into the past."[6]

This student came to my office for a conference, and we discussed the difficulty she was experiencing with the assignment. She told me she had suffered a chronic health condition as a child that required her to get frequent X-rays, a process that was understandably intimidating to her. Yet she came to know one technician who always managed to make her feel comfortable, an effect of so much relief, apparently, that the student partly attributes its influence for her present-day pursuit of radiological studies and a related desire to help others. The *Gatsby* quotation evoked for this student the powerful force of the past, the ever-changing dialectic of one's experience with it, and the need to free oneself from its grasp. But what beyond the obvious could she do for anyone else, she asked, with the encouragement she had found in this Fitzgerald line, no less as a radiologist? (Note: my assignment does not require students to choose a professional situation for their literary affordance; it is only a coincidence that both students in these sample cases did so.)

I asked the student to narrate for me what it had been like as a girl to undergo all those X-rays, to slow down and try to take me through the experience in vivid detail, which she did. Then we talked about what was at stake in those moments and what the relationship between technician and patient entailed in light of that and how drastically different the experience is for the provider and the recipient of the procedure. How easy it must be, over time, for the technician to become desensitized to the other's point of view, to the fact that this person's life could drastically change right then and there by what is or is not found in the X-ray. A cherished past narrative or a menacing future narrative could be halted instantly in that moment, a present moment that in such cases must press down on the patient like a great weight on his or her chest.

Following the conference, I emailed a summary of our conversation along with some related brainstorming to my student. Soon thereafter she had embarked on a significant project that called for compassionate mindfulness in radiological practice, an argument she packaged in the rhetorical temporal framing of Fitzgerald's repurposed famous last line. Here is an excerpt from my email.

> Being X-rayed is necessarily a solitary experience. It is not anything anyone ever does other than alone. Emphasizing the fact is the technician's leaving at the last minute to literally hide away out of sight in another room. If you are X-rayed at the dentist, you wear a huge heavy lead lump of a bib, pressing down on you like the importance of the moment. Hold still and don't budge even an inch. Someone is about to find out something about you that even you, who has indwelled your body your whole life, cannot determine. In the moment of being X-rayed, you are very specifically positioned between a past state of unknowing and a future state of knowledge. In life, we are, in fact, always positioned as such, in the swing of the hinge between past and future. But seldom are we so squarely put in the present moment as when we are holding still for an X-ray.
>
> Those of us unfortunate enough to have been X-rayed beyond the dentist's office know too well that what we will find out in the future might have us desperately longing for the lovely ignorance of the past. This bout with mortality is universal, and it is a current against which we will never win in beating back. But that is only one of a number of potential ways of viewing the relationship between life and death, past and future. Another way is to be there deeply, wholly in the moment now, and to realize oneself without concern for the past, which is gone, and the future, which is out of reach.
>
> "So we beat on, boats against the current, borne back ceaselessly into the past." Yes, we cannot help but "beat on," and in that act many of us are only "ceaselessly" pursuing "the past." But in each moment, aware or not, we are given an opportunity to pause between the strokes of our ultimately fruitless rowing and to realize *this is it.* This is what we get. It is beyond right or wrong, or simply beside the point of these ornaments we hang on the plain truth. It just is. As you wrote in your email to me: "things move forward and the past is not always important."

As an X-ray technician you may not quite be able to articulate to your patients this ethic stated above. But you can embody it and perhaps get across at least a sense of the sentiments of the quotation that you find most compelling, if not more than that. Somewhat similarly to how the technician of your youth eased your nerves in the X-ray room.

I can imagine your paper being a presentation delivered to an audience of professionals at a technicians' conference, or your delivery of a lesson to an aspiring group of health science students. The point of your paper would be to convince fellow and/or would-be technicians to take greater care toward easing the patient's nerves and to being more present in their work, and your central strategy in doing so would be the metaphorical reference to the conclusion of *Gatsby* that I described above.

PERMISSION AND INSPIRATION

Michel de Certeau is my favorite source of assurance to students that they are allowed to make literary affordances. Many students seem to want such permission before repurposing literary texts, perhaps because their educational histories have conditioned them to read passively. De Certeau can also be a source of *inspiration*, potentially partly because students perceive the deep admiration I have for his work. Unfortunately, I find that some of my undergraduate students are initially reluctant to do *anything* with a literary text (i.e., for school), let alone to actually *do* something with it other than conventional analysis, which is at least familiar if not particularly engaging to many of them. De Certeau provides an antidote by inviting and inspiring readers to "poach" texts for whatever purposes suit *them* (e.g., as opposed to "just" analyzing them to meet the teacher's, textbook's, or test's standards). De Certeau makes his case convincingly enough to empower students to give poaching a try—or, more accurately, to become aware of and expand on their unwittingly having somewhat already done so. Norman N. Holland's concept of identity themes (see also chapter 3 and interchapter 4) helps me trace patterns in students' active reading histories, though I always take care to emphasize the *theoretical* status of Holland's notion. Most of the other sources mentioned in chapter 3 can also be effectively employed for establishing permission, including affordance theory and metaphor theory.

I have also had success in permitting and inspiring students with Roland Barthes's work, especially the easily excerpted *Camera Lucida*. This essay theorizes the signifying power of photography and introduces a term that greatly facilitates autotextographic inquiry and thereby literary affordance making. This term is *punctum*, a neologism for an uncoded, subjective textual feature that productively interferes with or disturbs one's reading or viewing of a text. Contrast this with the coded *studium*, which is a text's general information or meaning, an "average affect" that comes "from a certain training." In Barthes's (1981, 26–27) words, the punctum "will break (or punctuate) the *studium*"; it "shoots out of [the text] like an arrow, and pierces me" with a "prick" or a "wound." For Barthes, this often takes the form of a photographic detail that "holds" him: a subject's fingernails, an unusual shirt collar, a dirt-road background, certain shoes, the exact degree of openness of a hand, and so on. In each case, the effect is "lightning-like" but carries "a power of expansion" (Barthes 1981, 45). The experience of a punctum is not guaranteed, nor does the text's creator intend it; rather, it occurs accidentally and may be inexplicable without scrutiny. Just like the theory of affordances I endorse in chapters 2 and 3, a punctum is not sought out per se, but rather it emerges. It "rises from the scene" of reading (Barthes 1981, 26); "it is what I [as a viewer] add to the photograph and *what is nonetheless already there*" (Barthes 1981, 55, original emphasis).

This idea combines very well with Michael Polanyi's difficult but rewarding work on tacit knowing, especially his notion of "indwelling," which can function as a kind of methodology for investigating one's experience of a punctum. Polanyi, a scientist turned philosopher, examines the phenomenon of embodied knowledge that is indisputable yet unaccountable, such as riding a bike without being able to explain the physical laws and mechanics of balancing, pedaling, and so forth. One of the ways Polanyi (1966b, 148, original emphases) seeks to understand this phenomenon is through contrasting external and internal experiences, or "the difference between looking *at* something and attending *from* it at something else." Polanyi continues: "We may say that when we learn to use language, or a probe, or a tool, and thus make ourselves aware of these things as we are of our body, we *interiorize* these things and *make ourselves dwell in them* . . . we may be prepared to consider the act of comprehending a whole *as an interiorization of its parts*, which makes us dwell in the parts . . . Such indwelling is not merely formal; it causes us to participate feelingly in that which we understand" (1966b, 148–49, original emphases). Being invited to "participate feelingly" with sustained intellectual focus on one's experiences of a textual punctum has been an exciting and rewarding prospect for my students and a practice that helps develop their awareness and capability in discussing what texts have done for them and what they can do with texts. These are the building blocks of literary affordance.

EXERCISES

The potential rewards of practicing the unconventional approaches to literature these exercises take include opening students' view of reading/writing to new worlds of possibilities in textual power and pleasure, practicing alternative rhetorics and thereby becoming more aware of rhetorical strategies in general, and rehearsing the universally significant and highly transferable skill of intellectual innovation. Among the potential risks involved in the corresponding written genres are narrating too much, not including enough conflict in the narrative, researching and analyzing too little, and not sufficiently narrowing down one's topic.

Autotextography

As I was writing this chapter, a BBC article appeared online about the author's former hosting of a surprisingly popular late-night call-in radio program literature segment. She writes of her audience, which included gentlewomen, truckers, and fantasy fans, "ask a listener how she first encountered a book, or where he was when he finished reading it, and in response you'd get a perfect sliver of autobiography" (Anderson 2016). I would add: then ask them to systematically analyze and present a theory or argument about that autobiography, supported with primary and secondary research, and you've got an autotextography on your hands.

In short, autotextography is both a method and a genre for investigating one's own prior (likely unintentional or un-/semi-conscious) literary affordances, in other words, what a text has done for oneself, including necessarily (as we are inherently social creatures) how that textual experience has somehow mediated one's participation in a particular situation or culture. This could be family, friendships, school or professional life, and any number of other subjectivity markers including race, class, gender, and so forth. Autotextography is a modification of autoethnography, which several major figures in that area have collaboratively explained as "an approach to research and writing that seeks to describe and systematically analyze (graphy) personal experience (auto) in order to understand cultural experience (ethno)" (Ellis, Adams, and Bochner 2011). The difference in my adaptation is that the writer has experienced the culture (better if a subculture) in terms of or through the lens of a significant "literary" text. I have found the researching and writing of autotextography to be an effective precursor assignment to the exploration of literary affordance for any student, regardless of his or her major. What follows are a corresponding original assignment and invention prompts and some quoted assessment criteria I have given to undergraduate and graduate students over the past few years to good effect, in various versions, combinations, and circumstances.

Assignment: Autotextography—What a Text Has Done for You

This assignment asks you to examine the functions and the significance of a role played in your life by a text that is *not* nonfictional: for example, a novel, story, poem, play, work of art or design, myth, graphic novel, comic, fairytale, feature film, TV show, song, fanfiction, or video game. Please take readers through the experience, and then examine the value of having participated in a specific subculture as deeply influenced by this text or some aspect of it—*preferably not exactly as intended by its author* (as best as you can tell). Remember that your subjectivity is socially constructed and performed; therefore, much of the impact your text has had on you has influenced your social being as well.

Your task includes explaining what your chosen text *has done for you* in significant, specific ways; where, when, and how that affect has occurred; and why your readers should care, and how they can benefit from abstractions you draw for them from your particular case. We are far less concerned here with what your text says on the page or what it means than with how this text has functioned (i.e., served some useful purpose) in a social context in your life. What was it like for you to have had that experience, *as mediated by your text*? What does any of this say about you, about the subculture in question, about how literary texts can be useful and not "just" meaningful? Your intention should be both to "instruct and delight" your readers, as the first-century Roman poet Horace famously advised.

Because your audience is academic or professional, the less obvious and more substantial the role your text played in your life, the better; the "lower" in culture your text is generally regarded, the harder your task of justifying its use may be. That is to say, your audience does not necessarily care about you or your text and in fact may be outright skeptical of your project, so you will have to work to win them over. For this, it will not nearly suffice merely to present facts or to reveal how you have been *entertained* by your text. That being said, you should still choose the text that has considerable personal resonance for you, regardless of its perceived status, because you will be more engaged and engaging that way. Depending on your level of engagement in this task and with your text, you could write an effective piece on the role of a children's book or an ineffective piece on that of a Shakespeare play in your life. The high degrees of authenticity and affinity you presumably associate with your subject matter will likely serve as powerful rhetorical tools for you.

Your other tools should include narration, research (primary and secondary), analysis, and proposals or arguments. Remember that autoethnography (our stylistic model) is both a genre *and* a research method, so seek a balance between the evocative (Ellis 1997) and analytical (Chang 2008) approaches to it. Recall the "aha" experiences narrated *and* analyzed by Marshall Gregory (2009) and Anna Quindlen (1998; see also, e.g., Adams 2015; Ostriker 1994; Freedman 1993) and the centrality of conflict to their pieces—without which your (and any such) piece will very quickly lose readers' interest. Collect and analyze primary research about yourself relevant to what your text has done for you and what you have done with it (e.g., helping you to overcome a challenge or to better understand something). See my non-exhaustive list of potential options. Collect and analyze secondary research on your text itself and on satellites of this text, including its author, context for creation, means of production and dissemination, popular and critical reception histories (e.g., published scholarship, user reviews), and so forth.

Autotextography Invention Prompts

- You don't just "read" (broadly defined) *any* text that comes your way; of course, you filter them. So can you detect any patterns in your past volitional reading that account for your filter? Can you predict any patterns in your future reading? Can you think of reasons why this knowledge would be useful to you? Now analyze your filter by theme, conflict, resolution, character, genre, key moment, key detail, and textual effects on you.
- Pick five or so texts with the richest content for you and/or the strongest effect on you [this works well when limited by medium, especially film; see interchapter 4]. Evocatively narrate your history of encountering these texts, as well as your initial and subsequent experiences with them. Focus on key moments in these histories.
- What do these texts and your experiences with them say about what your priorities or main issues in life are? What ideas or feelings are you and these texts working on?
- How have you *used* these texts, consciously, semi-consciously, or unconsciously? In other words, what value have you derived from them beyond "just" entertainment? In still other words, have you ever (figuratively) *produced* a text where it may have appeared you were only *consuming* a text?
- What most significant features of these texts and your experiences now stand out to you? In other words, figure out how and why a given *punctum* (Barthes) sticks with you and why it matters.
- What has your literary source text done for your that is significant enough for other people to be able to benefit from knowing about?

- What is the context in your life in which this effect or these effects occurred, including the conflict, characters, and setting?
- What are some key ideas, conflicts, scenes, characters, and/or images in your source text to which you can trace or attribute the significant effect(s) you have experienced?
- What has been at stake for you with this text?
- What would your experience of your subculture have been like *without* your text?
- Narratively retrace your steps with your text from first encountering it to today.
- Where will you look for secondary research to support your analytical or argumentative claims?
- In addition to relying on your own memory, which is limited if not biased or otherwise flawed, what kinds of primary research will you conduct to gather supporting data for your narrative accounts? Some options are interviews; surveys; participant observation; artifacts such as personal records, documents, photographs, family lore, felt sense compositions; personality indicators such as Myers-Briggs types; multiple intelligences theory strengths and preferences (Gardner 2006; Armstrong 2009); key metaphors for life or relationships (Lakoff and Johnson 1980); vertical and horizontal identity traits (Solomon 2012); and discourse community memberships such as race, class, gender, ethnicity, religion, ability, sexuality, age, and region.

Autotextography Assessment Criteria (quoted directly from autoethnography scholars)

- "What substantive contribution to our understanding of social life does it make" (Sparkes 2002, 211).
- "What is its aesthetic merit, impact, and ability to express complex realities" (Sparkes 2002, 211).
- "Does it display reflexivity, authenticity, fidelity, and believability" (Sparkes 2002, 211).
- "Does the account work for the reader and is it useful" (Sparkes 2002, 211).
- It "transcends mere narration of self to engage in cultural analysis and interpretation" (Chang 2008, 43).
- It "enhances cultural understanding of self and others" (Chang 2008, 52).
- It "transform[s] self and others to motivate them to work toward cross-cultural coalition building" (Chang 2008, 52).
- It "evokes in readers a feeling that the experience described is authentic and lifelike, believable and possible" (Ellis 1997, 133).
- It "speaks to readers about their experience" (Ellis 1997, 133).

Literary Affordance

As I was writing this chapter, *New York Times* chief film critic A. O. Scott (2016) published an analysis of the summer's blockbuster films that revealed them to be allegories of corporate management issues (e.g., *Star Trek* imparting lessons about office romances; *Captain America*, about drafting mission statements). As always, Scott's insights are clever and convincing, and in this case they also amount to literary affordance. The article can be instructive to learners of this approach (especially young ones, given the likely familiar subject matter) because it risks but eventually overcomes a common pitfall for newcomers to affordances, what I call *decoding*. Decoding entails the revelation (or creation, if you prefer) of analogical or allegorical parallels among texts, without a rhetorical purpose other than that revelation itself. It's kind of an extended declaration of "look what I found!" That can be valuable, but it does not amount to a literary affordance. So when Scott states—after having mostly revealed parallels for the first two-thirds of his essay—that "real and metaphorical workplaces are everywhere you look," I worried that the piece might only serve only to decode, as in: *in these movies, as in real life, workplaces are complicated.* What would be missing in that case is an answer to the question "so what?" Thankfully, Scott goes on to answer this question with rhetorical points about various workplace challenges (e.g., meaninglessness, race issues, teamwork) as well as about movies and entertainment, of course. My points in raising this example are threefold: (1) to remind readers that my theory already exists in practice, (2) to provide another example of how literary affordance functions by considering a target issue in terms of a literary source text, and (3) to warn that attempts at literary affordance sometimes stop where they ought to start: by concluding rather than beginning with an analogical code. Most readers would not be satisfied to know merely *that* workplace issues could be thought of in terms of *Star Trek* or *Captain America*; they would also want to know *how* and *why* to do so.

This leads me to one more piece of advice before I introduce a related assignment, as well as some invention prompts and assessment criteria. This advice is to look for opportunities (or opportunities to help students) to graduate from *apparent* affordances to *subtler* ones. The problem with the former kind is similar to what we have just seen above: insufficiently answering the question "so what." An example I like to use with students is the hypothetical case of making a literary affordance of Saul Bellow's *Seize the Day* to motivate readers to seize the day. This objective is not wrong or misguided; it's just apparent and probably redundant. I struggle to imagine a genuine rhetorical situation that calls for issuing such an affordance or practicing it in a writing and rhetoric course. I have found that when students cannot move past or replace an *apparent* literary affordance, it can be helpful to reconceive the task in terms of explaining a unique method, for example, of seizing the day in terms of *Seize the Day* (i.e., as opposed to any other text). In teaching your readers how (and why) to experience your *particular* experience with the text, the outcome may be somewhat apparent, but at least the process of achieving it may be unique enough to warrant expression of the affordance.

Assignment: Literary Affordance—What You Can Do with a Text

Advanced readers are accustomed to interpreting literary texts for meanings, but in this assignment we want to see what else or more can be done with them. You are asked to please choose and make extensive use of a "literary" text (i.e., not nonfiction) to achieve an outcome more (or equivalently but differently) effectively than you would do without use of that text. Your audience should be academic or professional and explicitly identified in your text. In Michel de Certeau's and Henry Jenkins's terms, you are being asked to "poach" your chosen text as a tactic in trying to valuably solve a problem or fashion a useful product (i.e., Howard Gardner's [2006] definition of intelligence) for this audience. The outcome should be different from—and may even have nothing at all to do with—what you believe to be the author's intentions in composing the literary source text you use. This source text is neither the subject of your literary affordance nor a mere reference in it but rather a central lens, tool, framework, keyword source, or extended metaphor you make use of to achieve your unique purpose.

REQUIRED COMPONENTS:

- A specific (academic or professional) audience and context. State both of these clearly and early in your composition. If you prefer to address a lay audience instead, then you must seek pre-approval, as this is discouraged in the present context (though fine elsewhere, of course).
- A problem you wish to solve or a product you wish to fashion that has value to you and your audience. State this clearly and consistently throughout your composition.
- A literary (i.e., not nonfiction) text of your choosing. If you wish to make affordances of multiple texts, then you must seek pre-approval, as this entails unique challenges.

RHETORICAL/CREATIVE MODES:

- Argumentation—to persuade, inspire, invite, establish constructive common ground, and so on
  - Note: your primary purpose and mode must be some form of argumentation corresponding to the solving of a problem (i.e., what the problem is and what to do about it) or fashioning of a product (i.e., that it is needed and effective). But you may involve other modes as well.
- Exposition—to explain, inform, describe, teach
- Description—to represent, depict, describe, express
- Narration—to tell a story, illuminate, entertain
- Performance—to express creative content, broadly understood
- Design—to plan and execute a work for specific purposes

REQUIREMENT FOR PROJECTS WITH CREATIVE EMPHASES:

- If your literary affordance emphasizes creativity or design over rhetoric—for example, by taking the form of fiction or poetry, music, dance, painting, sculpture, drawing, photography, screenplay, digital art, three-dimensional printing, animation, game design, wearable technology, animatronic/robotic creation, and so on—then you must also submit a statement (minimum 500 words) explaining the structure of your composition, how you made use(s) of your source text, challenges you faced and how you dealt with them, how creative decisions were made in its composition, and what particular additional assessment criteria are appropriate (e.g., standards for choreography in the case of a dance piece).
- Request a conference to determine whether your project emphasizes creative over rhetorical expression.

Literary Affordance Invention Prompts

- Explain the differences in your experiences of having "read" a text that has done something significant for you and a text that has been "merely" entertaining to you. How do you account for that difference? How does it manifest? How to describe it intelligibly and compellingly to other people?
- Look for themes in important texts from your life and in your experience of those texts. Consider starting with Holland's theory (but note that it is still "just" a theory) that when we read we recreate in texts our fears, desires, and fantasies and then branching out to other possibilities. Name and rank the themes you find, and explain the logic of your naming and ranking systems.
- Listen to and read along with the sample evocative passage I read aloud to the class. Next, quickly sketch a drawing or compose a very short poem in response. Then post a photo of your response to Instagram using the course hashtag, adding to an instant slideshow of

the class's impressions to discuss. Can you help the class understand how and why you responded the way you did?

- Try any of these sequence options to begin:
  - Decide on a source text you want to use, then try to achieve a purpose in terms of it for a specific audience in a particular context (e.g., discussion, debate, controversy, discipline, course, publication, meeting, forum, and so on).
  - Decide on an audience and context you want to address, then find a text to help achieve a purpose that is significant to them.
  - Decide on a purpose you want to achieve, then engage an appropriate audience through the lens of your chosen text.
- Think of your subject matter as the target domain and your literary text as the source domain of a metaphor, whereby you consider the one thing (target) in terms of the other thing (source).
  - Alternatives to "in terms of," above, include through the lens of, deriving keywords or ideas from, as an allegory of, with illustration from, by comparison or contrast with.
  - E.g., theorizing rhetoric in terms of *The Tempest*'s Miranda, urging reconciliation through a Prosperoan lens, critiquing social values through key ideas from Caliban.
- List the most interesting conflict, the character you most relate to, and at least one key scene and detail in your source text. Try to use one or some of these as a lens through which to help your readers see something differently, perhaps even better. Or use the same as terms through which to teach them something.
- What might you be able to do for/to other people with reference to your source text and the knowledge you have generated about it? Consider Lloyd Bitzer's (1968) elements of the rhetorical situation: what is the problem or need you're addressing, what makes it urgent, and whom will you address who both can be swayed by language and has at least some power to affect change?
- Reframe any unrelated argument (preferably one that interests you) in terms of your source text. How does that change things? In other words, argue an issue within the terms (incidentally) established by your source text, not to prove a point about the text itself but to more deeply consider the text's terms and your interest in them.
- Always consider the cultural appropriateness of any literary affordances you make. If you feel you may be at risk of misappropriating culturally sensitive material, then ask around. In our course I will be discussing this with each of you, but in other contexts you will have to make your own efforts to seek out input on this important matter.

Literary Affordance Assessment Criteria/Self-Assessment Checklist

- Clarity and appropriateness of audience and context identification
- Analysis and synthesis of personal and other kinds of information

- Effectiveness of rhetorical uses of the primary text
- Respectfulness or cultural appropriateness of these uses
- Strength of the argument, including proposals and conclusions
- Quality of research (primary and secondary)
- Application of research as evidence
- Have I done any of the following? If so, how well?
  - Increased/enhanced my readers' awareness of their roles in textuality
  - Inspired their performance of those roles
  - Heightened their perceived value of that
  - Understood affordance as an alternative mode of discovery
  - Communicated ideas more effectively (e.g., forcibly, memorably)
  - Deepened my relationship to my source text
  - Improved my understanding of the power and pleasure of texts generally
  - Accrued any potential cultural capital
  - Developed my ability to make affordances (a recursive benefit)
  - Improved as a figurative narrator, reader, or even author of my own life

SAMPLE TEXTS

Of course, students very much want exposure to samples of autotextographies and literary affordances because they have never read these kinds of texts before, at least not named as such. That makes them anxious, despite my assurances not to be, in anticipation of their being asked to compose such texts. So I have collected a number of examples of each genre, both from professional writers and from students of mine. As a policy, I always secure both individual and institutional permissions (non-coercively in the former case) for collecting and teaching with student texts. These are de-identified and only used and collected in hard copy to prevent their dissemination beyond the class period. In addition to the selections below, a number of samples of each genre exist throughout this book, written both by others and by me.

Autotextography

- The first chapter of Marshall Gregory's (2009) final book, *Shaped by Stories: The Ethical Power of Narratives*, is a clear and compelling autotextography that reflects on his early encounters with wordplay, biblical narratives, and Mickey Spillane (among other texts) while growing up in the rural, fundamentalist Midwest. Despite the mostly unfamiliar textual and historical references, my students have greatly enjoyed and benefited from Gregory's work.

- Several of Anna Quindlen's (1998) chapters in *How Reading Changed My Life* are smart, interesting, and autotextographic. I prefer to use the chapter that begins with a Chesterton epigraph (they are unnamed and unnumbered) because it's easier for students to relate to. Among many other compelling stories she tells and analyzes here, Quindlen includes an account of the birth of her feminist criticism. This came in a moment of embarrassment at her mention of a then-favorite book being shot down with a one-word scoff by her college literature professor (a man on the Great Books side of the canon wars).
- Poet/critic Alicia Ostriker's (1994) *The Nakedness of the Fathers: Biblical Visions and Revisions* is a remarkable book in general and also because it offers some of the best autotextographic material I have encountered so far. Evocative, funny, philosophical, and more, I have used two of her chapters to very good effect: "Entering the Tents," an account of Ostriker's deeply felt dissonance reading the Torah in general as a woman, and "Job, or a Meditation on Justice," about her inability to reconcile specifically with the Book of Job for its erasure of Job's wife.
- Other selections I have used for modeling autotextography include Ellis (1997, 116–17), Freedman (1993, 13–16), and several chapters in the edited collection *The Movie That Changed My Life* (Rosenberg 1991).
- As for student work, I have used (with permission) a number of moving and well-written autotextographies as models for subsequent classes. These include one undergraduate's account of using *The Sun Also Rises* to reconcile with a parent's mental illness and alcoholism and an accompanying sense of moral ambivalence and another undergraduate's existential awakening through experiences with specific passages in the contemporary novel *Shantaram.* At the graduate level I have received (and am seeking permissions to teach with) many compelling autotextographies, including one student's gripping mis-en-abyme account of coming to terms with a love of gothic and horror fiction through a version of Stephen King's eponymous concept of *shining* and another student's explanation of unexpectedly developing a Miltonian lens through which to see the entire world.

Literary Affordance

- Perhaps my favorite sample text for teaching literary affordance, a 2013 opinion piece by David Brooks, is certainly not my favorite work in the genre in terms of content. But this article is brief, clear, and illustrative of the approach. Brooks (2013) proposes that *The Searchers*—the "greatest movie ever made"—provides an apt metaphor for today's unemployed male labor force through the film's controversial protagonist, Ethan Edwards (John Wayne). Brooks does not need the cinematic reference to make his argument intelligible, but his handy work of this literary affordance improves his ability to provoke *New York Times* readers with a novel position and supporting case. It's also a surefire way to win over support from the demographic whose plight he is lamenting.

- Another *Times* opinion piece, by Carol J. Adams (2015), offers both an autotextography and a literary affordance (not under these names, of course). She narrates and analyzes how Jane Austen's *Emma* helped her cope with parental caregiving responsibilities: "I began a dialogue in my mind in which I used what I learned about Alzheimer's to deepen my understanding of the novel, and Emma's behavior to instruct me on caregiving . . . I needed Emma as an example, to inspire me to be more patient, less judgmental. Caregiving books tell us how to behave; Emma showed me." Adams's literary affordance takes the form of a concept and keyword that others can use as she did, a "Box Hill moment."
- Within its first six months, Donald Trump's presidency inspired a number of other (highly critical) literary affordances in *New York Times* articles, including comparisons of him to a dreary frog that brags of itself to "an admiring Bog" in Emily Dickinson's "I'm Nobody! Who Are You?" (Clines 2017); to the evil and impudent emperor Commodus (Joaquin Phoenix) in the film *Gladiator* (Blow 2017); and to Alexander Sebastian (Claude Rains), the effects of whose perilous blunder are unwittingly delayed by "the enormity of [his] stupidity," in Alfred Hitchcock's classic *Notorious* (Stephens 2017). In each of these cases, the literary affordance not only contributes effectively to the writer's content but also comprises the central framework for the structure of the article. That is to say, it does not merely serve as an embellishment or trick. With this in mind, it may be worth noting that each of these articles reached literally millions of readers.
- Kurt Spellmeyer (2014) creates a memorable literary affordance of the classic film *Casablanca* in arguing for definitively politicized composition pedagogy. He makes the highly rhetorically effective move of putting his readers in Rick's shoes when Rick is (or by extension, we are) no longer able to maintain a self-interested and content-neutral stance on a high-stakes controversial issue.
- Longer and more difficult models include Richard Rorty's (1992) lightly polemical affordance of *Foucault's Pendulum* (in his role as a speaking respondent to that text's author, Umberto Eco), Steven Mailloux's (2000) and Diane Davis's (2005) dense but rewarding rhetorical repurposings of a *Star Trek: The Next Generation* episode, Hegel's theoretical use of *Antigone* (Hegel 1977), and Freud's various heuristic appropriations of literary texts—my favorite being his work on Jensen's *Gradiva* (Jensen and Freud 1993)—and any number of Freud's respondents who have followed suit, such as Cathy Caruth (1996).
- As for student work, undergraduate examples I have used as models (with permission) include one student's proposal to use Kafka's *The Metamorphosis* as a biblio-therapeutic countermeasure to mental illness

> stigmas and another student's ever-popular application of the children's book *If You Give a Mouse a Cookie* to the issue of sexual consent and self-determination. I have also modeled an excellent piece by a graduate student who reconsidered the relationships among writing center tutor, tutee, and writing teacher in terms of the conflicted and ambiguous triangulation of characters in Hemingway's "The Short Happy Life of Francis Macomber." Other notable graduate-level literary affordances I am seeking permissions to teach with include one student's "redeeming" of texts from a Christian fundamentalist upbringing that had been used to marginalize queer identity and another student's "prescription" of *Hamlet* for substance-abuse addiction.

DISTINGUISHING AFFORDANCE FROM INTERPRETATION

Unless you are required (and you choose to honor that requirement) *only* to interpret or analyze a literary text's meaning or unless you are required to teach *only* this act (and you honor that requirement), you may want to consider affordance as a supplement or alternative approach. Generally, the more freedom to choose along these lines the better, I think, but that is not for me to decide except in my own classes; I can merely extend an invitation to others. Chapter 4 addresses the matter of who might accept this invitation and why, and chapter 3 provides essential related information. In this chapter section I address how affordance relates to interpretation (used here interchangeably with *analysis*). I do so by exemplifying a missed opportunity to fruitfully practice literary affordance where conventional interpretation has supposedly failed, and along the way I issue some constructive criticism of how curricular commonplaces may discourage the kind of creative, alternative approach to literary textuality that I am promoting. My sample case comes from the 2016 textbook *Digging into Literature*, whose prefatory content and subtitle, *Strategies for Reading, Analysis, and Writing*, indicate that it is intended for teachers and students in college composition and introduction to literature courses as well as high school English courses (Wolfe and Wilder 2016, xiii).[7] These happen to be my primary audiences, too.

Digging into Literature offers its readers many genuinely helpful resources, including eight strategies for conducting literary interpretation or analysis: surface/depth, patterns, opposites, context, genre, social relevance, theoretical lenses, and joining the critical conversation. I might not have otherwise drawn my example from this text because it clearly and consistently emphasizes fairly standard literary interpretive purposes and practices, but authors Joanna Wolfe and Laura Wilder (2016, xii) insist that their book embodies principles of writing-in-the-disciplines and "will be useful in general education courses serving nonmajors," as well as to English majors. So again, the textbook appears to match closely with my interests, particularly where the book's strategy called "social relevance" is concerned. But my comments are meant to address issues I have with conventional "writing-about-literature" pedagogy in general, not specifically this text itself, which I consider to be of high quality in ways I will not review here.

Wolfe and Wilder (2016, xxii, my emphasis) include social relevance in a particular category of "strategies for going *beyond the text,*" as distinguished from close reading strategies. This strategy functions by "using the text to understand the origins or nature of social problems in our own contemporary situation" (Wolfe and Wilder 2016, inside cover). The authors claim that observing and practicing social relevance teaches students to "move outward from the text to a statement about the relevance of [a given] problem beyond the text itself," an effect that "can give an exigency, or motivation . . . that goes beyond understanding the text itself to helping us understand larger social problems, forces, and issues" (Wolfe and Wilder 2016, 190). I was initially excited to come across this strategy, as it appears to align well with the approach to texts I am calling literary affordance, which also *uses* texts *beyond* close reading, very much in connection with readers' *exigency*. But I soon came to be disappointed by the marginal status social relevance receives here, as well as the textbook's definition of literary analysis as a practice that necessarily "argues for a thesis *about* the text" (Wolfe and Wilder 2016, 24, 60, my emphasis). What I find in *Digging*, repeatedly and explicitly, and which I see as widely applied to literary texts in education generally, is a somewhat paradoxical assumption that going *beyond* the text is valuable mostly for writing *about* the text. In other words, the text ultimately remains the center of attention, not the reader *beyond* the text, let alone the (rhetorical) situations *beyond* the reader in which she or he inextricably exists or the holistic or ecological interactions of all these things *beyond* the individual status of any one of them. To repeat what I said at the beginning of this section, I suppose text-centrism is justifiable where conventional literary interpretation is the only possible act, but such is a rare condition beyond the confines of literature classes, and it no longer reflects the objectives of many college writing programs. Deriving social relevance or making affordances from literary texts could be a way to keep literature relevant to writing instruction, but not if that strategy is to be subservient to conventional literary interpretation.

Consciously or not, Wolfe and Wilder (2016, x) seem to downgrade the status of social relevance even while claiming that their textbook is unique for including strategies like it. For one thing, their chapter on social relevance is only 38 percent as long as the average number of pages in the other strategies' chapters. Furthermore, the authors describe social relevance as "not essential to a literary analysis" (Wolfe and Wilder 2016, 190), and they seem to walk it back from full status as a strategy by repeatedly describing it as a concluding device for papers that are about other things. To be fair, Wolfe and Wilder (2016, 191–93) also seem to retract the latter of these points by stipulating that social relevance can sometimes be central, not only peripheral, to an analysis. But none of the other seven strategies receives any such treatment. By contrast, *surface/depth* is called "essential" (Wolfe and Wilder 2016, 40), and *patterns* is said to go "hand in hand" with that (Wolfe and Wilder 2016, 60). *Theoretical lens* is described as "powerful" (Wolfe and Wilder 2016, 199), there are "good reasons" for *joining the critical conversation* (Wolfe and Wilder 2016, 220), and *genre* is "special" and "so important" (Wolfe and Wilder 2016, 172). *Context* seems to be self-evidently valuable to the authors because it gets no commentary of this sort. The worst any other strategy receives in the way of disclaimers is *opposites*, which Wolfe and Wilder (2016, 122) say is "not always possible . . . but usually productive" as a strategy.

My critique may seem nitpicky on the micro-level, but I think it is necessary for revealing assumptions (some might say ideologies) on the macro-level that it is meant to reflect, which often go unnoticed and therefore unchallenged in curricular approaches to textuality, detectable as potential biases in instructional materials like textbooks.[8] Wolfe and Wilder (2016, x) say they have determined through interviews that literature professors "desire to see students insert their original perspectives into scholarly conversations," a need the authors claim to have met beyond the level of just "general guidance" with their aforementioned strategies for going *beyond the text.* In other words, the book's chapters on context, genre, social relevance, theoretical lens, and joining the conversation are meant to help students "insert their original perspectives" into their literary interpretation, among other things. But I wonder how effectively such materials (generally, not only in this textbook) motivate students to be truly original in analyzing literary texts in their coursework. We have already seen how social relevance has been marginalized, so let's move on to the other strategies.

For starters, in pursuing context, genre, and so forth, should students get to choose the literary texts they work with, and if so, does the choice come from a provided list (this seems to be Wolfe and Wilder's preference) or is it wide open, and how broadly shall we define *literature*?

These matters set the tone for the rest of the task, as it can be awfully difficult to deeply engage with someone else's choice of text, especially if that person is an expert on the text (and you are not) and holds the teacher's proverbial red pen. Furthermore, when I imagine myself researching a text's historical context, its author's personal life, or the text's genre, I don't think to myself "here are opportunities for my *original perspective*." I suspect many students would also fail to make that connection. To a lesser extent, the same may go for applying a critical lens and joining literary scholars in so-called conversation by means of the methods sanctioned by the textbook: adding new evidence, adding new interpretations, and disagreeing with previous interpretations (Wolfe and Wilder 2016, 225–26). Yes, adding or disagreeing as such requires original input *in name*, but *truly* achieving "original perspective" probably also requires a genuine desire to add or disagree (or undertake any number of other potential acts of originality in a composition).

Also consider the sequencing of each subsection of the textbook's strategy chapters and the influence this may have on student originality. The subsection called "Now Practice on Your Own" consistently appears at the end of each chapter, after subsections about general information; definitions of the strategy; primary texts; steps to follow; thinking-aloud transcript excerpts from professors; exercises to undertake; explanations at the conceptual, sentence, and word levels; notes; and review. This is all valuable material, and my aim is not to degrade its worth, but I do wish to question (1) how much students are motivated or able to work on their "own" here at the end of each chapter, after so much preceding instruction and content; and (2) whether there is room among such pedagogical commonplaces and the curricular and cultural assumptions that underwrite them for alternative or additional approaches to literary textuality. If there is room, then perhaps there is a place in our pedagogy for literary affordances, where "original perspective" possesses primary, not subordinate, status.

Let's take part in a thought exercise, and then return to *Digging into Literature* for one last argument in this section. Imagine that you, like at least 97.3 percent of bachelor's students, are not an English major,[9] and you have been required to take a first-year writing course in which you are given the following essay assignment:

> *Persuade other readers to accept a complex interpretation* of *the "Morning Song" poem* by Sylvia Plath. *The more surprising and nonobvious the interpretation, the better,* but you *must be faithful to the surface meaning of the text.* Do not *ignore the surface reading, ignore contextual information about the author and time period,* or *disregard information that the community of readers of the text agree on. Readings*

that stretch logic, contradict textual evidence, or disregard historical and social context will be met with great skepticism—and will likely be dismissed altogether.

Honestly, how much would you feel engaged in taking up these tasks (which will affect how well you carry them out), let alone doing all of this and inserting your original perspective into the essay? Don't forget that this is only one of four or five major projects in your writing course, you're taking four or five other courses, you're working a job to counteract school loan debt, and you're not very confident in your standard written academic English skills. In addition, let's say you have never heard of Sylvia Plath before, you don't particularly care for poetry, and you've never given birth to a baby (i.e., the surface meaning of the poem).

With sincere apologies to Wolfe and Wilder for manipulating their original materials, I compiled the assignment above by reordering and connecting verbatim excerpts (the italicized passages) from pages 52–54 of *Digging into Literature*, where the authors explain how to produce plausible and avoid implausible readings. Again, it is genuinely not my intention to single out this particular book for criticism so much as to borrow from it in making points about institutional treatment of literary texts generally, of which I think the textbook makes a representative case. What I find to be the biggest problem with assignments of the kind I mean to indicate here—*persuade others to agree with your interpretation of the meaning of a literary text*—is that the task is so removed from what many, if not most, people other than English specialists do or want to do with literary texts. I am aware that a lab experiment in Introduction to Biology, for example, is also removed as such, but a key difference is that people interact with literary texts (broadly defined, as in this book's introduction) nearly every day of their lives, but most of them will never encounter biological experimentation outside of BIO 101. In other words, a reader's relationship to literature is necessarily personal and embedded in the narrative and rhetorical course of his or her own life (which is necessarily social). With readers entering introductory coursework already possessing so much personal experience with literary texts, it is no wonder to me that Wolfe and Wilder attest that their students are often "puzzled" by the seemingly "idiosyncratic" objectives of literary theorists and "have trouble 'getting' what their literature instructors expect." I suspect this is true, but I am not sure the antidote can just be a "demystification" of those objectives, as the authors insinuate (Wolfe and Wilder 2016, viii–ix) because I don't believe such a move will inspire most students to want to join the "scholarly discourse community" of English studies, even provisionally for a semester. Yet these same students all have an intuitive sense of what at least their favorite literary texts (once more, broadly defined) have done for them, and I believe they can extrapolate from this what they might do (i.e., rhetorically) with these or other literary texts.

At the heart of the issue I have just identified, and perhaps where a better response to it may emerge, is the insistence on *meaning* as the gold standard in approaching texts, with interpretation as the means of approach. Most people, not just English specialists, probably do talk (and think) about literary texts in their lives, even fairly frequently. But I suspect this discourse revolves around function more than meaning per se. That is to say, what texts *do* to us and for us: thrill us, disappoint us, make us laugh or cry, remind us of somebody, teach us something, provide unique angles on familiar experiences, introduce us to new experiences, establish opportunities for growth, and so forth. If this is true, then where I see potential for more engaged learning through literary texts (at least for non-specialists and not to the exclusion of other approaches) is in taking advantage of such textual power by putting these texts to work for us, in other words, by making affordances of them. This is not such a leap from interpretation as it may appear; in fact, as I say elsewhere in the book, I see considerable overlap between the two acts. It's more a matter of shifting emphasis and reconceiving purposes, and I believe there is room enough in the curriculum for both activities, as complements or as alternatives. I will demonstrate by returning to an example from *Digging into Literature.*

One of the unique qualities of this textbook, say the authors, is that it presents samples of not only " 'good' student writing" but also student writing of "varying quality." It's hard for me not to read the latter of these as meaning *not good*, but nevertheless I agree that inclusion of this variety is a unique aspect of the book. One of Wolfe and Wilder's (2016, 53) examples of such writing of "varying quality" is an essay by a student from one of their classes in which he "tried to" interpret Sylvia Plath's poem "Morning Song" as a "statement protesting the Vietnam War." They do not provide the essay itself, only their own paraphrases of it (I know it can be difficult to secure permissions). But the authors pronounce the work to be (and one of them as a teacher presumably penalized it for being) "ultimately not persuasive" for three reasons: (1) it ignores the surface meaning of the poem about a mother and her newborn baby, (2) it ignores contextual information about the author and the period in which it was written, and (3) it is guilty of "symbol-hunting" (Wolfe and Wilder 2016, 53).

As someone who endorses the act of textual *poaching* (chapter 3), my attention perked up when I came across this last item, symbol-*hunting*.

Apparently, this is an analytical error wherein one "twists and forces the text into a series of symbols that are used to fit a preconceived interpretation" (Wolfe and Wilder 2016, 53). Wolfe and Wilder (2016, ix) warn students against both this mistake and that of "ignoring certain substantive aspects of the primary text or its cultural context." They advise use of their textbook's strategies instead to "make [one's] arguments more persuasive to the literary scholars and students who read them" (Wolfe and Wilder 2016, 39). I have nothing against this advice for application to specialized contexts, but for general ones like those for which Wolfe and Wilder say their textbook is partially intended (and at which many other curricular materials like it are targeted), I have significant reservations. In the four following indented paragraphs I will express some of these reservations in "think-aloud" format. A consistent feature of *Digging into Literature* is transcribed excerpts of recordings of professors "thinking aloud" while reading primary texts (Wolfe and Wilder 2016, 43–45, 63–64, 148–49, 192–93, 209–10). I endorse this technique, which is similar to freewriting or stream-of-consciousness writing (though I would like to have also seen examples from students in *Digging*), and here I will respond to the textbook in-kind. Following Wolfe and Wilder's format, italicized passages here reflect direct quotations from my primary source itself (i.e., their textbook).

> It's not just this book or textbooks in general that arouse my skepticism but any curricular artifact or pedagogy in the humanities that would seek to tell how and why *we* insiders (who know) do what we do without at least equally welcoming how and why *you* outsiders (who supposedly do not know but may very well know, just differently) do what you do. As my dad would say: teach the student, not the subject. But the labor chorus in my head sings "yes, but easier said than done with 100 students across several campuses." *Substantive aspects of the primary text or its cultural context* (Wolfe and Wilder 2016, 53). I can't help but think that instructions and examples are not particularly strong motivators, no matter how clear and abundant they may be (e.g., "I had no need to work on my car's engine, but the instruction manual was so good that I just couldn't help myself." [Is this Pirsig peeking in?]). Of course, *substantive aspects of the primary text* and its *cultural context* are important, but need they always or primarily occupy our attention? Who gets to decide that, and what are their stakes in deciding? I know the standard rationale—learn the basics and then innovate afterward—but I always worry that drilling of the basics drills out the will and means for innovating (except perhaps for a few resilient "experts," who then get to do the deciding). Wolfe and Wilder (2016, 39) want students in general education courses such as first-year composition to write papers that are *persuasive to the literary scholars and students who read them.* I'll give credit to anyone who can truly motivate a whole class of non–English majors to really want to address such an audience with their

essays, and I'll give a cigar to anyone who can truly get literary scholars to read these essays in such a way as to be persuaded by them.

Okay, on to symbol-hunting, a.k.a. *twists and forces* [of] *the text into a series of symbols that are used to fit a preconceived interpretation* (Wolfe and Wilder 2016, 53). Yikes, that could almost be a subtitle to my book! Like many aspects of my project, there are so many aesthetic, epistemological, ethical, and other associations that it's hard to know where to begin and what to leave out. Let's take the compound terms of the metaphor in order. First up, *symbol.* I object to the notion that the supposedly faulty acts of a symbol-hunter should be "preconceived" (this usage smacks of *premeditated,* by the way, as in *murder*). A student who has never read Plath's poem before and comes up with a Vietnam War interpretation can hardly be said to have conceived this interpretation *prior* to encountering the text. This is not just splitting hairs. Rather than dismiss the student's notion as implausible, why not explore this necessarily text-interactive experience to draw on and draw out his *original perspective* (Wolfe and Wilder 2016, x)? Perhaps this student is interested in war, or maybe war is an unwitting metonym for conflict for him. There is plenty of conflict in Plath's writing, as well as in life generally. Maybe what the poet has to say and how she says it can be helpful to this student in thinking about conflict or war or protest or something else associated that still needs teasing out. I agree that a mere drawing of equivalencies is likely to have little value in itself for many people other than the equivalency drawer. For example, the poem could also be said to be about a work of art or the experience of having a crush on somebody. So what? (There's that pesky preposition "about" again, always trying to insinuate meaning where function would do just fine.) But why assume there isn't potential for greater value to be found in the motivated starting point of equivalency drawing (i.e., if indeed it is motivated)? When a student puts something next to a text in the formulation of an equivalency, consider keeping them there next to each other but shifting the relationship from equivalence to juxtaposition. What do we get from viewing these things in light of each other, for both their similarities and their differences with each other? Doing so would not be a random act if the student had enough interest in the objects and outcomes of their own juxtaposition.

Let's move on to *hunting.* It seems to me that it's not technically hunting if there's no prey to hunt for. Imagine hunting for elephants in New England. If you had a license for the gun and could prove it was only elephants that you were stalking (and if we leave zoos out of the equation), then the crime would not be hunting but only trespassing because there are obviously no elephants to be found and shot. In fact, if you owned the property, then it's not even trespassing; it would just be walking around the woods with a gun. So crossing over to the other side of the metaphor, I have to ask: who owns the territory of a poem or its meaning or its potential use values in other contexts? Who gets to decide what you can or cannot look for or take shots at in the woods of a poem's lines, and again, what are their stakes in deciding? Robert Frost's woods-owning neighbor may not have minded his stopping by and finding a poem where

> there wasn't anything but snow. Are literary scholars now going to wall off that property against further poaching? "Something there is [in me] that doesn't love [such] a wall." I have just violated that line of poetry, a famous line from another much beloved poem by Frost. A poem I have spoken of with my father countless times (and now here another line from the same text: "He will not go behind his father's saying"). But that is a poem about lines—line-like walls—being inevitably violated. *Lines* of poetry indeed.
>
> But what if there *is* prey out there? Let's change the scene to hills now. What if there *is* a chance you might find what you are targeting in those hills? Then it's no longer a matter of *twists and forces* [of] *the text . . . into a preconceived interpretation,* is it? The symbols are really "there" (i.e., "there" in the relational way discussed in chapter 2, with help from Chemero). Should we say, then, that this is a prey-conceived interpretation? What if I see an elephant where you just see snowy white hills? Hills like white elephants. Must we abort such a conception? True, it might miscarry (see below for justification of this punning), but it might bear fruit, be fruitful. My vegetarian predilections seem to have nudged us from the faunal into the floral domain. The point is, I hope we can drop the charges of symbol-hunting and turn the conversation instead to what stands to be gained and lost in the act, whatever we call it, and how that might be fruitfully combined with other methods and put to other purposes, or when and why such combinations might not even be necessary, and how to determine these things.

So yes, competent readers can probably agree that on the surface, Plath's "Morning Song" is a poem about a mother and her newborn baby, and I am willing to believe, as Wolfe and Wilder (2016, 53) say, that their example student "could not create a plausible connection between the war imagery he saw in the poem and the surface reading of motherhood that most readers agree on." But highlighting one aspect of a textual encounter necessarily obscures other aspects of it, and at least I, as a writing teacher, would prefer to shine a light on whatever aspects seem most instructional for helping the student become a better producer of texts in response to texts in whatever contexts may be most significant to him (I'm sticking with the gender of Wolfe and Wilder's example student) in a given time and place. If we accept that this student's subjectivity is necessarily socially constructed, then we do not have to worry about charges of solipsism for this pedagogy; we only need to forge explicit connections with that student's lived rhetorical situations (you could say discourse communities here, if you prefer). If I can preserve or even grow his sense of textual pleasure along the way, then even better. Maybe there's a chance he will want to explore literary texts again more often and more deeply. Maybe a poem's plausible meanings have little or nothing to do with these values to be potentially derived from it.

With some minor adjustments to the example case Wolfe and Wilder have provided, we have a potentially very interesting and worthwhile subject on our hands to explore. Instead of saying that the poem *is* a statement against war, which is to argue for a particular *meaning* of the poem, how about saying that the poem can be effectively *used* as a statement against war, which is to argue for a particular *utility* of the poem? This is a shift from interpretation to affordance. Here is a revised version of my pastiche assignment from above, which retains much of the original language and seeks to make the adjustments to which I have just referred:

> Engage other readers* in your use of a literary text (broadly defined) of your choosing. The more surprising and non-obvious the usage, the better, but also consider the surface meaning of the text, contextual information about the author and time period, and information the community of readers of the text agree on. Readings that stretch logic, contradict textual evidence, or disregard historical and social context should account for doing so in terms of an appropriate set of standards for assessing your intentions. If you are not clear on your intentions or corresponding standards, then make trying to clarify them part of your task as well, perhaps in a metacognitive companion piece, marginal comments, or another method that seems effective.
>
> *Be sure it is apparent who your audience is and how you plan to engage them in your composition: for example, persuading, inspiring, inviting, informing, challenging, listening, establishing common ground, combining these or other aims, and so forth. You may state these things directly in your composition if you feel that is your best option. You will have opportunities to ask for feedback throughout our drafting and revising processes, and you can always also do that with friends and family.

How might Wolfe and Wilder's student with the implausible essay about Plath and war proceed with this assignment? Among other things, he could use the same strategies *Digging into Literature* recommends (e.g., context, patterns, opposites), but toward a modified end. Instead of arguing that the meaning of the text is war-related, the writer could argue how the use of "Morning Song" as a lens through which to consider wars like Vietnam helps us understand them better or at least usefully differently. In about an hour's worth of researching, I was able to learn the following about context, patterns, and opposites related to "Morning Song" (which I had never read prior to this occasion) with use only of Google, Wikipedia, and the MLA International Bibliography, the last of which most university libraries will have access to and which Wolfe and Wilder (2016, 231) recommend to their readers. With some guidance and perhaps a head start from their teacher, many undergraduates could be expected to produce similar findings over the course of, say, a weekend or a week.

It turns out that the poem was written during an extremely tumultuous period, both personally and globally. Intimate experiences of life and death were constantly alternating forces in Plath's life at the time: in 1960 her daughter, Frieda, was born; in 1961 she miscarried a second child and wrote "Morning Song," among many other poems; in 1962 her son, Nicholas, was born, she separated from her unfaithful husband, and at least her second documented failed suicide attempt occurred; and in 1963, after a long struggle with severe depression, she killed herself. A reader looking for a conflict from this context to juxtapose with military conflict could select any of the tragically many choices here. I chose birth and miscarriage for my own reasons; someone else might prefer infidelity or mental illness, for example.

During a prolific period from 1961 to 1962, Plath wrote a number of poems about or inspired by her contemporaneous reproductive experiences (for lack of a better phrase). As we already know, one of these poems was "Morning Song," about birth. Another was "Parliament Hill Fields," about miscarriage. This is a start to building some context. As for patterns, like "Morning Song," "Parliament Hill Fields" opens with an evocation of baldness and closes with balloons. Both poems also include imagery of cries, drafts, shadows, walls, clouds, wind, night, breath, pinkness, ears, scenes through glass (a window, a frame), bed, whiteness, swallowing, and hands. That's a lot of patterns for two short poems (totaling sixty-eight lines, combined) from the same period that unconventionally address motherhood. As for opposites, taken as a pair, these poems straddle the threshold of life and death, with one child just born and another unborn. Getting back to context now, is it not plausible that during this period, the extremely insightful and sensitive Plath would read connections between her personal battles and battles on the global scale, both figurative (as in the Cold War) and literal (as in deadly attacks occurring in Vietnam)? The children of mothers die, from natural as well as militaristic causes. Being the bearers of those lives, how do mothers cope with this fact, whether it manifests in their wombs or in the headlines or in both, as in Plath's case? By the time she was writing "Morning Song," the nuclear arms race had conspicuously escalated to the point of assured mutual destruction, with the United States, the Soviet Union, the United Kingdom, and France all possessing enough weapons to annihilate humanity. Imagine birthing a child into that context; then imagine failing to carry a child to birth right after that. Could it be valuable (variously understood) to us as parents, as citizens, as people born to mothers, to try to fathom these complex and emotional matters through the lens of works by one of the twentieth century's greatest poets? I think so.

Wolfe and Wilder (2016, 53) say the student in their sample case "ignores contextual information" about Plath and the year in which the poem was written, which they claim was "before the onset of the United States' involvement in the Vietnam War." It is not difficult to put a student on a path toward researching such things, especially if that student is engaged in the subject. If he were, then he would find that by 1961 the United States had actually been significantly involved in Vietnam, strategically and financially, for at least a decade, and US personnel had already been killed there as well as thousands of others, including large numbers of civilians. He might also come to suspect that it could be a mistake to equate Plath's interests solely with the American view of the war (of which there was, of course, no such singular thing anyway). After all, Plath had been living in the United Kingdom for over five years by that time, and it is reasonable to speculate that her point of view was informed by European attitudes toward the war, especially with neighboring France having ended its violent colonial enterprise there not long beforehand. Furthermore, in the fall of 1961 American and British counterinsurgency plans were at odds with each other, notably over the degrees of militaristic rather than diplomatic involvement. We can see again that there are complicating factors to consider.

So although "Morning Song" does not appear to be *about* the Vietnam War, I believe a plausible and valuable case could be made that Vietnam is in the air in the writing of the poem or at least that we could put the poem into orbit around the war or vice versa, to keep the imagery aerial (playing homonymically on the poem's collection title, *Ariel*). More than a few scholars have published studies of Plath's work in relation to war (e.g., Bayley 2007; Bradley 2005; Hwang 2007), and a number of dissertations have been written on the topic. Wolfe and Wilder's sample student may not have made a "persuasive" argument about the war connection, as these literary scholars have done, but I hope to have shown that unless he plans to be a literary scholar, he does not necessarily need to do so. I do not know what happened to Wolfe and Wilder's example student. He could have been given a bad grade and that was the end of it. Or he might have been (and I suspect he was) given the chance to revise his work to better align with the course's expectations. But he could have been encouraged to shift his goal from interpretation to affordance by applying Plath's poems to the context of today's somewhat Vietnam-like War on Terror. Among other benefits, this move would alleviate the need to establish war-related intentions on Plath's part and would potentially broaden and increase the interest of the student's readership. Frankly, relatively few contemporary readers are interested in Plath's views on war, but many are concerned about today's War on Terror and at least some of them would be receptive to considering this war and others like it from an artistic angle. Even better, if the student were developing his topic while I was writing the first draft of this chapter, then he could consider using Plath's poetry to address a controversy emerging in real time over a mother, the death of her son in a dubious war, and political rhetoric. That is the highly publicized feud between then-presidential candidate Donald Trump and Ghazala Khan over this mother's silent presence during her husband, Khizr Khan's, speech at the 2016 Democratic National Convention about their son, Humayun Khan, an immigrant Muslim US Army officer killed in the Iraq War.

I, for one, would be interested in reading a paper that uses Sylvia Plath's poetry to examine Donald Trump's campaign rhetoric, and I would even be open to being persuaded by such a paper, though persuasion in the usual, agonistic sense need not be the outcome (see chapter 5). Conducting and composing this kind of work might not be any easier for the student than would be writing an interpretation of the poem's meaning—it may even be harder—but the task might be more engaging and valuable to him and his readers. In fact, with a unique and engaging composition like this one in hand, the student might even attract more than just hypothetical readers. Of course, any affordance of this kind would be accountable to a number of legitimate challenges, including "why a poem instead of or in addition to nonfictional sources like a history book," "why *this* poem and not another one," "how does this poem help us better understand the other subject or at least usefully differently understand it," and so forth. But if a student who wanted to take this route were restricted to only interpreting the meaning of Plath's poems and staying within the bounds of what others agree on, then he likely could not undertake the project.

Finally, the completion of a "persuasive" literary analysis or even a "successful" literary affordance need not be the only or the best standard by which to judge the value of a reader's work done with a literary text. That is to say, it need not always be the *outcome* that makes the process worthwhile. I know this is a somewhat controversial proposal, but I will state anyway: it is not necessarily a bad thing to have to stop or pause work on a project, say, at the end of a semester without it being just right or finished or thoroughly convincing and so on, especially if a writer is engaged enough in the project to continue working on or at least thinking about it afterward. A typical fifteen-week semester is an arbitrary unit and a tiny fraction of a lifetime when it comes to developing one's relationship to textuality. Of course, it is a convenient unit (as would be other fixed numbers of weeks) for comparing student outcomes with each other for the sake of ranking. But relatively few people are interested in such ranked comparisons of textual engagement once students have graduated.[10] As Peter Elbow (1991, 136) reminds us, "Life is long and college is short."

Among any number of alternative criteria we could apply to unfinished or not completely traditionally persuasive compositions is the potential benefit of a student having done deep thinking, close reading, inference drawing, conferencing, extensive researching, experimenting, peer workshopping, innovating, revising, and even soul searching on a topic that, perhaps most important, has emerged from and prioritized his "original perspective" on a text he selected because it is important to him in his situated lived experience. Some or all of these activities may show up again in the student's life after this particular assignment has long since receded into the past. Deciding the value of these activities can be done relative to the student's personal desires instead of or in addition to impersonal curricular standards. Of course teachers, let alone students, may not always be free to determine these matters or to determine them entirely—including whether to pursue literary affordance at all—yet opportunities to influence or negotiate such matters will likely appear to those who seek them. This book hopes to have propelled your interest in such seeking and to serve as a humble guide and companion along that path, if you choose to take it.

NOTES

CHAPTER 1: INTRODUCTION

1 *The Tempest* (4.1.47–48). All references to *The Tempest* are from (Shakespeare 1987).

2 I take these elements from Lloyd Bitzer's (1968, 11) seminal essay, in which (relevantly to the present context) he writes "the fictive rhetorical discourse within a play or novel may become genuinely rhetorical outside fictive context—if there is a real situation for which the discourse is a rhetorical response. Also, of course, the play or novel itself may be understood as a rhetorical response having poetic form."

3 Scholars who conduct research in this area use terms like "stand-on-able" (Tolman 1932, 448), "sit-on-able" (Mark 1987, 364), "letter-mailing-with-able" (Scarantino 2003, 951), and "climb-on-able or fall-off-able or get-under-neath-able or bump-into-able" (Gibson 1979, 128).

CHAPTER 2: AFFORDANCE THEORY

1 There is some ambiguity in affordance theory about whether action is a definitive component. It usually, but not always, is. Michaels (2003, 137–38) points out that in Gibson's (1979, 131; see my next paragraph) example of substances affording nutrition, *nutrition* is not an action. I am interested in literary affordances that are both active and inactive.

2 Costall (2012) provides the useful term *canonical* for identifying the intended affordance of an object, and he even uses the example of the maker of a chair designing it for sitting on, not standing on. But because I am not aware of this term's widespread adoption, I will not employ it in this way here. Also, the word *canonical* has complicated other meanings in literary studies, which I do not wish to run the risk of evoking.

3 I am aware that this could be characterized as an affordance of affordance theory, but let's not get ahead of ourselves.

4 In an effort to emphasize this emergent quality, Noble (1993, 386) argues that the nounal form *affordance* creates unnecessary problems and should be avoided in favor of the verbal form *afford* whenever possible. Noble's proposal makes good sense, but I am not aware of its widespread adoption, so if only for the sake of familiarity I will not often abide by it.

5 It's debatable whether the experiences of laughter, levity, and similar emotions are mediated by representational cognition or not, but it seems feasible (if not more likely) that they are at least in part directly experienced (i.e., not the product of internal processes of representation).

6 Direct and indirect perception is a huge philosophical and psychological issue that I cannot take up here beyond crude appropriation of these terms and an occasional gloss. For excellent discussions of this issue with specific regard to Gibson, see Costall and Still (1989) and Noble (1993, 375–78). Also, McArthur and Baron (1983, 234) explain respective alliances between ecological/direct and information processing/indirect theories of social perception.

7 Predictably, some ecological theories have been critiqued for a lack of empirical research to support claims (e.g., Schmitt 1987, 269–75).

8 I recommend Alan Costall (2012, 88) along these lines, who sees a problem in the framing of discussions of affordance in terms of perception rather than action. Also see Chemero (2009, 143–45) for a well-researched retort to the tendency to assume that body scale is the only or best "relata" for studying affordances.
9 Noble (1981, 72–73) justly gives Gibson something of a pass, but he maintains his critique.
10 Even more interesting, Chemero (2009, 2013) offers radical embodied cognitive science as something of a corrective to the non-radical kind, but this goes beyond my ability to review here.
11 For another application of this theory to writing and rhetoric pedagogy, see Rule (2017).

INTERCHAPTER 2: WHEN SHALL I MARRY ME?

1 Incidentally, I recently consulted two distinguished scholars for help in understanding Scott's grammatical construction here. The literary scholar was certain that I am reading something into the poem that is not there. The linguist affirmed ambiguity here, adding that it seemed impossible to know for certain. My thanks to them both for their input.

CHAPTER 3: LITERARY AFFORDANCE

1 I take heart in Wayne C. Booth's similar prefatory apologia offered in *The Rhetoric of Fiction* (though, alas, I do not possess his brilliance to fall back on):

> I could not pursue this study at all without moving far from the secure harbor of my own special training. Careful as I have tried to be, I know that experts in each period or author are sure to find errors of fact or interpretation that no expert would commit. But I hope that my larger argument does not stand or fall on whether the reader agrees with all of my analyses. They are intended as illustrative, not definitive, and though the book includes, I think, some contributions to the reading of individual works, each critical conclusion could have been illustrated with many other works. If there is anything to my case, the experienced reader will be able to supply illustrations to replace those that seem to him faulty. (Booth 1961, xiv–xv)

2 This verb can be thought of as meaning both *to record* and *to support with references* (i.e., to other documents).
3 Perhaps in the future I will try to crowdsource an abundance of literary affordance examples and conduct an organized corpus analysis of them toward a typology. But for now, I prefer to keep the concept loose and open to innovation and revision.
4 As I have said, once one has an eye out for affordances, examples begin to appear more frequently. Some familiar examples are being watched as if by Big Brother, having opposing dispositions like Jekyll and Hide, and witnessing a chaotic group of children like *Lord of the Flies*. Of course, I am interested in working with cases that call for deeper investigation or meditation than these casual references offer.
5 For a counterargument, see Scholes (1998, 37–58).
6 Stout (1982, 5–6), following Donald Davidson, arrives at a similar point of reconciliation but through inverse means, claiming that that these various schools of thought are simply theorizing about different things: "The more you and I seem to differ on some topic, the less reason we have for thinking that we are discussing the same topic at all . . . Too much divergence ceases to be divergence altogether: it merely changes the subject." For a fascinating, if sad, real-world version of these issues, see Liptak (2016), who reports on a Texas judge who coined the phrase "the Lennie standard" after the *Of Mice and Men* character in calling for a mental

disability exception to the death penalty, which Steinbeck's son denounced in the name of his father's authorial intentions despite the fact that Lennie was based on a real person who was granted leniency in a real murder case.

7 Despite our overlapping views, I do not seek affiliation with declared pragmatists such as James, Rorty, and these others; nor do I subscribe to any other established school of thought. That's not for some fantasy of remaining impervious to critique; I suspect my odds of that happening fall to zero with even just my book's title. Rather, as I have stated above, that's because my approach does not originate or end in any particular camp, and I wish to emphasize its nomadic characteristics. But I also acknowledge that my approach, of course, is neither wholly original nor wholly nomadic.

8 See the section below on ethical criticism.

9 In his article "Hamlet: My Greatest Creation," Holland (1975c, 421) argues: "Each of us, as we experience not only plays and movies and novels but all of reality, uses the materials that reality gives us within our own personal style of experiencing. Thus each of us creates our own Hamlet from the words that Shakespeare gives us." I feel no need to call the poem Khost's "Lycidas," but I do want to make note of Holland's worthwhile position, which I see in more of a rhetorical than a philosophical light.

10 Subversion is a charge that often appears in discussions of textual appropriation, such as in a relatively favorable *New York Times* account of fanfiction behavior, which nevertheless states: "Fans seize control of characters or celebrities and *subvert* their narratives for their own ends" (Hess 2017, my emphasis). Unlike *afford*, the word *subvert* carries such negative connotations as overthrow, ruin, destruction, corruption, and undermining.

11 This has been demonstrated, for example, by my graduate students through original exercises they contribute to class, including one in which the student leader first trained the class in how to use a given fanfiction trope to analyze another fictional text and then asked each of us to replicate the act with another text of our individual choosing (to good effect).

12 I tend to think of one's life narrative (or lived experience or "experiences with the world") and one's rhetorical situations as more or less the same as each other or at least inextricably linked, so I use these terms interchangeably. See Corder (1985, 18, original emphasis): "Our narratives are the evidence we have of ourselves and of our convictions. Argument, then, is not something we *make* outside ourselves; argument is what we are . . . All the choices we've made, accidentally or on purpose . . . have also made us arguments." But this conflation of narrative and rhetoric is not essential to my theory, so readers can take an either/or view if need be.

13 I want to acknowledge several argumentative uses of dance in protests pertaining to recent tragic acts of violence, including the death of Freddie Gray in Baltimore ("Man Dances" 2015); a string of controversial shooting deaths in Dallas, Minnesota, and Louisiana (Kourlas 2016); and the mass shooting at a gay nightclub in Orlando (Kehrer 2016). Incidentally, it might be argued that the first two of these examples entail literary affordances, respectively, of songs by Michael Jackson and Beyoncé. To gain insight into this possibility, ask why the performers chose those particular songs.

14 Along similar lines, I resist designating certain descriptive terms as formal classifications because they exist on a continuum of degrees rather than as categorical opposites. These are subtle/apparent (i.e., the degree to which a given affordance corresponds to what is believed to have been intended by the source text's author or is sanctioned as correct or not by critical reception; see my *Seize the Day* example in chapter 6), creative/rhetorical (creative acts are often also rhetorical and vice

versa, but sometimes one aspect carries more emphasis than the other; see below in this chapter), personal/social (subjectivity is always already socially situated, and social phenomena are experienced personally), and intentional/unintentional (a.k.a., organic/created; I don't presume to know where and when motives originate, though I can speculate about degrees of awareness).

15 A note on usage: although affordance, metaphor, and simile are somewhat analogous *to each other*, that's not what I mean here. What I mean is each of these tropes is generally characterized by properties of analogy, that is, of relationality.

16 Though many of this book's reviewers did attack this point (Mailloux 1979, 211–13; Shechner 1979, 155; Tompkins 1978, 1072–75).

17 But I do believe that even an affordance that receives no public synthesizing or authorizing—that is to say, a seemingly wholly personal affordance—still can yield significant indirect public effects by virtue of influencing the affordance maker's worldview, rhetorical tactics, and so forth.

18 Incidentally, Sontag (1966, 5) uses similar language, "a certain code, certain 'rules'" in making a similar point against the insistence on interpretation as the only or best thing to do with art.

19 I invoke Bloom only because Rorty does, on multiple occasions, not because I believe this is a necessary comparison to make. In fact, to a degree I think it's a faulty comparison because Bloom's (1973) theory of misreading, at least in its initial formulation, applied to poets, not to critics.

20 Once the necessary changes have been made

21 See also Avital Ronell (1992, 11): "'Literature' . . . has a tradition of uncovering abiding structures of crime and ethicity with crucial integrity; one need only think of what Hegel drew from *Antigone* or Freud from *Oedipus Rex*."

22 Coincidentally, as I was writing this passage, the release of the book *Conceding Composition: A Crooked History of Composition's Institutional Fortunes* (Skinnell 2016) was announced, whose subtitle gave me further heart in pursuing this particular imagistic affordance. Chapter 4 of my book examines that crooked history in some detail.

23 Former students of mine (who have studied rhetor response theory) often ask me: what ever happened to your crooked neighbor? Here is an update as of my book's final revisions. Although, unfortunately, she still smokes in her apartment, she has been banned from doing so on the building's stoop, only in part, I think, because of a little campaigning I did behind the scenes with my superintendents (a crooked move, it could be said). I have seen her smoking and reading on a nearby bus stop bench while clearly not awaiting a bus. Meanwhile, the Auden poem and my associations with it described above have only deepened their already profound place in my heart and found further application to disagreeable social situations through assimilation into my general ethos. To me, this last point may be the key takeaway: that my literary affordance continues to find applications as an abiding aspect of my worldview.

24 As I was revising this passage, the BBC published an article questioning whether use of artwork for any purposes at all amounts to misappropriation, the sample case being a reproduced *Mona Lisa* used in a Polish protest to support abortion rights. Although this BBC article begins with the framework of textual meaning, "Can art mean anything we want it to?" it ends on a note similar to literary affordance theory by declaring the *Mona Lisa* to be an "endlessly convertible" icon and "a map that can lead us anywhere we want to go" (Grovier 2016). Some productive questions I recommend users or would-be users of the *Mona Lisa* ask themselves, then, are where might this icon more productively (or enjoyably, and so forth) lead us than other destinations, how might it lead us where we're going better than other texts

would do, who seems more likely to be drawn to this affordance than others, and what in particular makes the *Mona Lisa* so effective (again, or enjoyable, and so forth) as a "map" for us?

25 Lessig may or may not agree with my applications of his ideas to the revision of undergraduate education, as he appears to be somewhat ambivalent on that matter by way of promoting Read/Write pedagogy for graduate law curricula (Lessig 2009, 85).

26 Although I do not employ this phrase elsewhere, it might be helpful to some readers to think of literary affordance as a kind of "fan *nonfiction.*"

CHAPTER 4: INSTITUTIONAL PRACTICE

1 For excellent shorter versions of this history I recommend Farris's (2014), McComiskey's (2006), and Lauer's (2006) accounts. For longer, theoretical, and pedagogical accounts, see Bergmann and Baker (2006); Berlin (1984, 1987, 1996); Connors (1997); Crowley (1998); Gaughan and Khost (2007, 1–18); Graff (2007); Horner (1983); Ianetta (2010); Miller (1991b); Schilb (1996); Young and Fulwiler (1995).

2 It is common today to see advertisements for NTT writing jobs that *require* applicants to hold a PhD. Even worse are cases like one that appeared on a listserv while I was writing this book: an ad for an adjunct job teaching a single section of writing that read "recent PhDs are especially welcome to apply" (deliberately anonymized). I suspect that relatively few PhDs in writing are taking these jobs; more likely, they are being taken by PhDs in English and other fields.

3 It goes without saying that internal and external advocacy, unionizing, and exposure of contingent labor exploitation must also be continued and intensified in the effort to improve working conditions in writing programs. Employment issues in higher education are finally making headlines these days, and most of this discourse absolutely rightly foregrounds material concerns such as salary, benefits, and job security. But these subjects should not comprise the entire story. Many NTTFs also have scholarly agendas—of various kinds and motives—and this often-neglected fact deserves more attention than it typically receives. Scholarship and working conditions do not conform to a cart-before-horse dichotomy. Rather, they are inextricably and reciprocally related such that the lamentable compensation, working conditions, and professional disrespect NTTF often endure can inhibit their performance as scholars, and their consequent lack of scholarly production can exacerbate their difficulty in securing better employment.

4 See Gunner (1993); McDonald and Schell (2011); McLeod and Schwarzbach (1993); Robertson, Crowley, and Lentricchia (1987); Sledd (1991); Tuman (1991); Wyche-Smith and Rose (1990).

5 I think of Shakespeare's Prospero relinquishing his angst, exchanging one form of power for another, and demonstrating the emotional bonds one forges with one's subjects of study: "And deeper than ever did plummet sound / I'll drown my book" (*The Tempest* 5.1.57–58).

6 I eventually co-wrote a history of this program (Khost and Belanoff 2014).

7 Change is extremely difficult to effect at the disciplinary or departmental levels, but it can be enacted easily on a smaller scale, such as at the pedagogical level, and perhaps an accumulation of these instances may result in what Scholes (2011, xiv) recognizes is more characteristic of the Kuhnian view of paradigm shift. Richard E. Miller (1998) has compellingly demonstrated this point with a number of detailed case studies.

8 In his review of *Textual Power*, however, Gerald Graff (1986, 179) *distinguishes* between Scholes and Eagleton.

9 Again I think of Prospero's renunciation of angst and powers upon accepting entanglement in what he could have controlled with detachment: "With nobler reason 'gainst my fury / Do I take part. The rarer action is / In virtue than in vengeance" (5.1.27–29).

10 *Naming* editors Linda Adler-Kassner and Elizabeth Wardle (2016, 4, original emphasis) do acknowledge that the collection reflects just "*some* of what our field knows," but they mention this only in passing in their introduction. How different a rhetorical effect it would have yielded to have specified this in the book's title instead: *Naming Some of What We Know*. That's certainly not as catchy, but it sends a far different message to disciplinary outsider-insiders about how they are encouraged to interact with the book's content.

11 Samuels (2016, A4) expands this issue beyond just disciplinary expertise to the need for corresponding improvements in material conditions of employment: "The question remains whether a move to adopt a writing studies approach in the teaching of composition courses can be achieved without collective action dedicated to transforming our institutions of higher education." For Samuels (2016, A6–A7), the problem includes the hypocritical practice of staffing composition courses with graduate students specializing in subjects other than writing.

12 That is, wonderfully.

13 I am not suggesting that voluntary NTTF—a diverse group in their own right—would not prefer tenure if it were available to them. This classification, in my usage at least, intends only to highlight their intention not to pursue TT employment at a given time, a decision that may or may not be permanent or in their control. For example, for varying reasons I fluctuated between voluntary and involuntary attitudes while working for twelve continuous years as a full-time NTT writing teacher.

14 In 2013 I surveyed NTTF with PhDs in literature who primarily teach undergraduate writing (i.e., not literature or creative writing), using the Writing Program Administrators listserv to recruit participants nationally. Given the small number of qualified selectees from my subject pool (n = 21) and my limited means of recruitment, I do not claim the results of this IRB-approved study to be generalizable. But it may still be worth noting a few findings because they could resemble the kinds of results found by a local assessment, which is the level at and method by which I recommend this issue be addressed. Roughly half of the participants (48%) were very likely or likely to pursue TT employment, roughly a quarter of them (27%) were unlikely or very unlikely, and a remaining quarter (26%) were undecided. Yet nearly all participants (95%) were interested in submitting work for publication in refereed venues, and over half of them (55%) admitted they do not submit scholarship for publication in refereed venues as often as they would like to. Insufficient time was the most common reason cited for this lack of submission. This group's top three ranked motives for seeking publication in refereed venues were to "pursue interest in the subject regardless of other reasons," to "advance knowledge of the subject," and to "improve teaching/students' learning." These were ranked above options for seeking tenure, pursuing promotion off the tenure track, gaining respect, earning merit pay, and write-in answers. As for desired support in conducting scholarship, the option "freedom to teach literary subject matter and to write about that" ranked fourth (with a count of 7 selections), after funding (10), promotion (10), and course release (8), above many other options. See Khost (2016b) for more.

15 See Cassuto (2015) for an excellent account of this view.

16 Barbara Tovey also interprets *The Tempest* as Shakespeare's response to Plato's critique of art in *The Republic*, in which Socrates bans imitative poetry and drama from his ideal society, allowing exceptions only for such works that benefit the republic and its people. Shakespeare, says Tovey (1983, 278), "intended *The Tempest* to exem-

plify precisely the kind of poetry of which Socrates here speaks, poetry which is not merely pleasant but which is beneficial to 'regimes and human life.' He conceived of *The Tempest* . . . as a dramatic and poetic imitation of *The Republic* itself," not only rising to meet all of Socrates's challenges but also affectionately teasing him along the way.

17 This point comes from John X. Evans (1981, 82), who also makes clear that More's *Utopia* "was well-known during Shakespeare's lifetime."

18 This is also why Plato's philosopher king returns to the cave, post-enlightenment, in *The Republic.*

19 Others have also derived titles of original literary works from *The Tempest*—a minor form of affordance—including "Full Fathom Five" by Sylvia Plath, *Into Thin Air* by Jon Krakauer, and *The Isle is Full of Noises* by Derek Walcott.

20 That is, fine.

21 Prospero is repeatedly tempted to seek vengeance rather than reconciliation with this party, so it is possible that Miranda has persuaded him here, as Ariel arguably appears to do later in the play (5.1.17–21).

22 It is also reasonable to suspect that in the three or so hours of their acquaintance, Ferdinand has told Miranda that his ship was wrecked in voyaging home from Tunis, where his sister was married to the king there for diplomatic reasons.

23 One counterargument to my reading of "brave new world" would point out Prospero's aside that immediately follows his daughter's exclamation: " 'Tis new to thee" (5.1.184). This usage of "new" is generally taken to mean something cynical like: not yet known for its darker aspects. But there are several reasons not to settle so easily for this standard interpretation. For one thing, as I have shown, Miranda is already aware of life's darker elements, not only in abstraction (e.g., Caliban's existence has made her aware of rape, enslavement, and corporal punishment) but also specifically in terms of the treacherous individuals she is addressing with these lines. Furthermore, in a literal sense, Miranda is indeed about to enter a new world: of marriage, political rule, and luxury; perhaps Prospero is merely commenting on the fruits of his and Miranda's effective performances (as in this emphasis: " '*Tis* new to thee"). Or on the contrary and most to my point about Miranda's rhetorical savvy, it is possible that Miranda's artful strategic disingenuousness has convinced even her unwitting father. Ferdinand, Alonso, and Prospero all have reasons for wishing to believe that Miranda is pure, innocent, and naive, so it may be no wonder that they perceive these traits in her. Perhaps the same applies to the play's interpreters throughout history, except for feminist readers such as those I have cited in this chapter.

CHAPTER 5: AFFORDANCE, AUDIENCE, AND ARGUMENT

1 The pairing of *agonistic* (meaning competitive) with *monologic* (meaning isolated from engagement with others) may appear to be contradictory; after all, how can one compete if not with others? But the kind of argumentation I am critiquing makes some of the moves of genuine debate with others in the name of winning (e.g., stating claims, offering evidence) without genuinely engaging anyone. It is a monologue without an audience, let alone an interlocutor. For a good critique of other falsities underlying argumentation as the "dominant mode" in secondary and postsecondary instruction, see DeStigter (2015).

2 I want to be clear that I do not denounce assessment or object altogether to measures of student achievement, including methods that are replicable, aggregated, and data-driven (Haswell 2005). I do believe, however, that these matters should be entrusted to trained, practicing educators according to our vetted scholarly lit-

erature, to the stated values of our professional organizations, and in some cases to our local institutional contexts. While we advocate for this ideal, teachers can and should take pedagogical steps to offset the ongoing pernicious influences of the current high-stakes testing regime.

3 Putting aside for present purposes the worthy but highly philosophical counterargument to this point posed by the work of Emmanuel Levinas, as he has a different kind of compulsory relationship in mind.

4 Notwithstanding Louise Rosenblatt's (1995, xvi, 26) insightful distinction between these terms, I will use them interchangeably for present purposes.

5 See John R. Edlund's (2013) excellent blog post for a good place to begin learning more about the long-standing, ongoing debate that distinguishes argument from persuasion.

6 It is apposite to note here comments dismissing feelings in favor of argumentation made by CCSS chief architect and champion and now president of the College Board, David Coleman (2011, 10), in a 2011 speech at a New York State Education Department event: "The only problem with [personal] writing is as you grow up in this world you realize people really don't give a sheet [*sic*] about what you feel or what you think. What they instead care about is can you make an argument with evidence . . . It is rare in a working environment that someone says, 'Johnson, I need a market analysis by Friday but before that I need a compelling account of your childhood.'" I want to draw attention not to Mr. Coleman's now famous expletive and its "blunt" context, as he put it, but rather to the nature of the rhetorical audience he poses in this statement. His first hypothetical entails "care" on the audience's part; the second involves direct interaction between an audience and a writer named Johnson. Putting aside the dispute about personal or argumentative writing for now, my point is that Coleman is assuming as foundational the value of a writer's authentic relationships with audiences, yet under his CCSS, students are constantly tested and test-prepped on writing for nobody at all, let alone for somebody they "care" about or have exigency in engaging, as "Johnson" does.

7 Today, high-stakes tests and their attendant high-cost preparatory courses play significant influences on placement into schools, programs, and even jobs for many Americans. Consider the respective 2010 and 2014 *New York Times* reports on a burgeoning "test-prep industry for 4-year-olds" (Winerip 2010) and on businesses screening post-undergraduate job applicants by their SAT scores (Dewan 2014).

8 The National Council of Teachers of English's 2016 president-elect agrees: "Teachers sometimes forget that every day they go to class they are advocates not only for their students but for our profession" (Houser 2015).

9 I am included in both categories. Like many other composition instructors, I regularly use Perl's "guidelines" in my teaching. Furthermore, my first experience of the exercise was as a graduate student in Professor Perl's class as she was refining the guidelines for her book.

10 Insert here any preferred metaphor: loop, spiral, Möbius strip, tangent, fractal, and so on.

11 Both Jeffrey Carroll (1989, 66) and William Strong (1987, 25) quote this passage in their essays, which otherwise make relatively minor reference to felt sense.

12 To be clear, these characterizations somewhat stray from Perl's (2004, xvi) understanding of her guidelines exercise, as she writes: "Seen from this [mechanistic] angle, the Guidelines are another tool . . . . But when they are connected to felt sense, they offer us a way to examine larger issues of composing."

13 Again, or loops, spirals, Möbius strips, tangents, fractals, and so on, metaphorically speaking.

14 I am deliberately alluding to Michael Polanyi's (1966a, 10) related notion of *indwelling*: "When we learn to use language, or a probe, or a tool, and thus make ourselves aware of these things as we are of our body, we interiorize these things and make ourselves dwell in them."

INTERCHAPTER 5: NO VAMPIRES

1 I cannot pursue the connection here, but I suspect these notions align with Diane Davis's (2010) project in *Inessential Solidarity*, in which she writes, for example, "communication can take place only among existents who are given over to an 'outside,' exposed, open to the other's affectation and effraction" (2010, 2), and "solidarity is at least the rhetoricity of the affect as such, of the 'individual's' irreparable openness to affection/alteration" (2010, 4).

CHAPTER 6: TEACHING AUTOTEXTOGRAPHY AND LITERARY AFFORDANCE

1 I have just made a rather mild literary affordance of Rumi's poem, of *apparent* and *extending* varieties. Both Rumi and I are obviously inviting our respective readers, and by quoting and interjecting in his poem as I have done, I am hoping to suggest that I have adopted his method of detaching expectations and value judgments from the act of invitation. It could be said that in a way I have accepted Rumi's offer, if we take his orchard to be an attitude rather than a place, which seems a safe bet. But have I been "culturally respectful" in making this affordance? I hope so. Frankly, I am at a loss on how to be certain. Whom to appeal to for validation? I certainly won't get consensus from scholars, who can't agree on anything, but anyway, which ones to ask and how? Neither is it feasible to ask all Afghans, Persians, and Turks, each of whose cultures lays some claim to Rumi's legacy (he was born 800 years ago in present-day Afghanistan, did his composing mostly in Persian, and eventually settled in what is today Turkey, all of which at the time was part of a Persianate or Turko-Persian society). Rumi is also an important spiritual figure, having been the founding figure of an order of Sufism (posthumously). But the Sufis are not a singular group either, and my literary affordance doesn't really entail the mystical side of Rumi's work, and besides, I suspect the Sufi answer would be to look into my heart, and if my actions are done lovingly (n.b., they *are*), then that is sufficient validation. I have cherished and studied Rumi's work for decades, including by learning (slowly; I still have a long way to go) to read it in the original Persian. I have made a pilgrimage to Rumi's mausoleum in Konya, Turkey, where I paid my respects at his sarcophagus, literally in a dizzy reverie—perhaps because it may be a place where, for me, the line between the physical and spiritual is "thin," as a friend of mine used to say. Furthermore, although I have not sought initiation as a "darvish," I have periodically regularly participated in weekly Sufi Majlis ceremonies (this roughly translates as group contemplative sitting sessions). Does all this accrue to enough street cred for me to be able to make the seemingly innocuous affordance of Rumi's stanza that I have made without guilt (or worse), despite my not sharing the author's geographical, ethnic, or spiritual background?

2 Contemporary playwright Sarah Ruhl reverses the usual assignments of Orpheus's and Eurydice's rhetorical agency in her ingenious creative/dramatic affordance titled *Eurydice*. In this version of the story the eponymous wife fully knows of the one condition set on her release from the afterlife and deliberately causes her husband, Orpheus, to turn around during their ascension. A rhetorically mismatched pair, she says she appreciates words and "interesting arguments" for making her "a larger part of the human community," whereas he obsesses over his own internal music and admits "I didn't know an argument should be interesting" (Ruhl 2006, 1.25–

1.35). This Eurydice, who has agency (unlike in nearly every other version over the millennia), opts against returning from hell to her former life with Orpheus, whom she may still love but perhaps not enough to tolerate his alienating solipsism.

3 *The Card Players.* Not the version at the Met that I see fairly often but the rougher one that had been stolen for a while in the 1960s, which I saw in the Orsay three years ago, which made me think of my brother and that museum's having been closed when he and I wandered there together more than two decades ago.

4 See Seitz (1999, 121–28) for an important discussion of this danger.

5 Speech act theory analyzes this and other such functions of language in extensive detail. For starters, readers can consult Austin (1962) and Searle (1969) or their reviewers.

6 To get you into the mood, I highly recommend that you go back and reread a few of those extraordinary final pages of the novel—or more if you have the time.

7 In the preface the authors reverse their subtitular ordering of priorities: "writing" precedes "analytic abilities," and "composition courses" precedes "literature courses" (Wolfe and Wilder 2016, xiii). Perhaps it is just a coincidence or a sign of marketing pressures, but if this reordering *does* reflect the book's real ranking of priorities, then all the more reason for my following critique. Though it is certainly better than many other textbooks in this way, I still find *Digging* to privilege the text and its consumption (analysis) over the reader and production (writing), thus making the textbook (and as a symbol for many other curricular materials like it, thus making these materials, too) a questionable fit for the many composition courses out there that are no longer meant to be introduction to literature courses.

8 In a similar vein, A. Abby Knoblauch (2011) published the results of her comprehensive study of best-selling composition textbooks, revealing a pervasive bias favoring persuasive argumentation over other modes of discourse (*Digging* prominently announces its allegiance to persuasion, by the way). Even in the supposedly diverse approach taken by the textbook *Everything's an Argument* (Lunsford, Ruszkiewicz, and Walters 2012), Knoblauch found only lip-service treatment of alternative modes of argumentation. Chapter 5 of my book explores some implications of this curricular and cultural bias.

9 This statistic is as of the 2013–14 academic year. According to the National Center for Education Statistics, 50,404 of the 1,869,814 bachelor's degrees conferred in 2014 were in English language and literature/letters (US Department of Education 2016, table 322.10). In fact, the situation today may even be worse than this for English departments. A 2017 study found a 17 percent decline in the number of English bachelor's degrees conferred from 2012 to 2015 (American Academy of Arts and Sciences 2017).

10 In fact, at least insofar as US employers are concerned, we know that their top interests include, in order: effective oral communication, teamwork, effective written communication, ethical judgment, critical and analytical reasoning, and application of learning "to real-world settings" (Hart Research Associates 2015, 4). I don't see a good reason to believe that literary interpretation necessarily upholds these values any better than does literary affordance. In fact, I can even imagine—*but I am not making*—a case that organically motivated literary affordances may correlate better with some of these outcomes than does compulsory interpretation. As I have stated numerous times above, my book does not propose either/or or better/worse formulations here; rather, it appeals for room for both approaches to literature and for further inquiry into the places, purposes, and possibilities of each one.

REFERENCES

Adams, Carol J. 2015. "Jane Austen's Guide to Alzheimer's." *NYTimes.com*, December. https://www.nytimes.com/2015/12/20/opinion/jane-austens-guide-to-alzheimers.html?_r=0.

Adler-Kassner, Linda. 2012. "The Companies We Keep or the Companies We Would Like to Keep: Strategies and Tactics in Challenging Times." *WPA: Writing Program Administration* 36 (1): 119–40.

Adler-Kassner, Linda, and Elizabeth Wardle, eds. 2015. *Naming What We Know: Threshold Concepts of Writing Studies.* Logan: Utah State University Press.

Allison, Marisa, Randy Lynn, and Victoria Hoverman. 2014. *Indispensible but Invisible: A Report on the Working Climate of Non–Tenure-Track Faculty at George Mason University.* http://www.chronicle.com/items/biz/pdf/GMU-Contingent-Faculty-Study.pdf.

American Academy of Arts and Sciences. 2017. "Bachelor's Degrees in the Humanities." Humanities Indicators. https://humanitiesindicators.org/content/indicatordocaspx?i=34.

Anderson, Hephzibah. 2016. "The Book That Changed Jane Eyre Forever." BBC. http://www.bbc.com/culture/story/20161019-the-book-that-changed-jane-eyre-forever.

Anderson, W. S. 1982. "The Orpheus of Virgil and Ovid: *Flebile nescio quid.*" In *Orpheus: The Metamorphoses of a Myth*, ed. John Warden, 25–50. Toronto: University of Toronto Press.

Applebee, Arthur N. 2013. "Common Core State Standards: The Promise and the Peril in a National Palimpsest." *English Journal* 103 (1): 25–33.

Aristotle. 1984. *The Rhetoric and the Poetics of Aristotle.* Trans. W. Rhys Roberts. New York: Modern Library.

Armstrong, Thomas. 2009. *Multiple Intelligences in the Classroom*, 3rd ed. Alexandria, VA: ASCD.

Arnold, Lisa. 2011. "Forum on the Profession." *College English* 73 (4): 409–27.

Austin, J. L. 1962. *How to Do Things with Words.* Cambridge, MA: Harvard University Press.

Barks, Coleman. 2004. *The Essential Rumi: New Expanded Edition.* New York: HarperOne.

Barthes, Roland. 1981. *Camera Lucida: Reflections on Photography.* Trans. Richard Howard. New York: Hill and Wang.

Barthes, Roland. 1986. *The Rustle of Language.* Trans. Richard Howard. New York: Hill and Wang.

Bayley, Sally. 2007. "'I Have Your Head on My Wall': Sylvia Plath and the Rhetoric of Cold War America." *European Journal of American Culture* 25 (3): 155–71. https://doi.org/10.1386/ejac.25.3.155_1.

Bell, Barbara Courier. 1975. "'Lycidas' and the Stages of Grief." *Literature and Psychology* 25: 166–74.

Benjamin, Walter. 1968. "The Work of Art in the Age of Mechanical Reproduction." In *Illuminations: Essays and Reflections*, ed. Hannah Arendt, trans. Harry Zohn, 217–51. New York: Schocken.

Bergen, Benjamin K. 2012. *Louder than Words: The New Science of How the Mind Makes Meaning.* New York: Basic Books.

Bergmann, Linda S., and Edith M. Baker, eds. 2006. *Composition and/or Literature: The End(s) of Education.* Urbana, IL: National Council of Teachers of English.

Berlin, James A. 1984. *Writing Instruction in Nineteenth-Century American Colleges.* Carbondale: Southern Illinois University Press.

DOI: 10.7330/9781607327769.c007

Berlin, James A. 1987. *Rhetoric and Reality: Writing Instruction in American Colleges, 1900–1985*. Carbondale: Southern Illinois University Press.
Berlin, James A. 1996. *Rhetorics, Poetics, and Cultures: Refiguring College English Studies.* Urbana, IL: National Council of Teachers of English.
Berthoud, Ella, and Susan Elderkin. 2014. *The Novel Cure: From Abandonment to Zestlessness: 751 Books to Cure What Ails You.* New York: Penguin.
Bitzer, Lloyd. 1968. "The Rhetorical Situation." *Philosophy and Rhetoric* 1 (1): 1–14.
Bleich, David. 1978. *Subjective Criticism.* Baltimore: Johns Hopkins University Press.
Bloom, Harold. 1973. *The Anxiety of Influence: A Theory of Poetry*. New York: Oxford University Press.
Blow, Charles M. 2017. "Senators Save the Empire." *NYTimes.com,* May 4. https://www.nytimes.com/2017/05/04/opinion/senator-donald-trump.html?smid=pl-share.
Booth, Wayne C. 1961. *The Rhetoric of Fiction.* Chicago: University of Chicago Press.
Booth, Wayne C. 1988. *The Company We Keep: An Ethics of Fiction.* Berkeley: University of California Press.
Borges, Jorge Luis. 1962. "Pierre Menard: Author of the *Quixote*." In *Ficciones,* trans. S. A. Emecé Editores, 45–56. Buenos Aires: Grove.
Bousquet, Marc, Tony Scott, and Leo Parascondola, eds. 2004. *Tenured Bosses and Disposable Teachers: Writing Instruction in the Managed University*. Carbondale: Southern Illinois University Press.
Bradley, Amanda J. 2005. "A Vicious American Memory: Sylvia Plath's Feminist Criticism of Wars, Wars, Wars." *Xchanges* 4 (2). http://xchanges.org/xchanges_archive/xchanges/4.2/bradley.html.
Brancazio, Peter J. 1985. "Looking into Chapman's Homer: The Physics of Judging a Fly Ball." *American Journal of Physics* 53 (9): 849–55. https://doi.org/10.1119/1.14350.
Brooks, David. 2013. "Men on the Threshold." *NYTimes.com,* July 15. https://www.nytimes.com/2013/07/16/opinion/brooks-men-on-the-threshold.html?smid=pl-share.
Burke, Kenneth. 1969. *A Rhetoric of Motives.* Berkeley: University of California Press.
Burke, Kenneth. 1973. *The Philosophy of Literary Form: Studies in Symbolic Action,* 3rd ed. Berkeley: University of California Press.
Burn, Katharine. 2007. "Professional Knowledge and Identity in a Contested Discipline: Challenges for Student Teachers and Teacher Educators." *Oxford Review of Education* 33 (4): 445–67. https://doi.org/10.1080/03054980701450886.
Carillo, Ellen C. 2016. "Reimagining the Role of the Reader in the Common Core State Standards." *English Journal* 105 (3): 29–35.
Carroll, Jeffrey. 1989. "Disabling Fictions: Institutionalized Delimitations of Revision." *Rhetoric Review* 8 (1): 62–72.
Caruth, Cathy. 1996. *Unclaimed Experience: Trauma, Narrative, and History*. Baltimore: Johns Hopkins University Press.
Cassuto, Leonard. 2015. *The Graduate School Mess: What Caused It and How We Can Fix It.* Cambridge, MA: Harvard University Press. https://doi.org/10.4159/9780674495593.
Chang, Heewon. 2008. *Autoethnography as Method.* Walnut Creek, CA: Left Coast Press.
Chemero, Anthony. 2003. "An Outline of a Theory of Affordances." *Ecological Psychology* 15 (2): 181–95. https://doi.org/10.1207/S15326969ECO1502_5.
Chemero, Anthony. 2009. *Radical Embodied Cognitive Science.* Cambridge, MA: MIT Press.
Chemero, Anthony. 2013. "Radical Embodied Cognitive Science." *Review of General Psychology* 17 (2): 145–50. https://doi.org/10.1037/a0032923.
Cleary, Linda Miller. 1996. "'I Think I Know What My Teachers Want Now': Gender and Writing Motivation." *English Journal* 85 (1): 50–57. https://doi.org/10.2307/821123.
Clifford, John. 1987. "A Response from the Margin." *College English* 49 (6): 692–706. https://doi.org/10.2307/377812.

Clines, Francis X. 2017. "Trumpian Characters Are the Stuff of Fiction." *NYTimes.com*, January 30. https://www.nytimes.com/2017/01/30/opinion/trumpian-characters-are-the-stuff-of-fiction.html?smid=pl-share&_r=0.

Coleman, David. 2011. "Bringing the Common Core to Life." *NYSED.gov*, April 28. http://usny.nysed.gov/rttt/resources/bringing-the-common-core-to-life.html.

Coles, Robert. 1989. *The Call of Stories: Teaching and the Moral Imagination*. Boston: Houghton Mifflin.

Common Core State Standards Initiative. 2010. *Common Core State Standards for English Language Arts and Literacy in History/Social Studies, Science, and Technical Subjects*. June 2. http://www.corestandards.org/wp-content/uploads/ELA_Standards1.pdf.

Connors, Robert J. 1997. *Composition-Rhetoric Backgrounds, Theory, and Pedagogy*. Pittsburgh: University of Pittsburgh Press.

Corder, Jim W. 1985. "Argument as Emergence, Rhetoric as Love." *Rhetoric Review* 4 (1): 16–32. https://doi.org/10.1080/07350198509359100.

Costall, Alan. 2012. "Canonical Affordances in Context." *Avant (Torun)* 3 (2): 85–93.

Costall, Alan, and Ole Dreier. 2012. *Doing Things with Things: The Design and Use of Everyday Objects*. New York: Routledge.

Costall, Alan, and Arthur Still. 1989. "Gibson's Theory of Direct Perception and the Problem of Cultural Relativism." *Journal for the Theory of Social Behaviour* 19 (4): 433–41. https://doi.org/10.1111/j.1468-5914.1989.tb00159.x.

Council for Higher Education Accreditation. 2014. "An Examination of the Changing Faculty: Ensuring Institutional Quality and Achieving Desired Student Learning Outcomes." January. https://www.chea.org/userfiles/Occasional%20Papers/Examination_Changing_Faculty_2013.pdf.

Council of Writing Program Administrators, National Council of Teachers of English, and National Writing Project. 2011. *Framework for Success in Postsecondary Writing*. http://wpacouncil.org/framework.

Crowley, Sharon. 1998. *Composition in the University: Historical and Polemical Essays*. Pittsburgh: University of Pittsburgh Press. https://doi.org/10.2307/j.ctt5hjpc7.

Cunningham, Jennifer M. 2010. "Actively and Critically Learning: The Pedagogical Importance of Student Affinity." *Journal of Teaching Writing* 25 (2): 223–37.

D'Angelo, Frank J. 2009. "The Rhetoric of Intertextuality." *Rhetoric Review* 29 (1): 31–47. https://doi.org/10.1080/07350190903415172.

Davis, Diane. 2005. "Addressing Alterity: Rhetoric, Hermeneutics, and the Nonappropriative Relation." *Philosophy and Rhetoric* 38 (3): 191–212. https://doi.org/10.1353/par.2005.0018.

Davis, Diane. 2010. *Inessential Solidarity: Rhetoric and Foreigner Relations*. Pittsburgh: University of Pittsburgh Press. https://doi.org/10.2307/j.ctt5vkfx1.

De Certeau, Michel. 1984. *The Practice of Everyday Life*. Trans. Steven Rendall. Berkeley: University of California Press.

DeStigter, Todd. 2015. "On the Ascendance of Argument: A Critique of the Assumptions of Academe's Dominant Form." *Research in the Teaching of English* 50 (1): 11–34.

Dewan, Shaila. 2014. "How Businesses Use Your SATs." *NYTimes.com*, March 29. https://www.nytimes.com/2014/03/30/sunday-review/how-businesses-use-your-sats.html?_r=0.

DiMaggio, Dan. 2010. "The Loneliness of a Long-Distance Test Scorer." *Monthly Review* 62 (7): 31–40. https://doi.org/10.14452/MR-062-07-2010-11_3.

Doherty, Tim. 1995. "Strictly Ballroom? Dancing along the Borders of Movement and Writing." *Journal of the Assembly for Expanded Perspectives on Learning* 1 (1): 16–25.

Downs, Douglas, and Elizabeth Wardle. 2007. "Teaching about Writing, Righting Misconceptions: (Re)Envisioning 'First-Year Composition' as 'Introduction to Writing Studies.'" *College Composition and Communication* 58 (4): 552–84.

Eagleton, Terry. 1983. *Literary Theory: An Introduction*. Minneapolis: University of Minnesota Press.

Eco, Umberto. 1990. *The Limits of Interpretation.* Bloomington: Indiana University Press.

Ede, Lisa, and Andrea A. Lunsford. 1984. "Audience Addressed/Audience Invoked: The Role of Audience in Composition Theory and Pedagogy." *College Composition and Communication* 35 (2): 155–71. https://doi.org/10.2307/358093.

Ede, Lisa, and Andrea A. Lunsford. 2001. "Collaboration and Concepts of Authorship." *PMLA* 116 (2): 354–69.

Edlund, John R. 2013. "Argument versus Persuasion: A False Dichotomy." *Teaching Texts Rhetorically*, November 23. https://textrhet.com/2013/11/23/argument-versus-persuasion-a-false-dichotomy/.

Elbow, Peter. 1991. "Reflections on Academic Discourse: How It Relates to Freshmen and Colleagues." *College English* 53 (2): 135–55. https://doi.org/10.2307/378193.

Elbow, Peter, and Pat Belanoff. 1989. *A Community of Writers: A Workshop Course in Writing.* New York: Random House.

Ellis, Carolyn. 1997. "Evocative Autoethnography: Writing Emotionally about Our Lives." In *Representation and the Text: Re-Framing the Narrative Voice*, ed. William G. Tierney and Yvonna S. Lincoln, 115–39. Albany: State University of New York Press.

Ellis, Carolyn, Tony E. Adams, and Arthur P. Bochner. 2011. "Autoethnography: An Overview." *Forum: Qualitative Social Research* 12 (1). http://www.qualitative-research.net/index.php/fqs/article/view/1589/3095.

Evans, John X. 1981. "*Utopia* on Prospero's Island." *Moreana* 18 (69), issue 1: 81–84. https://doi.org/10.3366/more.1981.18.1.9.

Fahnestock, Jeanne, and Marie Secor. 1991. "The Rhetoric of Literary Criticism." In *Textual Dynamics of the Professions: Historical and Contemporary Studies of Writing in Professional Communities*, ed. Charles Bazerman and James Paradis, 77–96. Madison: University of Wisconsin Press.

Farley, Todd. 2009. *Making the Grades: My Misadventures in the Standardized Testing Industry.* San Francisco: Polipoint.

Farrar, Julie M. 1991. "Counterstatement." *College Composition and Communication* 42 (4): 493–94. https://doi.org/10.2307/358003.

Farris, Christine. 2014. "Literature and Composition Pedagogy." In *A Guide to Composition Pedagogies*, ed. Gary Tate, Amy Rupiper Taggart, Kurt Schick, and H. Brooke Hessler, 163–76. New York: Oxford University Press.

Fetterley, Judith. 1978. *The Resisting Reader: A Feminist Approach to American Fiction.* Bloomington: Indiana University Press.

Fish, Stanley. 1970. "Literature in the Reader: Affective Stylistics." *New Literary History* 2 (1): 123–62. https://doi.org/10.2307/468593.

Fish, Stanley. 1976. "Interpreting the 'Variorum.'" *Critical Inquiry* 2 (3): 465–85. https://doi.org/10.1086/447852.

Fish, Stanley. 1980. *Is There a Text in This Class? The Authority of Interpretive Communities.* Cambridge, MA: Harvard University Press.

Fleckenstein, Kristie S. 2005. "Cybernetics, Ethos, and Ethics." *JAC* 25 (2): 323–46.

Foss, Sonja K., and Cindy L. Griffin. 1995. "Beyond Persuasion: A Proposal for an Invitational Rhetoric." *Communication Monographs* 62 (1): 2–18. https://doi.org/10.1080/03637759509376345.

Freedman, Diane P. 1993. "Border Crossing as Method and Motif in Contemporary American Writing, or, How Freud Helped Me Case the Joint." In *The Intimate Critique: Autobiographical Literary Criticism*, ed. Diane P. Freedman, Olivia Frey, and Frances Murphy Zauhar, 13–22. Durham, NC: Duke University Press.

Freud, Sigmund. 1985. *The Complete Letters of Sigmund Freud to Wilhelm Fliess, 1887–1904.* Trans. Jeffrey Moussaieff Masson. Cambridge, MA: Belknap.

Freud, Sigmund. 1999. *The Interpretation of Dreams.* Trans. Joyce Crick. Oxford: Oxford University Press.

Friedman, Sandie. 2013. "This Way for Vampires: Teaching First-Year Composition in 'Challenging Times.'" *Currents in Teaching and Learning* 6 (1): 77–84.

Gaillet, Lynée Lewis, and Letizia Guglielmo. 2014. *Scholarly Publication in a Changing Academic Landscape: Models for Success.* New York: Palgrave. https://doi.org/10.1057/9781137410764.

Gallup. 2014. "Teachers Favor Common Core Standards, Not the Testing." *Education* 29 (October). http://news.gallup.com/poll/178997/teachers-favor-common-core-standards-not-testing.aspx.

Gardner, Howard E. 2006. *Multiple Intelligences: New Horizons in Theory and Practice.* New York: Basic Books.

Gaughan, Frank, and Peter H. Khost, eds. 2007. *Collaborating(,) Literature(,) and Composition: Essays for Teachers and Writers of English.* Cresskill, NJ: Hampton.

Gaver, William W. 1991. "Technology Affordances." In *Proceedings of the SIGCHI Conference on Human Factors in Computing Systems,* 79–84. New York: ACM. https://doi.org/10.1145/108844.108856.

Gendlin, Eugene. 1962. *Experiencing and the Creation of Meaning: A Philosophical and Psychological Approach to the Subjective.* New York: Free Press of Glencoe.

Gendlin, Eugene. 1978. *Focusing.* New York: Bantam.

Gibson, James J. 1966. *The Senses Considered as Perceptual Systems.* Boston: Houghton Mifflin.

Gibson, James J. 1977. "The Theory of Affordances." In *Perceiving, Acting, and Knowing: Toward an Ecological Psychology,* ed. Robert Shaw and John Bransford, 62–82. Hillsdale, NJ: Lawrence Erlbaum.

Gibson, James J. 1979. *The Ecological Approach to Perception.* Boston: Houghton Mifflin.

Gibson, Walker. 1950. "Authors, Speakers, Readers, and Mock Readers." *College English* 11 (5): 265–69.

Gilbert, Sandra M., and Susan Gubar. 1979. *The Madwoman in the Attic: The Woman Writer and the Nineteenth-Century Literary Imagination.* New Haven, CT: Yale University Press.

Ginsburg, G. P. 1990. "The Ecological Perception Debate: An Affordance of the *Journal for the Theory of Social Behaviour.*" *Journal for the Theory of Social Behaviour* 20 (4): 347–64. DOI: 10.1111/j.1468-5914.1990.tb00193.x.

Glenn, Cheryl. 2004. *Unspoken: A Rhetoric of Silence.* Carbondale: Southern Illinois University Press.

Graff, Gerald. 1986. "Teaching Power." *NOVEL: A Forum on Fiction* 19 (2): 179–82. https://doi.org/10.2307/1345553.

Graff, Gerald. 2007. *Professing Literature: An Institutional History.* 20th Anniversary ed. Chicago: University of Chicago Press. https://doi.org/10.7208/chicago/9780226305257.001.0001.

Graff, Gerald. 2008. "President's Column: How 'bout That Wordsworth!" *MLA Newsletter* 40 (4): 3–4.

Greeno, James G. 1994. "Gibson's Affordances." *Psychological Review* 101 (2): 336–42.

Gregory, Marshall. 2009. *Shaped by Stories: The Ethical Power of Narratives.* Notre Dame, IN: University of Notre Dame Press.

Grovier, Kelly. 2016. "Is This the Painting That Can Mean Anything?" *BBC,* October 7. http://www.bbc.com/culture/story/20161007-is-this-the-painting-that-can-mean-anything.

Gunner, Jeanne. 1993. "The Fate of the Wyoming Resolution: A History of Professional Seduction." In *Writing Ourselves into the Story: Unheard Voices from Composition Studies,* ed. Sheryl I. Fontaine and Susan Hunter, 107–22. Carbondale: Southern Illinois University Press.

Hairston, Maxine. 1985. "Breaking Our Bonds and Reaffirming Our Connections." *College Composition and Communication* 36 (3): 272–82. https://doi.org/10.2307/357971.

Hall, Stuart. 1980. "Encoding/Decoding." In *Culture, Media, Language,* ed. Stuart Hall, Dorothy Hobson, Andrew Love, and Paul Willis, 117–27. London: Hutchinson.

Halpern, Faye. 2015. "Strategic Disingenuousness: The WPA, the 'Scribbling Women,' and the Problem of Expertise." *College Composition and Communication* 66 (4): 643–67.

Harari, Yuval Noah. 2015. *Sapiens: A Brief History of Humankind*. New York: HarperCollins.

Harris, Joseph. 2006a. "Déjà Vu All over Again." *College Composition and Communication* 57 (3): 535–42.

Harris, Joseph. 2006b. *Rewriting: How to Do Things with Texts*. Logan: Utah State University Press.

Hart Research Associates. 2015. *Falling Short? College Learning and Career Success*. American Association of Colleges and Universities. https://www.aacu.org/sites/default/files/files/LEAP/2015employerstudentsurvey.pdf.

Haswell, Richard. 2005. "NCTE/CCCC's Recent War on Scholarship." *Written Communication* 22 (2): 198–223. https://doi.org/10.1177/0741088305275367.

Hays, Ryan. 2015. "Grow Your Own Plants." *Inside Higher Ed*, July 17. https://www.insidehighered.com/views/2015/07/17/colleges-should-teach-students-engage-real-dialogue-essay.

Heft, Harry. 2001. *Ecological Psychology in Context: James Gibson, Roger Barker, and the Legacy of William James's Radical Empiricism*. Mahwah, NJ: Lawrence Erlbaum.

Hegel, Georg Wilhelm Friedrich. 1977. *Phenomenology of Spirit*. Trans. A. V. Miller. Oxford: Oxford University Press.

Hess, Amanda. 2017. "When Fanfiction and Reality Collide." *New York Times*, June 21. https://www.nytimes.com/2017/06/21/arts/when-fan-fiction-and-reality-collide.html?emc=edit_th_20170622&nl=todaysheadlines&nlid=55469325.

Hirsch, E. D. 1976. *The Aims of Interpretation*. Chicago: University of Chicago Press.

Hofstadter, Douglas. 2006. "Analogy as the Core of Cognition." Presidential Lecture. *Stanford Humanities Center*, February 6. http://shc.stanford.edu/multimedia/analogy-core-cognition.

Hofstadter, Douglas, and Emmanuel Sander. 2013. *Surfaces and Essences: Analogy as the Fuel and Fire of Thinking*. New York: Basic Books.

Holbrook, Sue Ellen. 1991. "Women's Work: The Feminizing of Composition." *Rhetoric Review* 9 (2): 201–29. https://doi.org/10.1080/07350199109388929.

Holland, Norman N. 1975a. *5 Readers Reading*. New Haven, CT: Yale University Press.

Holland, Norman N. 1975b. "Unity Identity Text Self." *PMLA* 90 (5): 813–22. https://doi.org/10.2307/461467.

Holland, Norman N. 1975c. "Hamlet: My Greatest Creation." *Journal of the American Academy of Psychoanalysis* 3 (4): 419–27. https://doi.org/10.1521/jaap.1.1975.3.4.419.

Horne, Janet. 1989. "Rhetoric after Rorty." *Western Journal of Speech Communication* 53 (3): 247–59. https://doi.org/10.1080/10570318909374305.

Horner, Winifred Bryan, ed. 1983. *Composition and Literature: Bridging the Gap*. Chicago: University of Chicago Press.

Houser, Susan. 2015. "Faces of Advocacy: Intro to the 2016 NCTE Annual Convention." By Shekema Silveri. YouTube, December 17. https://www.youtube.com/watch?v=ZnUj4Z4PloA.

Human Readers. 2013. "Professionals against Machine Scoring of Student Essays in High-Stakes Assessment." *Human Readers*, March 12. http://humanreaders.org/petition/.

Hwang, Joon Ho. 2007. "Women's Space and Silenced Voices during the Cold War in Sylvia Plath's Poetry." *Feminist Studies in English Literature* 15 (2): 65–86. https://doi.org/10.15796/fsel.2007.15.2.003.

Ianetta, Melissa. 2010. "Disciplinarity, Divorce, and the Displacement of Labor Issues: Rereading Histories of Composition and Literature." *College Composition and Communication* 62 (1): 53–72.

Irwin, William. 2000. *Intentionalist Interpretation: A Philosophical Explanation and Defense*. Westport, CT: Greenwood.

Iser, Wolfgang. 1989. *Prospecting: From Reader Response to Literary Anthropology*. Baltimore: Johns Hopkins University Press.

Iser, Wolfgang. 1993. *The Fictive and the Imaginary: Charting Literary Anthropology*. Baltimore: Johns Hopkins University Press.

James, William. 1910. *Pragmatism: A New Name for Some Old Ways of Thinking*. New York: Longmans, Green.

Jamison, Christine, and Forest Scogin. 1995. "Outcome of Cognitive Bibliotherapy with Depressed Adults." *Journal of Consulting and Clinical Psychology* 63 (4): 644–50. https://doi.org/10.1037/0022-006X.63.4.644.

Jenkins, Henry. 1992. *Textual Poachers: Television Fans and Participatory Culture*. New York: Routledge.

Jensen, Wilhelm, and Sigmund Freud. 1993. *Gradiva and Delusion and Dream in Wilhelm Jensen's Gradiva*. Ed. Helen M. Downey. Los Angeles: Sun and Moon Press.

Johnson, Dan R., Brandie L. Huffman, and Danny M. Jasper. 2014. "Changing Race Boundary Perception by Reading Narrative Fiction." *Basic and Applied Social Psychology* 36 (1): 83–90. https://doi.org/10.1080/01973533.2013.856791.

Jones, Jonathan. 2014. "Who's the Vandal: Ai Weiwei or the Man Who Smashed His Han Urn?" *The Guardian*, February 18. https://www.theguardian.com/artanddesign/jonathanjonesblog/2014/feb/18/ai-weiwei-han-urn-smash-miami-art.

Jost, Walter. 2004. *Rhetorical Investigations: Studies in Ordinary Language Criticism*. Charlottesville: University of Virginia Press.

Kaufman, Geoff F., and Lisa K. Libby. 2012. "Changing Beliefs and Behavior through Experience-Taking." *Journal of Personality and Social Psychology* 103 (1): 1–19. https://doi.org/10.1037/a0027525.

Kehrer, Lauron. 2016. "Dancing as Queer Resistance." *Inside Higher Ed*, June 17. https://www.insidehighered.com/views/2016/06/17/white-queer-woman-scholar-describes-her-concerns-following-orlando-shootings-essay.

Kezar, Adrianna, and Daniel Maxey. 2015. *Adapting by Design: Creating Faculty Roles and Defining Faculty Work to Ensure an Intentional Future for Colleges and Universities*, 2nd ed. The Delphi Project. https://www.insidehighered.com/sites/default/server_files/files/DELPHI%20PROJECT_ADAPTINGBYDESIGN_EMBARGOED%20(1).pdf.

Khost, Peter H. 2016a. "'Alas Not Yours to Have': Problems with Audience in High-Stakes Writing Tests, and the Promise of Felt Sense." *Journal of the Assembly for Expanded Perspectives on Learning* 21 (1): 47–68.

Khost, Peter H. 2016b. "Survey of Postsecondary Writing Teachers' Publishing and Plans." *REx* 1. http://rex1.comppile.org/search/full_report.php?EntryID=44%20target=.

Khost, Peter H., and Pat Belanoff. 2014. "Community through Collaborative Self-Reflection: Reports on a Writing Program History and Reunion at Stony Brook University." *Composition Forum* 30. http://compositionforum.com/issue/30/stony-brook.php.

Khost, Peter H., Debra Rudder Lohe, and Chuck Sweetman. 2015. "Rethinking and Unthinking the Graduate Seminar." *Pedagogy* 15 (1): 19–30. https://doi.org/10.1215/15314200-2799132.

Kidd, David Comer, and Emanuele Castano. 2013. "Reading Literary Fiction Improves Theory of Mind." *Science* 342 (6156): 377–80. https://doi.org/10.1126/science.1239918.

Kiefer, Kate. n.d. "What Is Rogerian Argument?" *Writing@CSU*. Colorado State University. https://writing.colostate.edu/guides/teaching/co300man/com5e1.cfm.

Kirlik, Alex. 2004. "On Stoffregen's Definition of Affordances." *Ecological Psychology* 16 (1): 73–77. https://doi.org/10.1207/s15326969eco1601_10.

Knapp, Steven, and Walter Benn Michaels. 1982. "Against Theory." *Critical Inquiry* 8 (4): 723–42. https://doi.org/10.1086/448178.

Knoblauch, A. Abby. 2011. "A Textbook Argument: Definitions of Argument in Leading Composition Textbooks." *College Composition and Communication* 63 (2): 244–68.

Kourlas, Gia. 2016. "This Is a Protest Dance: Alvin Ailey Performs to Beyonce's 'Freedom.'" *New York Times*, July 14. https://www.nytimes.com/2016/07/15/arts/dance/freedom-alvin-ailey-dancers-make-a-protest-move.html?_r=0.

Lakoff, George, and Mark Johnson. 1980. *Metaphors We Live By*. Chicago: University of Chicago Press.

Lamb, Catherine E. 1991. "Beyond Argument in Feminist Composition." *College Composition and Communication* 42 (1): 11–24. https://doi.org/10.2307/357535.

Lamos, Steve. 2011. "Credentialing College Writing Teachers: WPAs and Labor Reform." *WPA: Writing Program Administration* 35 (1): 45–72.

Lauer, Janice M. 2006. "Rhetoric and Composition." In *English Studies: An Introduction to the Discipline(s)*, ed. Bruce McComiskey, 106–52. Urbana, IL: National Council of Teachers of English.

Lawrence, D. H. 1994. *The Complete Poems of D. H. Lawrence*. London: Wordsworth Poetry Library.

Leininger, Lorie Jerrell. 2001. "The Miranda Trap." In *The Tempest: Critical Essays*, ed. Patrick Murphy, 223–30. New York: Routledge.

LeMesurier, Jennifer Lin. 2014. "Somatic Metaphors: Embodied Recognition of Rhetorical Opportunities." *Rhetoric Review* 33 (4): 362–80. https://doi.org/10.1080/07350198.2014.946868.

Lessig, Lawrence. 2009. *Remix: Making Art and Commerce Thrive in the Hybrid Economy*. New York: Penguin.

Liptak, Adam. 2016. "Supreme Court to Consider Legal Standard Drawn from 'Of Mice and Men.'" *NYTimes.com*, August 22. https://www.nytimes.com/2016/08/23/us/politics/supreme-court-to-consider-legal-standard-drawn-from-of-mice-and-men.html.

Long, Russell C. 1980. "Writer-Audience Relationships: Analysis or Intervention?" *College Composition and Communication* 31 (2): 221–26. https://doi.org/10.2307/356377.

Lunsford, Andrea A., John J. Ruszkiewicz, and Keith Walters. 2012. *Everything's an Argument*, 6th ed. New York: Bedford/St. Martin's.

Lynch, Dennis A., Diana George, and Marilyn Cooper. 1997. "Moments of Argument: Agonistic Inquiry and Confrontational Cooperation." *College Composition and Communication* 48 (1): 61–85. https://doi.org/10.2307/358771.

Lyon, Arabella. 2013. *Deliberative Acts: Democracy, Rhetoric, and Rights*. State College: Penn State University Press.

Mailloux, Steven. 1979. "Review." *Journal of Aesthetics and Art Criticism* 38 (2): 211–13. https://doi.org/10.2307/430734.

Mailloux, Steven. 1989. *Rhetorical Power*. Ithaca, NY: Cornell University Press.

Mailloux, Steven. 1997. "Articulation and Understanding: The Pragmatic Intimacy between Rhetoric and Hermeneutics." In *Rhetoric and Hermeneutics in Our Time: A Reader*, ed. Walter Jost and Michael J. Hyde, 378–94. New Haven, CT: Yale University Press.

Mailloux, Steven. 1998. *Reception Histories: Rhetoric, Pragmatism, and American Cultural Politics*. Ithaca, NY: Cornell University Press.

Mailloux, Steven. 2000. "Making Comparisons: Making Contact, Ethnocentrism, and Cross-Cultural Communication." In *Post-Nationalist American Studies*, ed. John Carlos Rowe, 110–28. Berkeley: University of California Press. https://doi.org/10.1525/california/9780520224384.003.0006.

Mancuso, Carolina. 2006. "Bodies in the Classroom: Integrating Physical Literacy." *Journal of the Assembly for Expanded Perspectives on Learning* 12 (1): 25–35.

"Man Dances Like Michael Jackson in Middle of Baltimore Riots." 2015. By SanVic. YouTube, April 28. https://www.youtube.com/watch?v=51WsWXfRwA0.

Mark, Leonard S. 1987. "Eyeheight-Scaled Information about Affordances: A Study of Sitting and Stair Climbing." *Journal of Experimental Psychology: Human Perception and Performance* 13 (3): 361–70. https://doi.org/10.1037/0096-1523.13.3.361.

Markell, Kathryn A., and Marc A. Markell. 2008. *The Children Who Lived: Using Harry Potter and Other Fictional Characters to Help Grieving Children and Adolescents*. New York: Routledge.

Marzano, Robert J. 2012. "Art and Science of Teaching / Teaching Argument." *Educational Leadership.* ASCD, September. http://www.ascd.org/publications/educational-leadership/sept12/vol70/num01/Teaching-Argument.aspx.

Maynard, Douglas C., and Todd Allen Joseph. 2008. "Are All Part-Time Faculty Underemployed? The Influence of Faculty Status Preference on Satisfaction and Commitment." *Higher Education* 55 (2): 139–54. https://doi.org/10.1007/s10734-006-9039-z.

McArthur, Leslie Zebrowitz, and Reuben M. Baron. 1983. "Toward an Ecological Theory of Social Perception." *Psychological Review* 90 (3): 215–38. https://doi.org/10.1037/0033-295X.90.3.215.

McComiskey, Bruce, ed. 2006. *English Studies: An Introduction to the Discipline(s).* Urbana, IL: National Council of Teachers of English.

McDonald, James C., and Eileen E. Schell. 2011. "The Spirit and Influence of the Wyoming Resolution: Looking Back to Look Forward." *College English* 73 (4): 360–78.

McLeod, Susan H. 2006. " 'Breaking Our Bonds and Affirming Our Connections,' Twenty Years Later." *College Composition and Communication* 57 (3): 525–35.

McLeod, Susan H., and Fred S. Schwarzbach. 1993. "What about the TAs? Making the Wyoming Resolution a Reality for Graduate Students." *WPA: Writing Program Administration* 17 (1–2): 83–87.

Michaels, Claire F. 2003. "Affordances: Four Points of Debate." *Ecological Psychology* 15 (2): 135–48. https://doi.org/10.1207/S15326969ECO1502_3.

Miller, Richard E. 1998. *As if Learning Mattered: Reforming Higher Education.* Ithaca, NY: Cornell University Press.

Miller, Susan. 1984. "The Student's Reader Is Always a Fiction." *JAC* 5 (1): 15–29.

Miller, Susan. 1991a. "The Feminization of Composition." In *The Politics of Writing Instruction: Postsecondary*, ed. Richard Bullock and John Trimbur, 39–54. Portsmouth, NH: Boynton/Cook.

Miller, Susan. 1991b. *Textual Carnivals: The Politics of Composition.* Carbondale: Southern Illinois University Press.

Mitchell, Ruth, and Mary Taylor. 1979. "The Integrating Perspective: An Audience-Response Model for Writing." *College English* 41 (3): 247–71. https://doi.org/10.2307/376441.

MLA Office of Research. 2014. *MLA Issue Brief: The Academic Workforce.* Modern Language Association. https://apps.mla.org/pdf/awak_issuebrief14.pdf.

Monahan, Mary Beth. 2013. "Writing 'Voiced' Arguments about Science Topics." *Journal of Adolescent and Adult Literacy* 57 (1): 31–40. https://doi.org/10.1002/JAAL.204.

National Governors Association (NGA) Center for Best Practices and the Council of Chief State School Officers (CCSSO). 2010. *Common Core State Standards for English Language Arts and Literacy in History/Social Studies, Science, and Technical Subjects—Appendix A: Research Supporting Key Elements of the Standards, Key Terms.* http://www.corestandards.org/assets/Appendix_A.pdf.

National Governors Association (NGA), Council of Chief State School Officers (CCSSO), and Achieve. 2008. "Benchmarking for Success: Ensuring US Students Receive a World-Class Education." http://www.corestandards.org/assets/0812BENCHMARKING.pdf.

Neel, Jasper P. 1984. "Writers, Readers, and Texts: Writing in the Abyss." *JAC* 5: 87–106.

New York State Education Department. 2013. *Regents Examination in English Language Arts (Common Core) Sample Questions Fall 2013.* October 10. https://www.engageny.org/resource/regents-exams-ela-sample-items.

Noble, William. 1981. "Gibsonian Theory and the Pragmatist Perspective." *Journal for the Theory of Social Behaviour* 11 (1): 65–85. https://doi.org/10.1111/j.1468-5914.1981.tb00023.x.

Noble, William. 1993. "Meaning and the 'Discursive Ecology': Further to the Debate on Ecological Perceptual Theory." *Journal for the Theory of Social Behaviour* 23 (4): 375–98. https://doi.org/10.1111/j.1468-5914.1993.tb00541.x.

Nussbaum, Martha. 1985. "Finely Aware and Richly Responsible: Literature and the Moral Imagination." *Journal of Philosophy* 82 (10): 516–29.

Nussbaum, Martha. 1998. "Exactly and Responsibly: A Defense of Ethical Criticism." *Philosophy and Literature* 22 (2): 343–65. https://doi.org/10.1353/phl.1998.0047.

Ong, Walter J.S.J. 1975. "The Writer's Audience Is Always a Fiction." *PMLA* 90 (1): 9–21. https://doi.org/10.2307/461344.

Ostriker, Alicia. 1994. *The Nakedness of the Fathers: Biblical Visions and Revisions.* New Brunswick, NJ: Rutgers University Press.

Park, Douglas B. 1986. "Analyzing Audiences." *College Composition and Communication* 37 (4): 478–88. https://doi.org/10.2307/357917.

Penrose, Ann M. 2012. "Professional Identity in a Contingent-Labor Profession: Expertise, Autonomy, Community in Composition Teaching." *WPA: Writing Program Administration* 35 (2): 108–26.

Perl, Sondra. 1980. "Understanding Composing." *College Composition and Communication* 31 (4): 363–69. https://doi.org/10.2307/356586.

Perl, Sondra. 1994. "A Writer's Way of Knowing: Guidelines for Composing." In *Presence of Mind: Writing and the Domain beyond the Cognitive*, ed. Alice Brand and Richard Graves, 77–87. Portsmouth, NH: Boynton/Cook.

Perl, Sondra. 2004. *Felt Sense: Writing with the Body*. Portsmouth, NH: Boynton/Cook.

Petraglia, Joseph. 1995. "Spinning Like a Kite: A Closer Look at the Pseudotransactional Function of Writing." *JAC* 15 (1): 19–33.

Pfister, Fred R., and Joanne F. Petrick. 1980. "A Heuristic Model for Creating a Writer's Audience." *College Composition and Communication* 31 (2): 213–20. https://doi.org/10.2307/356376.

Pinter, Robbie Clifton. 2002. "The Landscape Listens—Hearing the Voice of the Soul." *Journal of the Assembly for Expanded Perspectives on Learning* 8 (1): 71–78.

Polanyi, Michael. 1966a. "The Logic of Tacit Inference." *Philosophy* 41 (155): 1–18. https://doi.org/10.1017/S0031819100066110.

Polanyi, Michael. 1966b. *The Tacit Dimension.* Garden City, NY: Doubleday.

Popken, Randall. 2001. "Felt Sensing of Speech Acts in Written Genre Acquisition." *Journal of the Assembly for Expanded Perspectives on Learning* 7 (1): 10–19.

Porter, James E. 1992. *Audience and Rhetoric: An Archaeological Composition of the Discourse Community*. Englewood Cliffs, NJ: Prentice-Hall.

Quindlen, Anna. 1998. *How Reading Changed My Life.* New York: Ballantine.

Rafoth, Bennett. 1988. "Discourse Community: Where Writers, Readers, and Texts Come Together." In *The Social Construction of Written Communication*, ed. Bennett Rafoth and Donald Rubin, 131–46. Norwood, NY: Ablex.

Rapee, Ronald M., Maree J. Abbott, and Heidi J. Lyneham. 2006. "Bibliotherapy for Children with Anxiety Disorder using Written Materials for Parents: A Randomised Controlled Trial." *Journal of Consulting and Clinical Psychology* 74 (3): 436–44. https://doi.org/10.1037/0022-006X.74.3.436.

Ratcliffe, Krista. 2005. *Rhetorical Listening: Identification, Gender, Whiteness.* Carbondale: Southern Illinois University Press.

Ravitch, Diane. 2015. "Who Is Grading Common Core Tests? It Is Worse than You Thought." *Diane Ravitch's Blog*, June 23. https://dianeravitch.net/2015/06/23/who-is-grading-common-core-tests-it-is-worse-than-you-thought/.

Reed, Edward. 1996. *Encountering the World: Toward an Ecological Psychology*. Oxford: Oxford University Press.

Reid, E. Shelley. 2004. "Uncoverage in Composition Pedagogy." *Composition Studies* 32 (1): 15–34.

Reiff, Mary Jo. 1996. "Rereading 'Invoked' and 'Addressed' Readers through a Social Lens: Toward a Recognition of Multiple Audiences." *JAC* 16 (3): 407–24.

Rice, Jenny. 2015. "Para-Expertise, Tacit Knowledge, and Writing Problems." *College English* 78 (2): 117–38.

Rich, Motoko. 2015. "Grading the Common Core: No Teaching Experience Required." *New York Times*, June 22. https://www.nytimes.com/2015/06/23/us/grading-the-common-core-no-teaching-experience-required.html.

Robertson, Linda R., Sharon Crowley, and Frank Lentricchia. 1987. "The Wyoming Conference Resolution Opposing Unfair Salaries and Working Conditions for Post-Secondary Teachers of Writing." *College English* 49 (3): 274–80. https://doi.org/10.2307/377922.

Ronell, Avital. 1992. *Crack Wars: Literature Addiction Mania*. Lincoln: University of Nebraska Press.

Rorty, Richard. 1982. *Consequences of Pragmatism: Essays, 1972–80*. Minneapolis: University of Minnesota Press.

Rorty, Richard. 1985. "Philosophy without Principles." *Critical Inquiry* 11 (3): 459–65. https://doi.org/10.1086/448299.

Rorty, Richard. 1992. "The Pragmatist's Progress." In *Interpretation and Overinterpretation*, ed. Stefan Collini, 89–108. Cambridge: Cambridge University Press.

Rosenberg, David, ed. 1991. *The Movie That Changed My Life*. New York: Viking.

Rosenblatt, Louise. 1994. *The Reader the Text the Poem: The Transactional Theory of the Literary Work*. Carbondale: Southern Illinois University Press.

Rosenblatt, Louise. 1995. *Literature as Exploration*, 5th ed. New York: Modern Language Association.

Ruhl, Sarah. 2006. *The Clean House and Other Plays*. New York: Theatre Communications.

Rule, Hannah J. 2017. "Sensing the Sentence: An Embodied Simulation Approach to Rhetorical Grammar." *Composition Studies* 45 (1): 19–38.

Salvatori, Mariolina, and Patricia Donahue. 2010. "Citation Difficulties." *International Journal for the Scholarship of Teaching and Learning* 4 (1): 1–5. https://doi.org/10.20429/ijsotl.2010.040102.

Samuels, Robert. 2016. "Contingent Labor, Writing Studies, and Writing about Writing." *FORUM: Issues about Part-Time and Contingent Faculty* 20 (1): A1–A16.

Sargent, M. Elizabeth. 2003. "Felt Sense in the Composition Classroom: Getting the Butterflies to Fly in Formation." *ADE Bulletin* 134–35: 57–67. https://doi.org/10.1632/ade.134.57.

Scarantino, Andrea. 2003. "Affordances Explained." *Philosophy of Science* 70 (5): 949–61. https://doi.org/10.1086/377380.

Schell, Eileen E. 1998. *Gypsy Academics and Mother-Teachers: Gender, Contingent Labor, and Writing Instruction*. Portsmouth, NH: Boyton/Cook.

Schilb, John. 1996. *Between the Lines: Relating Composition Theory and Literary Theory*. Portsmouth, NH: Heinemann-Boynton/Cook.

Schmitt, Bernd. H. 1987. "The Ecological Approach to Social Perception: A Conceptual Critique." *Journal for the Theory of Social Behaviour* 17 (3): 265–78. https://doi.org/10.1111/j.1468-5914.1987.tb00099.x.

Scholes, Robert. 1982. *Semiotics and Interpretation*. New Haven, CT: Yale University Press.

Scholes, Robert. 1983. "Who Cares about the Text?" *NOVEL: A Forum on Fiction* 17 (2): 171–80.

Scholes, Robert. 1985. *Textual Power: Literary Theory and the Teaching of English*. New Haven, CT: Yale University Press.

Scholes, Robert. 1998. *The Rise and Fall of English: Reconstructing English as a Discipline*. New Haven, CT: Yale University Press.

Scholes, Robert. 2011. *English after the Fall: From Literature to Textuality*. Iowa City: University of Iowa Press.

Schwarz, Daniel R. 2001. "A Humanistic Ethics of Reading." In *Mapping the Ethical Turn: A Reader in Ethics, Culture, and Literary Theory*, ed. Todd F. Davis and Kenneth Womack, 3–15. Charlottesville: University Press of Virginia.

Scott, Andrea. 2013. "Response to Faye Halpern's 'The Preceptor Problem: The Effect of "Undisciplined Writing" on Disciplined Instructors.'" *WPA: Writing Program Administration* 37 (1): 214–19.

Scott, A. O. 2016. "Even Superheroes Punch the Clock." *NYTimes.com*, August 10. https://www.nytimes.com/2016/08/14/movies/even-superheroes-punch-the-clock.html.

Searle, John R. 1969. *Speech Acts: An Essay in the Philosophy of Language*. London: Cambridge University Press. https://doi.org/10.1017/CBO9781139173438.

Sebek, Barbara Ann. 2001. "Peopling, Profiting, and Pleasure in *The Tempest*." In *The Tempest: Critical Essays*, ed. Patrick M. Murphy, 426–81. New York: Routledge.

Sedgwick, Eve Kosofsky. 2003. *Touching Feeling: Affect, Pedagogy, Performativity*. Durham, NC: Duke University Press.

Seitz, James E. 1999. *Motives for Metaphor: Literacy, Curricular Reform, and the Teaching of English*. Pittsburgh: University of Pittsburgh Press.

Selzer, Jack. 1992. "More Meanings of Audience." In *A Rhetoric of Doing: Essays on Written Discourse in Honor of James L. Kinneavy*, ed. Stephen Witte, Neil Kakadate, and Roger Cherry, 161–77. Carbondale: Southern Illinois University Press.

Shakespeare, William. 1987. *The Tempest*. New York: Signet Classics.

Shechner, Mark. 1979. "Review." *Criticism* 21 (2): 153–56.

Sherwood, Steve. 1995. "Tutoring and the Writer's 'Felt Sense': Developing and Safeguarding the Mind's Ear." *Writing Lab Newsletter* 19 (10): 10–14.

Sirc, Geoffrey. 2005. "Composition's Eye/Orpheus's Gaze/Cobain's Journals." *Composition Studies* 33 (1): 11–30.

Skinnell, Ryan. 2016. *Conceding Composition: A Crooked History of Composition's Institutional Fortunes*. Logan: Utah State University Press. https://doi.org/10.2307/j.ctt1d4tzt5.

Sledd, James. 1991. "Why the Wyoming Resolution Had to Be Emasculated: A History and a Quixoticism." *JAC* 11 (2): 269–81.

Slights, Jessica. 2001. "Rape and the Romanticization of Shakespeare's Miranda." *Studies in English Literature 1500-1900* 41 (2): 357–79. https://doi.org/10.2307/1556193.

Smith, Ashley A. 2015. "Common Core Gets a Footing." *Inside Higher Ed*, April 28. https://www.insidehighered.com/news/2015/04/28/colleges-begin-take-notice-common-core.

Smith, Jeff. 1997. "Students' Goals, Gatekeeping, and Some Questions of Ethics." *College English* 59 (3): 299–320. https://doi.org/10.2307/378379.

Smith, Nancy M., Mark R. Floyd, Forest Scogin, and Christine Jamison. 1997. "Three Year Follow Up of Bibliotherapy for Depression." *Journal of Consulting and Clinical Psychology* 65 (2): 324–27. https://doi.org/10.1037/0022-006X.65.2.324.

Solomon, Andrew. 2012. *Far from the Tree: Parents, Children, and the Search for Identity*. New York: Scribner.

Sontag, Susan. 1966. *Against Interpretation*. New York: Dell.

Sparkes, Andrew. 2002. "Autoethnography: Self-Indulgence or Something More?" In *Ethnographically Speaking: Autoethnography, Literature, and Aesthetics*, ed. Arthur P. Bochner and Carolyn Ellis, 209–32. Walnut Creek, CA: Altamira.

Spellmeyer, Kurt. 2014. "Fighting Words: Instrumentalism, Pragmatism, and the Necessity of Politics in Composition." *Pedagogy* 14 (1): 1–25. https://doi.org/10.1215/15314200-2348893.

Stephens, Bret. 2017. "How Trump May Save the Republic." *NYTimes.com*, May 12. https://www.nytimes.com/2017/01/30/opinion/trumpian-characters-are-the-stuff-of-fiction.html?smid=pl-share&_r=0.

Stoffregen, Thomas A. 2003. "Affordances as Properties of the Animal-Environment System." *Ecological Psychology* 15 (2): 115–34. https://doi.org/10.1207/S15326969ECO1502_2.

Stoffregen, Thomas A. 2004. "Breadth and Limits of the Affordance Concept." *Ecological Psychology* 16 (1): 79–85. https://doi.org/10.1207/s15326969eco1601_11.

Stoffregen, Thomas A., and Bruno Mantel. 2015. "Exploratory Movement and Affordances in Design." *Artificial Intelligence for Engineering Design, Analysis, and Manufacturing* 29 (3): 257–65. https://doi.org/10.1017/S0890060415000190.

Stout, Jeffrey. 1982. "What Is the Meaning of a Text?" *New Literary History* 14 (1): 1–12. https://doi.org/10.2307/468954.

Strickland, Donna. 2001. "Taking Dictation: The Emergence of Writing Programs and the Cultural Contradictions of Composition Teaching." *College English* 63 (4): 457–79. https://doi.org/10.2307/378890.

Strickland, Donna. 2011. *The Managerial Unconscious in the History of Composition Studies.* Carbondale: Southern Illinois University Press.

Strong, William. 1987. "Language as Teacher." *College Composition and Communication* 38 (1): 21–31. https://doi.org/10.2307/357583.

Sword, Helen. 1989. "Orpheus and Eurydice in the Twentieth Century: Lawrence, H. D., and the Poetics of the Turn." *Twentieth Century Literature* 35 (4): 407–28. https://doi.org/10.2307/441894.

Theater of War Productions. 2017a. "About." *Theater of War Productions.* http://theaterofwar.com/about/mission.

Theater of War Productions. 2017b. "Overview." *Theater of War Productions.* http://theaterofwar.com/projects/theater-of-war/overview.

Thompson, Ann. 1998. "'Miranda, Where's Your Sister?': Reading Shakespeare's *The Tempest.*" In *Critical Essays on Shakespeare's* The Tempest, ed. Virginia M. Vaughan and Alden T. Vaughan, 234–43. New York: G. K. Hall.

Thug Notes. 2013. "Hamlet (Shakespeare)—Thug Notes Summary and Analysis." By Wisecrack. YouTube, August 13. https://www.youtube.com/watch?v=A98tf9krihg.

Tolman, E. C. 1932. *Purposive Behavior in Animals and Men.* New York: Appleton-Century.

Tompkins, Jane P. 1978. "Review." *Modern Language Notes* 93 (5): 1068–75.

Tompkins, Jane P. 1980. *Reader-Response Criticism: From Formalism to Post-Structuralism.* Baltimore: Johns Hopkins University Press.

Tovey, Barbara. 1983. "Shakespeare's Apology for Imitative Poetry: *The Tempest* and *The Republic.*" *Interpretation* 11 (3): 275–316.

Tuman, Myron C. 1991. "Unfinished Business: Coming to Terms with the Wyoming Resolution." *College Composition and Communication* 42 (3): 356–65. https://doi.org/10.2307/358078.

Turner, Phil. 2005. "Affordance as Context." *Interacting with Computers* 17 (6): 787–800. http://dx.doi.org/10.1016/j.intcom.2005.04.003.

Turvey, M. T. 1992. "Affordances and Prospective Control: An Outline of the Ontology." *Ecological Psychology* 4 (3): 173–87. https://doi.org/10.1207/s15326969eco0403_3.

Tzu, Lao. 1961. *Tao Teh Ching.* New York: St. John's University Press.

US Department of Education. 2016. "Table 322.10 Bachelor's Degrees Conferred by Postsecondary Institutions, by Field of Study: Selected Years, 1970–71 through 2013–14." Institute of Educational Sciences, National Center for Education Statistics. https://nces.ed.gov/programs/digest/d13/tables/dt13_322.10.asp.

Walker, Clay. 2015. "Composing Agency: Theorizing the Readiness Potentials of Literacy Practices." *Literacy in Composition Studies* 3 (2): 1–21. https://doi.org/10.21623/1.3.2.2.

Wardle, Elizabeth. 2008. "Continuing the Dialogue: Follow-Up Comments on 'Teaching about Writing, Righting Misconceptions.'" *College Composition and Communication* 60 (1): 175–81.

Wardle, Elizabeth, and Doug Downs. 2013. "Reflecting Back and Looking Forward: Revisiting 'Teaching about Writing, Righting Misconceptions' Five Years On." *Composition Forum* 27. http://compositionforum.com/issue/27/reflecting-back.php.

Wardle, Elizabeth, and J. Blake Scott. 2015. "Defining and Developing Expertise in a Writing and Rhetoric Department." *WPA: Writing Program Administration* 39 (1): 72–93.

Warren, William H. 1984. "Perceiving Affordances: The Visual Guidance of Stair Climbing." *Journal of Experimental Psychology: Human Perception and Performance* 10 (5): 683–703. https://doi.org/10.1037/0096-1523.10.5.683.

Wilson, Andrew D., and Sabrina Golonka. 2013. "The Affordances of Objects and Pictures of Those Objects." *Notes from Two Scientific Psychologists*, February 28. http://psychsciencenotes.blogspot.com/2013/02/the-affordances-of-objects-and-pictures.html.

Winerip, Michael. 2010. "Equity of Test Is Debated as Children Compete for Gifted Kindergarten." *NYTimes.com*, July 25. https://www.nytimes.com/2010/07/26/education/26winerip.html.

Wolfe, Joanna, and Laura Wilder. 2016. *Digging into Literature: Strategies for Reading, Analysis, and Writing.* Boston: Bedford/St. Martin's.

Wyche-Smith, Susan, and Shirley K. Rose. 1990. "One Hundred Ways to Make the Wyoming Resolution a Reality: A Guide to Personal and Political Action." *College Composition and Communication* 41 (3): 318–24. https://doi.org/10.2307/357659.

Yancey, Kathleen Blake. 2015. "Coming to Terms: Composition/Rhetoric, Threshold Concepts, and a Disciplinary Core." In *Naming What We Know: Threshold Concepts of Writing Studies*, ed. Linda Adler-Kassner and Elisabeth Wardle, xviii–xxvii. Logan: Utah State University Press. https://doi.org/10.7330/9780874219906.c000a.

Young, Art, and Toby Fulwiler, eds. 1995. *When Writing Teachers Teach Literature: Bringing Writing to Reading.* Portsmouth, NH: Boyton/Cook Heinemann.

ABOUT THE AUTHOR

PETER H. KHOST (pronounced *coast*), PhD, is an assistant professor in the independent Program in Writing and Rhetoric (PWR) and a faculty affiliate in the Department of English at Stony Brook University. In the PWR Peter serves as associate director and is founding co-principal investigator of the Writing Research Lab. He co-edited *Collaborating(,) Literature(,) and Composition: Essays for Teachers and Writers of English* (Hampton Press) and has published essays in *Composition Forum*; *Pedagogy: Critical Approaches to Teaching Literature, Language, Composition, and Culture*; *English Journal*; and numerous other journals and edited collections. Peter is co-editor of the *Journal of the Assembly for Expanded Perspectives on Learning*. He lives in New York City with his wife and their son.

INDEX